John O'Connor

# The Workhouses of Ireland

*The fate of Ireland's poor*

ANVIL BOOKS, DUBLIN
IRISH BOOKS & MEDIA, MINNEAPOLIS

First published 1995 by
Anvil Books
45 Palmerston Road, Dublin 6
in association with
Irish Books and Media, Minneapolis
Reprinted 1997
© Text John O'Connor 1995

ISBN  0  947962  71  9  pbk

Library of Congress Catalog Card Number
94-79809

ISBN  0  937702  15  3  pbk

Printed by Colour Books, Dublin

*To my wife Mary Josephine,*
*my book's first reader*

# Contents

# Illustrations

## Sources

Architectural Archive of Ireland, 96, 105; Commissioners
of Public Works in Ireland, 21; Cork Examiner, 78-9;
Department of Health and Social Services, Northern
Ireland, 106, 205; Halls' Ireland, 112, 117; *The Illustrated
London News*, 45, 109, 125; National Library of Ireland,
41, 138; from *The Illustrated London News*, 3, 50, 53, 99,
128, 133, 135, 148-9, 153, 154, 156, 157, 162, 175.

# Prologue

When I first began to write this book I was concerned with facts and figures – the background to the poverty of Ireland, the laws that created the workhouse system, the estimates of planners and architects, the logistics of an operation that involved thousands of men in a gigantic building programme, the statistics of starvation, disease and death.

Then, slowly, imperceptibly, the pages became peopled with ghosts from the past. Not with names – these people were seldom named. Not with voices – they left little record. But shadowy though they were they left an indelible impact on the events through which they lived. They emerge fleetingly but powerfully, like the features of a distant landscape illuminated momentarily by a sudden burst of sun through the clouds. They were glimpsed by other people and it is thus that they come alive ...

The man who carried his wife from the workhouse to their old home, mile after weary mile, and was discovered next morning dead, his wife's feet held to his breast as if he were trying to warm them. The parties of orphan girls departing, bible in hand, for Australia. The girl, noted by a worker at Grosse Ile, whose golden hair moved in the slight breeze as her body was lowered from the ship that had become her grave. The batches of wild mountainy men and women, two hundred strong, from the Kenmare workhouse, who appeared on the dockside at Cork, week after week, on the first part of their journey to America. The woman, separated from her family, who hid behind bushes as she tried to catch a glimpse of her sons and daughters among the workhouse children as they filed into the yards once a day. The men, women and children who, refused admittance to the workhouse at Louisburg, had to turn away and on that 'trail of tears' back to their cabins, watch as their companions died from starvation or exposure in the bitter March of 1847. The women and children, recorded by the *Illustrated London News,* scattered over the turnip fields, 'like a flock of famished crows'. The fatalism of those who lay down near the closed gates of some workhouse and were discovered next morning, 'some stirring and some who were quiet enough'.

One name recorded is that of Connor McInerney, found by Spencer Hall by the side of a green lane, having crawled from the workhouse in Limerick where his wife had died. He himself was mortally ill but he longed 'to breathe once more the fresh air . . . and die near his home and among his people'.

The voices in this book are those of the politicians, the planners, the administrators, the commentators. Only rarely does that of a workhouse 'inmate' break through. Understandably. 'Paupers' were often uneducated. Personal memoirs and records are scant. But as the excerpt from *Mo Sceal Féin* shows, they were not without feelings and emotions – and they could display great generosity of spirit. Their voices have not been fully heard. Not yet. My hope is that should a second edition of this book be produced some now unknown accounts from those who experienced life in the workhouse may be included.

As the commemorative plaque on the old Magherafelt workhouse says: 'It will be good to remember these things.'

*Beatha an Staraidhe Firinne* – 'Truth is the Life of History.'

From *Leabhar na gCeart* (The Book of Rights),
a tenth-century Gaelic manuscript

# Introductory Note

The workhouse was the most feared and hated institution ever established in Ireland. The horror of life – and death – within its grim walls left such bitter memory in the folk-mind of the Irish people that one of the first actions of the newly formed Dáil Éireann after adopting the Declaration of Independence in 1919 was to order the abolition of the 'odious, degrading and foreign workhouse system of poor relief.'

*The Workhouses of Ireland* begins in the eighteenth century and traces, through documentary material, the development of the workhouse system in the nineteenth century, its impact on the lives of the people, its phasing-out and eventual abolition in the more enlightened social awareness of the twentieth century. It embraces the period from the old Irish Parliament to the new Dáil Éireann – over two hundred fateful years – and it covers the whole thirty-two counties of Ireland. In this way the history of the workhouses – long deferred – will be recorded as an essential element of the social and economic history of Ireland and its people. It is hoped that it will also prove useful as a source book for future research workers, students, local historians and heritage studies, for the workhouse is undoubtedly part of Irish history. A historical outline of the poor laws is also given; and there is a chapter on the workhouses in England and Wales and the poor-houses in Scotland.

Perhaps I might add a word on how this book came to be written. As a boy growing up in Kerry, I had heard tales from the older people of the grim days of the workhouses and 'the sheds'. This was the seed of my interest in the

13

subject. Then when I started my working life in the National Library of Ireland I was encouraged to delve into the wealth of archival material on the workhouse and the closely related field of poor law. Later still, in the Department of Health, I was involved in the programme for the renovation and replacement of the County Homes (formerly workhouse buildings) and the provision of modern welfare homes. The book then has had a long gestation period but will, I hope, fulfill a need in the historical studies of Ireland.

My thanks are due to the staff of the National Library of Ireland for their helpful and courteous service in the course of my work. Thanks, too, to the staff of the Raheny Public Library, who were so obliging in facilitating my research. And of course, I am indebted to the works and documents of the many scholars and authorities listed in the Bibliograpy and References, which made my researches over the years so pleasurable and rewarding.

The Department of Health and Social Services in Northern Ireland was an essential link in my work on this project. It gives me great pleasure, therefore, to place on record the ready and friendly co-operation I received when seeking information on the workhouses in Northern Ireland. In this regard, Mr Brian W. Parker, Principal Information Officer of the Department, was most helpful, and I am particularly grateful to the Department and to Mr Cahal Dallat for permission to utilise information and illustrations from the Department's publication *Caring by Design: The Architectural Heritage of Health and Social Services in Northern Ireland, 1985,* which Mr Dallat wrote in his capacity as Chairman of the Federation for Ulster Studies.

Finally, I wish to acknowledge with gratitude and appreciation the expert advice, encouragement and assistance I received from Rena Dardis of Anvil Books.

Many of the illustrations are from the *Illustrated London News* of the years 1847 to 1850. Photography was then only in its infancy and history is indebted to this paper for sending artists to Ireland who travelled throughout the country to record for posterity, in graphic pictorial representations, the conditions of life in Ireland in those times.

Most of the prints reproduced are by courtesy of the National Library of Ireland and to the staff there and at the Irish Architectural Archive, my thanks for their knowledgeable help.

Séan Ó Suilleabháin, Leitrim County Librarian, kindly provided the excerpts from the Minute Books of the Carrick-on-Shannon and Mohill Unions.

John O'Connor
January 1995

# 1

# Breakdown of the
# Irish System of Care

*'Let a thoughtful care be had for the reception of the poor and strangers from afar; for in these do we most truly welcome Christ.'*

THE RULE OF ST BENEDICT

In pre-conquest Ireland there had been a very long and honourable tradition and custom of caring for the sick and poor. Under Brehon law there was an obligation on the ruler of every territory to provide *briugu*, 'hospitaller facilities for the sick and the homeless, and a welcome to every face'. There are many references to these 'hospitals', with 'four doors and a stream of water running through', which had beds for patients as well as having a physician in attendance.

One of the earliest hospitals on record was founded about BC300 at Eamhain Macha near Armagh by Princess Macha. It was known as *Broin Berg* or the 'house of sorrow' and formed part of the chief royal residence in Ulster until its destruction in AD332. It comprised a form of 'hospital' service which had been established there and elsewhere by the druids in pre-Christian Ireland, who practised a primitive type of surgery and healing.

The advent of Christianity in the late fourth and early fifth centuries and the subsequent establishment of monasteries led to the sick and destitute coming under the care of religious orders, a system that struggled to survive in the face of the wars of native Irish kings and the raids of the Norse invaders (which was the most destructive it is hard to say).

The Welsh historian Giraldus Cambrensis (Gerald of

Wales), who came to Ireland with King John in 1185, mentions the monastic settlement at Monaincha in County Tipperary (founded in the sixth century), which had two islands. On the greater was a 'church of the ancient religion', on the lesser a chapel served by Culdees (followers of Saint Columba): this was known as 'the island of the living' and he notes; 'People who are grievously afflicted with diseases, when all hopes of life are at an end, are put into a little boat and wafted over to the larger isle where, as soon as they land, they expire'.[1] Whatever about their latter end, there is a clear indication that the care of the sick was a tenet of monastic life.

Gradually, as the Norse became traders rather than pirates and despite the return to inter-tribal warfare which followed the death, in 1014, of Brian Boru (the only king who might have succeeded in making the kingship of all Ireland a reality) there was a flowering of cultural activity and the arts and an increase in the number of religious foundations, of which there were already some hundreds.

A reform of Irish church life and its structures took place from the end of the eleventh century and as a result Ireland became closely associated with advanced developments in monasticism taking place on the continent. In the summer of 1140 St Malachy of Armagh (1113–1148) visited the Cistercian monastery of Clairvaux in France on his way to

*Irish scribe*

Rome and this was the beginning of a close personal friendship with St Bernard. He left four of his companions there to be trained as Cistercians, among them Christian O Conarchy who was to become abbot of Mellifont, the first Irish Cistercian house, which was founded in 1142. It prospered and the Cistercians took root in Ireland. Seven further houses were added by 1153 and eight more by 1172, among them Bective (1147), Boyle (1161) and Holy Cross (1180).

Malachy also visited the regular canons at the abbey of Arrouaise in the diocese of Arras, who followed the rule of St Augustine with observances borrowed from the Cistercians. The progress of the Augustians in Ireland was even more rapid than that of the Cistercians, sixty-three monasteries being established before the Norman invasion of 1169. Some of them were new foundations, including that at Ferns (by Dermot MacMurrough in 1158); others, perhaps most, conversions of Gaelic foundations.

The Normans built monasteries as enthusiastically as they built castles. Among those they founded were Dunbrody (Harvé de Monte Marisco), Ardfert (Thomas Fitzmaurice), Kells in Meath (Hugh de Lacy), Athassel (William de Burgh), Youghal (Maurice FitzGerald), and Inistioge (Thomas FitzAnthony).

The Cistercians followed the Rule of St Benedict which laid down, among other things, that anyone arriving at a monastery was to receive shelter and care. The poor were to be given suitable food and drink and a third part of the clothing of the brethern – there was even a special instruction that the man in charge of the guest-house was to be very kind to the poor: 'Let a thoughtful care be had for the reception of the poor and strangers from afar; for in these do we must truly welcome Christ.' All Cistercian monasteries had infirmaries and many had houses for lepers. A medieval poem says of Holy Cross: 'Thou art the holy house for care of the sick; saved is every sick  man who enters thee; sorrow to all who frequent not that house

– the house which cares for all sufferers."

The rule of St Augustine, too, was increasingly adapted to the care of the old and the sick. One of the first proper hospitals, the priory and hospital of St John the Baptist at Thomas Street outside the New Gate in Dublin, was established by Ailred the Palmer some time before 1188, when Pope Clement III confirmed it. It was known as Palmer's Hospital, and was one of the fourteen priory-hospitals set up by the Augustinian Hospitallers, the *Fratres Cruciferi* (cross-bearing brothers) as they became known, a name derived from their practice of carrying a staff surmounted by a cross. Three of their houses had sisters as well as brethern and the title of 'sister', which continues to be used for nurses, came into use then.

The role of the monastery in caring for the sick and elderly is clearly set out by William Marshall, Strongbow's son-in-law, who founded St John's Abbey for the Augustinians in Kilkenny. The original record refers to it as 'the priory or hospital of St John the Evangelist', and the lands and benefits it received, including 'tithes of my mills, fisheries, orchards and dove-cotes', were 'to build a religious house, in honour of God and St John, for the support of the sick and indigent.'[2]

Herbs were well known to the monks of old and in her book on Holy Cross, Geraldine Carville identified the herb garden which was situated beside the infirmary. Here they grew foxglove, dandelions, penny royal, sow thistle, hyssop and monk's rhubarb, which were used as potions or ointments to treat skin diseases, heart conditions, jaundice, burns and chest complaints. Laurel leaves were boiled down and applied to numb pain.[3]

Bleeding, bonesetting and surgery were practised in the monastery infirmaries but a papal order of 1163 and a canon law of 1215 decreed that, henceforth, surgery was to be left to the *barbitonsores* – the lay brothers who carried out barbering and tonsoring of the monks. As a result the barber's craft was dignified with the title of profession, being conjoined with that of surgery. The Dublin Guild of Barber Surgeons was incorporated by Henry VI in 1446, nearly a hundred years before the London Guild.

That there was a general interest in medical matters is clear from the Irish-language manuscript section of Trinity College library, which includes several translations of medical texts dating from the early fifteenth century – one is a text on materia medica, compiled from the antidotaries and herbals of some European schools in France and Italy.

How effective monastic medicine was it is difficult to say. Herbal remedies were certainly successful in curing some diseases, and no doubt the *barbitonsores* had some competence in surgery (though at Holy Cross major cures were attributed to the relic which gave the abbey its name). But whatever about curing patients it is clear that the monasteries offered beds to the sick, as well as comfort and support. The monastic ruins of Ireland bear silent witness to centuries of hospital care, during a time often disparaged as one of the most backward periods of civilization.

*Dunbrody Abbey*

One must turn to Ireland's history in the fifteenth, sixteenth and seventeenth centuries to understand how such vast numbers of the population became pauperised and how the poor law became necessary to provide a system of relief.

Since the Norman invasion and the submission of the Cambro-Normans to Henry II in 1171, Ireland had been nominally the fief of the English Crown. But the conquest was in name only. When the Tudors came to the throne at the end of the fifteenth century, only a narrow thirty-mile strip stretching from Dublin to Dundalk and inland to Kells, Trim and Naas was under direct English rule. In the south, the great Norman families of the Geraldines and the Butlers, and in Connacht the de Burgoes held sway over vast territories, becoming over the centuries 'more Irish than the Irish themselves', adopting Irish dress, Irish customs, even the Irish language. In the north the ancient Irish clans of O'Neill and O'Donnell ruled a territory which was isolated and remote. Other Irish clans included the Maguires of Fermanagh, the O'Rourkes of Breffni, the MacCarthys in south Munster, the MacMahons, the O'Reillys, the O'Byrnes and the O'Tooles in the areas around the Pale. The relationship of both native Irish and Norman-descent lords with the Crown was an uneasy combination of surface loyalty and deep-rooted hostility. If forced, they made token submission, while still maintaining Gaelic structures and customs.

Then there occurred an event – the Reformation – which was to have far-reaching consequences and sweep away the old way of life for ever. The various monastic orders had become by this time feudal proprietors of substantial lands. These were seized on the suppression of the monasteries (which began in 1535) and given to rapacious royal favourites or sold at a nominal price to adventurers and soldiers of fortune, who drove out the hereditary subtenants, occupied their lands and combined their holdings into large tracts of land. With the dissolution of the monasteries the support system they provided came to an end, leaving the country with virtually no effective means or structures for providing for the sick and the poor over the next few centuries.

The loss of the monasteries was not the only consequence of the Reformation. The majority of Irish people remained loyal to the Catholic faith, as did the countries of Spain and France. England was now faced with the possibility of Ireland being used as a backdoor for foreign invasion, so the subjection of the entire country became the main aim of English policy in Ireland; the native Irish clans and the old Norman families had to be brought under control. Discontent with the new regime led to rebellions which were ruthlessly put down. Land seizure inevitably followed. After the collapse of the Geraldine rebellion (1563–1583) nearly a million acres in Munster were confiscated and the Plantation of Munster, which cleared the owners off their lands and planted English settlers, commenced in 1585.

In the north of Ireland, O'Neill and O'Donnell swore fealty to the Crown but, supported by the Spaniards, they rose in rebellion. A five-year war ended in final defeat at the battle of Kinsale in 1601. Unable to accept the conditions imposed by England, O'Neill and O'Donnell went into exile in 1607, the 'Flight of the Earls' that left Ulster defenceless. Nearly all the fertile land of six counties – Armagh, Cavan, Derry, Donegal, Fermanagh and Tyrone – was confiscated. The Plantation of Ulster, the most ambitious to date, dispossessed the native Irish in favour of 'thrifty' Lowland Scots.

Another rising, in 1641, led to the Cromwellian war, which ended in 1652. In August that year, the English Parliament passed an Act which professed to consider the whole of Ireland forfeited. There followed yet another plantation, the Cromwellian. The Irish who had taken part in the rising were transported abroad and their estates confiscated. Even those who hadn't, found themselves being dispossessed and moved to inferior land west of the Shannon. 'To Hell or to Connacht' was the grim joke.

All these various plantations and confiscations transferred the ownership of Irish land to English and Scottish
settlers who held it as loyal servants of the Crown. It was
part of the continuing but unavailing efforts of England to
complete the conquest of Ireland.

With the restoration of the Stuarts, especially James II
who was determined to restore the Catholic faith, Ireland
must have experienced a surge of hope. But James was
deposed and the bloodless revolution of 1688 brought his
son-in-law, William of Orange, to the English throne. In
the Williamite war that followed, the Irish supported James
and were defeated decisively at the battle of the Boyne in
1690. There followed the Penal Laws (1695–1829) which
effectively barred Catholics from regaining possession of
the land. The ancient system of land tenure was changed,
with profound and lasting effect, and the inheritance of
land in Ireland was made subject to English law. Among
other provisions, Catholics could not buy land and they
were forced to distribute any land they might have equally
among all their sons.

(As this is a book about workhouses, not land confisca-
tion, the preceding paragraphs give only a broad general
picture of the situation, ignoring the intricacies of land
tenure in Gaelic Ireland, the ways in which Catholics
sought to retain title to their lands, and the fact that
English settlers often had to sublet to the original Irish
tenants because of a shortage of 'thrifty' English and
Scottish prepared to risk life and limb in a foreign land
which, had they troubled to consult any authority, would
have been described to them as 'savage and barbarous'.)

The statistics relating to land ownership in Ireland are
startling. In 1643 Catholics owned 59% of all Irish land.
By 1703 this had dropped to 14% and even that was to be
halved by the middle of the century. Edmund Burke
summarised the changeover: 'The exploiting colonials had
devised a plan as well fitted for the oppression, impoverish-
ment and degradation of a people, and the debasement in

them of human nature itself, as ever proceeded from the perverted ingenuity of man.'[4]

In his *Tour of Ireland* (1776), Englishman Arthur Young noted that:

> On the whole, nineteen-twentieths of the Kingdom of Ireland changed hands from Catholic to Protestant. The lineal descendants of the great Irish families are now to be found all over Ireland in the lowest situation, working as cottiers. It must be apparent to every traveller through Ireland that the labouring poor are treated with harshness. A landlord can scarcely invent an order which a servant labourer or cottier dares to refuse to execute. Nothing satisfies but unlimited submission.[5]

The peasantry still worked the land; their lot had not changed noticeably. They were still at the bottom of the heap – and it must have seemed immaterial to them whether the land was owned by Irish clan, Norman overlord, Anglo-Irish earl, Cromwellian adventurer or plantation settler. But in some important aspects there had been a disastrous downturn in their condition. The collapse of the clan structure removed an age-old support system in which they had a place, lowly though that may have been. The suppression of the monasteries meant that the poor, the sick and the elderly had now no avenue of escape from the harsh reality of deprivation.

The result of the widespread confiscations, religious persecutions and social disturbances of those centuries left the country exhausted and desolate. The vast majority of the Irish people was now poverty-stricken, with no rights, no hope of help, justice or compassion, hewers of wood and drawers of water, virtual slaves in their own land.

# 2

# Origins of the
# Poor Law System

*'The authors of this law (the Poor Relief Act of 1601) seem to have been ashamed to state the grounds for it, for (contrary to traditional usage) the Act has no preamble whatever.'*

HISTORY OF THE PROTESTANT REFORMATION, W. COBBETT

Every generation looks at history afresh; its own prevailing concerns and attitudes tend to colour its understanding of past events. It is appropriate, therefore, in a book about the workhouses of Ireland to consider the evolution of the poor laws in England which led to the establishment of the workhouse system.

The Poor Relief Act of 1601 (43 Elizabeth I, 1558–1603) – 'An Acte for the Reliefe of the Poore' – is regarded as the foundation of the poor law system. But the practice of regulating the relief of the poor has a much older origin, being of common-law genesis. For the two preceding centuries parochial responsibility had been accepted as the basis, under common law, for regulating the relief of the poor 'so that no one should die from lack of sustenance'. The suppression of the monasteries and a breakdown in the medieval social structure of western Europe, which both destroyed the traditional framework of charity and produced new types of poverty, accelerated the process by which charity for the poor became a compulsory tax. This solicitude was not, as we shall see, entirely philanthropic.

An Act of 1564 (14 Elizabeth I) sought, by a measure designed for the local care of the aged and the destitute, to suppress 'the roaming beggar'. Justices of the Peace and parish officers were empowered to 'appoint meet and convenient places for the habitations and abidings' of these classes; those who refused to be lodged in 'the appointed and abiding places', or who left them to beg, were to be punished as vagabonds. This Act also deserves mention as recognising the principle of non-resident relief, though this was of a limited and restrictive character.

The importance of the Act of 1601, which was really the culmination of a series of enactments, was that it introduced the means by which relief would be granted. Under the Act parish overseers were directed to raise the money required according to the ability to pay of the inhabitants of the parish. This was the origin of the rating system. Originally the poor rate was in the nature of a local income tax; in time, however, the practice was followed of rating only real estate. Thus the poor-rate became a tax on property.

The main objectives of the Act were:

1. The establishment of parochial responsibility – church-wardens or overseers were to decide what was 'reasonable' in the way of relief.
2. The suppression of begging.

*Great Seal of Elizabeth I*

3. The provision of work as a means of assistance – the Act directed parochial authorities 'to raise weekly or otherwise by taxation, sums of money for a convenient stock of hemp, wool, thread, iron and other ware and stuff, to set the poor on work.'
4. The use of the House of Correction for 'those who refused or spoilt work or went abroad begging or lived idly.'
5. The setting to work and apprenticeship of children.

Thus in the reign of Elizabeth I, England officially recognised pauperism, laying down secular and legal obligations to aid the poor, which were to be financed by the new poor rate. Many amendments and alterations were made to the English system of poor laws subsequent to this Act but the principle was maintained of treating the poor as a thriftless section of society to be feared, strictly controlled, and, where necessary, punished.

Even at that time, the idea of a system of relief based on work was attractive to many landed proprietors and well-to-do farmers in the southern counties of England. Through a celebrated jurist, Sergeant Snigge, a friend of King James I who ascended the throne in 1604, they petitioned the Crown as follows:

Some of the more wealthy farmers in the parishes have devised a skilful mode by which all the trouble of executing this Act of 1601 might be avoided. This it is hoped will prevent persons in distress from wanting relief, and be the means of keeping down demands on parishes. We are apprehensive that the present Act will not warrant a prudential measure of this kind; but you are to learn that the rest of the freeholders of the county, and the adjoining county, will very readily join in instructing their members to propose an Act to enable the parish to contract with a person to lock up and work the poor; and to declare that if any person shall refuse to be so locked up and worked, he shall be entitled to no relief;

this, it is hoped, will prevent persons in distress from wanting relief and be the means of keeping down the poor rate.[1]

This view was endorsed in an essay by Jacob Vanderlint, published in London in 1734:

To this end and for extirpating idleness, debauchery and excess, promoting a spirit of industry, lowering the price of labour in our manufactures and easing the land of the heavy burden of poor rate, we suggest the device of shutting up such labourers as become dependent on public support – in a word, paupers – in 'an ideal workhouse', such ideal workhouse to be made a House of Terror and not an asylum for the poor. In this House of Terror, this 'ideal workhouse', the poor shall work fourteen hours in a day, allowing proper time for meals, in such manner that there shall remain twelve hours of neat labour.[2]

The Elizabethan recognition of pauperism evolved over the next century into a ground swell of support for a work-house system.

The Poor Relief Act of 1601 did not apply to Ireland where the masses of destitute poor were left unaided and had to subsist as best they could by charity – or die. The prevailing official attitude was one of unconcern; the solution – to get them to move on somewhere else. According to Benn's *History of Belfast*, Black George McCartney proposed at the court of the Assembly of the Borough of Belfast in 1675 that 'all the inmates and beggars, who come into and secretly convey themselves into ye towne, may be diligently sought after and speedy course taken to discharge the towne of such.'

# 3

# Relief Measures in Ireland in the Eighteenth Century

*'The poor, being restrained by Law from exercising many of its Rights of State of Nature for the support of Life itself, should be provided by Law with a subsistence in Time of Distress.'*

PROPOSAL FOR COUNTY POOR-HOUSES (1768)

The socio-political writings relating to the past state of Ireland bear ample witness to the extreme poverty of the mass of the population during the century before the introduction of the workhouses. Writing in 1727, Dean Swift observed:

Whoever travels this country and observes the face of nature, or the faces and habits and dwellings of the natives, will hardly think himself in a land where law, religion or common humanity is expressed. The miserable dress and diet and dwelling of the people, the general desolation of most parts of the kingdom; the families living in filth and nastiness upon buttermilk and potatoes, without a single shoe or stocking to their feet, or a house so convenient as an English hog-sty to receive them . . . [1]

Population figures for medieval Ireland are difficult to establish but it is estimated that by the year 1700 the population was over two million. Growth accelerated rapidly during the 1700s, reaching an estimated three million by 1720. It continued to rise, compounding the widespread poverty then existing. Charitable organisations did what they could but they were too few and badly organised to cope with the enormous problem. Public provision for the relief of the poor and destitute sick became an urgent necessity. There must have been debates and discussions on the matter because we find Dublin Corporation passing a resolution in 1688 that a workhouse was 'intended to be built and begun near the citie'.

The first relevant enactment was that of the Irish Parliament in 1703, which provided for the erection of a 'House of Industry' in the city of Dublin 'for the employing and maintaining the poor thereof'. The preamble fills in the background:

> The necessities, number, and the continual increase of the poor within the city of Dublin and liberties thereto adjoining are very great and exceeding burdensome for want of workhouses to set them to work and a sufficient authority to compel them thereto; and whereas the Lord Mayor, sheriffs, commons, and citizens of Dublin, for the encouragement of so charitable and necessary a work, are willing not only to appropriate a piece of ground for a workhouse within the city, but also to endow the same with lands of inheritance to the value of £100 per annum.

And so, in due course, a workhouse was erected 'on the ground walled at the south-west of James's Street and a parcel of land adjoining thereto called the Pipes, containing about fourteen acres, on which are built several small houses called George's Folly.'[2]

The administration of the workhouse was in the hands of a new body which had been established within the county and city of Dublin, with the title 'The Governor and Guardians of the Poor'. It consisted of the chief governor (or Lord Lieutenant), the Lord Mayor, the Lord Chancellor, the Protestant Archbishop of Dublin, the sheriffs, the Justices of Peace, the members of the corporation and many others named, who were to have a perpetual succession as a corporate body. They were to assemble on the first Thursday in every month 'to examine, search and see what poor persons are coming into, inhabiting or residing within the said city and liberties or any part thereof, and to apprehend any idle vagrants and beggars and to cause them to be set and kept at work in the said workhouse for any time not exceeding seven years.'[3] It also came within their terms of reference to inflict 'reasonable punishment or correction' from time to time on all persons within the workhouse who did not conform to the established regulations.

The main classes provided for were 'sturdy beggars', 'disorderly women', the old and infirm, and orphan children. In his *Brief History* Wodsworth records the details. The accommodation for the inmates consisted of 'vaults and other convenient places' under the hall of the workhouse. These vaults or cellars were specified as having been 240 feet long by 17 feet wide and they had a double row of beds, 'two-tier' high, to admit of sleeping a hundred men and sixty women; presumably those who didn't work spent the day there as well. The diet consisted of gruel, bread, milk, porridge and 'burgoo' (oatmeal stirred in cold water and seasoned with salt and pepper).[4]

The law required the vagrants and sturdy beggers 'to be employed' and to work 'voluntarily'. When there was no work or employment to be had for them, or if the 'voluntary' effort lagged, they were liable to be flogged, imprisoned, receive 'severe usage' and be treated with 'proportionate vigour'. If they died their bodies were buried without coffins (though round about 1731 it was ordered that they be allowed that luxury). If they proved seriously recalcitrant, they were liable to be transported beyond the seas 'without trial or traverse'.

One of the provisions of the 1703 Act allowed the Governors 'to detail and keep in the service of the said corporation until the age of sixteen any poor child or children found or taken up within the said city or liberties above five years of age, and to apprentice out such children to any honest person (ie. Protestants); a male child until the age of twenty-four and a female child until the age of twenty-one'. Homeless children up to five years of age were regarded as the responsibility of the parish church authorities.

The task of providing for the care and maintenance of abandoned children became so great a burden on the resources of the parish authorities that the Irish Parliament passed an Act in 1730 obliging the governors of the workhouse to receive from the churchwardens of the parishes of Dublin all foundling children then in their care and coming into their hands in the future. A part of the workhouse was accordingly reserved as a Foundling Hospital and the workhouse became the Foundling Hospital and Workhouse of the City of Dublin.

As well as admitting orphaned and deserted children in the normal way, there was, at one of the gates, a basket fixed to a revolving door.[5] Those who wished to abandon a child anonymously placed it in the basket, rang a bell and departed, leaving the child to be collected by the porter. The churchwardens also engaged 'lifters', who made nightly rounds of the city and 'lifted' any abandoned infants and children found lying in public places. They were either removed to the Foundling Hospital or given 'the bottle', which consisted of a dose of narcotic and had the twin effect of preventing crying and putting the children out of their misery.

(It must be remembered that what seem to us now to be savage practices were widespread in eighteenth-century Europe. Jean Jacques Rousseau, the philosopher, famous among other things for *The Social Contract* (1762) and the phrase 'Man is born free, and everywhere he is in chains', had apparently no compunction about consigning his five children to foundling institutions.)

The Act of 1703 is important as being the first in which

direct provision was made for the relief of poverty in
Ireland. It was, however, limited in scope and only applied
to Dublin. But it recognised the principle of taxing the
public by a form of poor rate for the prevention of
vagrancy and begging and the relief of the destitute. In
1728 the governing body was reconstituted and its powers
extended to include children of all ages.

In 1735, following a petition to the Irish Parliament by
Cork Corporation, an Act was passed for 'erecting a workhouse in the city of Cork for employing and maintaining
the poor, punishing vagabonds and providing for and
educating foundling children.' In its main provisions the
Cork Act was similar to the one passed for Dublin. A
board of governors was created to administer the
workhouse and it was supported by the revenue of one
shilling on every ton of coal and culm (anthracite) import-
ed into Cork. The governors met for the first time in  May
1736; they selected a site on Watercourse Road in January
1737 and the workhouse eventually opened in April 1747.
While it was originally intended to be used as a combined
workhouse and foundling hospital, in practice it was used
entirely as a foundling hospital and no part of it was set
aside as a workhouse.

The setting up of a voluntary organisation, the Belfast
Charitable Society in 1752, marked the beginning of services for the poor of Belfast. The Society arranged for the
building of a poor-house and infirmary, and though the
raising of the necessary funds by subscriptions and from
local people took much longer than had been expected the
poor-house was opened on 24 December 1774. It was not
elaborate but it provided accommodation for medical and
surgical cases in the infirmary, and some comfort for those
who, though not ill, were suffering from poverty and
destitution. Medical care was free, as the 'Gentlemen of
the Faculty of Physicians and Surgeons' had 'generously
resolved to attend such patients *gratis* and have been
pleased to undertake to make regulations with respect to

A

# SCHEME

For ESTABLISHING

## County Poor-Houfes,

IN THE

# KINGDOM

OF

# *IRELAND.*

Publifhed by Order of the DUBLIN SOCIETY,

D U B L I N :

Printed by S. POWELL and SON, Printers to
the SOCIETY, M DCC LXVI.

*Title page of the Dublin Society's Proposals*

the diet and treatment of such poor.'

In what must be recorded as a progressive and compassionate move the Royal Dublin Society published, in 1768, proposals for a comprehensive scheme for establishing county poor-houses in or near each county town in the 'Kingdom of Ireland', 'as no provision hath been hitherto made for the poor of country parishes. The poor, being restrained by Law from exercising many of its Rights of State of Nature for the support of life itself should be provided by Law with a subsistence in Time of Distress.'[6]

These enlightened proposals went unheeded as far as Parliament was concerned, though a few foundations known as alms-houses were privately provided in some locations in Ireland by charitably disposed rich people as a means of helping the poor.

Four years after the Royal Dublin Society proposals, the Irish Parliament, no doubt responding to pressure about what must have been an increasing problem, passed an Act for 'badging such poor as shall be found unable to support themselves by labour and otherwise providing for them and for restraining such as shall be found able to support themselves by labour or industry from begging.'

Under this Act of 1772 corporations were to be established throughout the country. They were empowered to accept subscriptions and donations and acquire land 'for the sites of houses to be built for the reception of the helpless poor and for keeping in restraint sturdy beggars and vagabonds.' As soon as they possessed sufficient funds they were required 'to build hospitals, to be called workhouses or houses of industry, for the relief of the poor, as plain, as durable, and at as moderate expense as may be.'

The control of the begging classes also came under their brief. They could grant badges to such of the helpless as had resided for one year in their respective counties, cities or towns, with a licence to beg within such limits for such time as might be thought fit. Every man above fifteen years of age found begging without a badge was to be committed to the stocks for a period not exceeding three hours for the first offence and six hours for every subseqeuent offence.

The double functions assigned to the Dublin workhouse of dealing both with vagrants and foundling children were deemed to be inconsistent and a rough scheme of class-ification of inmates was provided for in the Act. Grand Juries were required to present certain sums annually, and all rectors, vicars and incumbents were required to permit such clergymen as the respective corporations might appoint to preach sermons in their churches annually and to permit collections to be made for the objectives contemplated by the Act.

A further Act, passed in 1774, amended and extended the provisions of previous poor relief Acts but did not effect any real improvements. This was the last effort by the Irish Parliament to come to terms with the rampant poverty which existed.

It must be stated that the state of Ireland at that time was such that it by no means followed that because Acts were passed that their provisions would be implemented. In fact the enactments of the Irish Parliament dealing with the relief of the poor were only brought into operation to a very limited extent. There was neither the political will to enforce the provisions nor the availability of the necessary funds – the ratepayers were only liable for a portion and the contributions which were to have made up the shortfall never materialised in sufficient quantities.

To summarise progress in the eighteenth century: Houses of Industry (workhouses) were authorised by law, but were actually only provided to a very limited extent, in 1703 for Dublin and in 1735 for Cork. Only two other Acts dealing with the poor were passed and they can be dismissed as ineffectual. By combining two objectives of an opposite nature, punitive and ameliorative, neither was accomplished.[7] As Sir George Nicholls in his history of the poor laws observes, 'The training up and educating poor children as Protestants and the repression of vagabondism appear to be the objects chiefly sought to be attained.'[8]

The eighteenth century ended on an ominous note. In 1798 there was yet another rising and the French promised help to the Irish rebels. The appearance of a fleet in Bantry Bay concentrated the mind of the English authorities wonderfully. Ireland as a colony was a threat; the rising was savagely put down and the Irish Parliament was persuaded, by bribery and corruption, to vote itself out of office. Under the Act of Union of 1800 Ireland became part of Great Britain. Ireland was bereft of a parliamentary assembly to legislate, however inadequately, for the economic and social affairs of the country. And the general principle of non-interference by governments known as *laissez-faire*, then prevailing in Britain, meant that the misery of the Irish people would continue.

# 4

# English Legislation Leading to the Introduction of Workhouses

*'The lot of the able-bodied inmate (of the workhouse) should be less tolerable than that of the lowest labourer outside.'*

THE POOR RELIEF ACT OF 1834

Legislation relating to the relief of the poor in the eighteenth and nineteenth century led eventually to the establishment of a nation-wide system of workhouses in England and subsequently in Ireland.

The Act of 1772 (9 George III) was notable for the fact that it incorporated what became known as the 'workhouse test'. Under the Act, parishes, either singly or in combination, were empowered to provide houses and to contract with any persons 'for the lodging, keeping, maintaining and employing of poor persons and to take the benefit of their work, labour and services.' It added that 'no poor who refuse to be lodged and kept in such houses shall be entitled to parochial relief.' This, in essence, was the genesis of the workhouse system.

The Act of 1782 (22 George III) recognised the failure of the previous Act, both in curbing the increase in expenditure and relieving the condition and sufferings of the poor. Under this Act parishes could combine to form a 'union' and build a workhouse. It was stipulated that no persons should be sent to such workhouses except those who had become indigent by old age, sickness or infirmities and were unable to maintain themselves by their labour. However, as the able-bodied poor were the main problem, a requirement of the Act was that employment be found for them near their own homes and that landowners, larger farmers and employers be encouraged to provide such employment by a system of supplementary allowances to bring wages up to what was considered subsistence level. This was known as the Speedhamland system, after the place in Berkshire where it was first introduced. But the Act was unsatisfactory and difficult to operate.

A further Act was passed in 1796 (36 George III) repealing the earlier statute of 1782, which had restricted outdoor relief. This reversal of policy, which encouraged relief to able-bodied persons in their own homes, resulted in the cost of relief rising with frightful rapidity. This led to constant public agitation for measures to reduce both the growing numbers of paupers and the expenditure involved.

One of the keenest supporters of the workhouse test (as opposed to relief in the home) was Jeremy Bentham (1748–1832), the jurist, legal reformer and utilitarian philosopher, whose fame reached its peak in the closing decades of the eighteenth century. His philosophy is laid bare in the most startling way in his scheme for what he called 'pauper management', published in 1796. A huge National Charity company should be floated, he suggested, with as many small shareholders as possible, which would build in England a chain of 250 colossal workhouses to accommodate all the poor of the country (half a million to begin with, but rising to a million). These paupers would be housed and fed in as spartan a manner as possible and put to work. Thus not only would the problem of Britain's poverty be solved at a stroke, by a combination of nationalising and privatising the poor; the scheme would produce profitable dividends for thousands of shareholders. Bentham worked out his scheme to the tiniest loving detail, from the number of people to a room (hundreds) to the hours of sleep they would be allowed (minimal).[1]

Bentham's solution apparently fell on deaf ears. Expenditure kept on rising, whether as outdoor relief or in supplementing wages. Labourers preferred to receive allowances

# MANAGEMENT OF THE POOR:

O R,

# *A   P L A N,*

CONTAINING THE

PRINCIPLE AND CONSTRUCTION OF AN ESTABLISHMENT,
IN WHICH PERSONS OF ANY DESCRIPTION ARE
TO BE KEPT UNDER *INSPECTION.*

AND IN PARTICULAR

| | |
|---|---|
| PENITENTIARY-HOUSES, | POOR-HOUSES, |
| PRISONS, | MANUFACTORIES, |
| HOUSES OF INDUSTRY, | MAD-HOUSES, |
| WORK-HOUSES, | HOSPITALS, |

AND  SCHOOLS.

*WITH A PLAN OF MANAGEMENT.*

IN A SERIES OF LETTERS.

BY  J E R E M Y   B E N T H A M,
OF *LINCOLN'S-INN*, ESQ.

ILLUSTRATED WITH COPPER-PLATES.

D U B L I N:
J A M E S   M O O R E.
1796.

*Title page of Bentham's 'pauper management'*

# P R E F A C E.

*M*O *R A L S reformed—health preserved—industry invigorated—instruction diffused—public burthens lightened—Economy seated as it were upon a rock—the Gordian knot of the Poor-Laws not cut but untied—all by a simple idea.* —————————Thus much I ventured to fay on laying down the pen—and thus much I should perhaps have faid on taking it up, if at that early period I had feen the whole of the way before me.—A new mode of obtaining power, of mind over mind, in a quantity hitherto without example: and that, to a degree equally without example, fecured by whoever choofes to have it fo, againft abufe.--Such is the engine: fuch the work that may·be done with it.—How far the expectations thus held out have been fulfilled, the Reader will decide.

The Letters which compofe the body of this tract, were written at Crecheff in Ruffia, and from thence fent to England in the year 1787. The attention of the public in Ireland having been drawn to one

*Preface to Bentham's tract*

from 'the parish', while farmers used the poor law allowance as a supplement to the wages of their workers. In many parts of the country, all agricultural labourers and some tradesmen were paid wholly or in part out of the poor rate. Lord Castlereagh, then Leader of the House of Commons, stated in 1817 that 'in cases where nineteen shillings or twenty shillings in the pound is paid in poor rates, fifteen shillings will be found to be wages paid.'

Under mounting public pressure the British Government appointed a Royal Commission in 1832 to enquire into the practical application of the laws for the relief of the poor in England and Wales, and into the manner in which those laws were administered. Ireland, which at this period had become one of the most densely populated countries in Europe (the 1820 figure was about six and a half million), with hundreds of thousands of people without means of support for themselves and their dependents, was excluded from the Commission's enquiry; this in spite of the fact that the English Poor Relief Acts of 1772, 1782 and 1796, inadequate though they were, did not apply to Ireland.

Sir Edwin Chadwick, a disciple of Bentham and employed by him as his assistant, became a member of the Royal Commission on the poor laws and, in conjunction with Nassau W. Senior, he was responsible for drafting the Commission's report which led to new poor laws. These were to be the foundation of the workhouse system.

The Commission reported in 1834. On the evidence presented it found that the most pressing problem in England and Wales was that connected with the relief of the able-bodied. It appeared to the Commission that the provision of outdoor relief to this class (which had hitherto, through misinterpretation and maladministration, been given in an unchecked manner) should come to an end and that the remedy was to accommodate them in well-managed workhouses. As a secondary consideration other classes – the aged, the infirm, and children – were also to be catered for in the workhouse. As regards 'the dreaded evil of congregating large bodies of sturdy beggars together in  workhouse', the Commission was of the opinion that this might be avoided by better management and super-intendence of the workhouse: 'Each class might thus receive appropriate treatment; the old might enjoy their indulgence without torment from the boisterous; the children be educated; and the able-bodied subjected to such courses of labour and discipline as would repel the indolent and vicious.'

Concern for the needy was tempered with fear that the sturdy beggar might share in the welfare windfall. So, to claim relief, the able-bodied were to be subjected to stringent conditions that would separate the deserving poor from their undeserving brethren.

The report also recommended, in accordance with its terms of reference, a tightly organised system for the relief of the poor, based on a network of Unions administered by elected district authorities, styled Boards of Guardians, under the direction and central control of three Com-missioners appointed by the Government.

An Act, based on the report, entitled 'An Act for the Amendment and Better Administration of the Laws re-lating to the Poor in England and Wales', was passed on 14 August 1834. This was a composite Act, firmly based on the workhouse principle, and it effectively put under the direction and central control of the three Commissioners the administration of the existing laws for the relief of the poor, from the 1601 Act down to and including the 1834 Act itself.

The main principles may be summarised as follows:

1. Workhouses were to be established 'for relieving and setting to work therein such destitute poor persons as by reason of Old Age, Infirmity, or Defect may be unable to support themselves, and destitute Child-

ren, and such other Persons as shall be deemed destitute Poor and unable to support themselves by their own Industry or by other Lawful Means.'

2. Relief would only be offered in the workhouse.
3. The able-bodied person seeking relief would be compelled to earn it in a workhouse where his condition 'should be less tolerable than that of the lowest labourer outside.' (Presumably, though not specified, this condition applied to all workhouse inmates.)

The Commissioners suggested classification, pointing to the impropriety of herding all classes of indoor persons under one roof, and recommended a greater utilisation of charitable effort. However, in the implementation of the workhouse system no practical classification of the different classes of inmates was operated, so the workhouses became general mixed institutions.

*Attack on an English workhouse*

Thus, in 1834, a centralised system of poor relief was provided in England and Wales but in a harsh and inflexible form. Relief was to be determined by destitution and provided only within a workhouse.

The poor law relief system that was to be applied in Ireland derived from that of England, so only a passing reference is necessary to Europe. Institutions for the relief of indigence had long been a feature in countries such as Holland, Belgium, France and Germany. These consisted of hospices for the aged and infirm, regional workhouses, charitable institutions, and depots known as 'poor colonies'. The continental countries also had a classification system under which the various classes were housed in appropriate institutions. This differed from the English system of the general mixed workhouse. A more radical and beneficial difference was that the 'workhouse test', which was an essential feature of the English poor law system, did not apply on the continent.

In America in the nineteenth century, Government-supported institutions took in those who had no money or had lost everything – job, land, home, hope – and who would have faced starvation without help. They became known as poor-houses. But a high price was exacted for such shelters – the breaking up of families. Basic accommodation was for adults only, though husbands and wives were separated; children were taken away and placed in orphanages. Little wonder that poor families rejected a move to the poor-houses, except as a last resort when their spirits as well as their bodies were weakened beyond endurance. Eventually the Government took the initiative – a giant step forward in social progress – of providing the poor with a maintenance allowance instead of committing them to a custodial institution. The poor-houses were remodelled to become county homes and used to house those who required temporary accommodation.

# 5

# Developments Leading to
# the Irish Poor Laws

*'It thus appears that the workhouse system in England is used as a means, not so much of setting the able-bodied directly to work as of putting them upon their own resources. The difficulty in Ireland is not to make the able-bodied look for employment, but to find it profitably for the many who seek it.'*

REPORT OF THE ROYAL COMMISSION, 1836

In the century between 1720 and 1820 the Irish population more than doubled. In 1720 it was only three million; by 1820 the figure was six and a half million. In the towns, where employment was virtually non-existent, the only resource of the poor was begging. In the country the answer was land, rented or hired from an often absentee landlord, at rents that were higher than in England. The Irish labourer and cottier (small tenant farmer) relied on growing enough potatoes to feed their families and leave a small surplus to be sold. It was a hand to mouth existence.

At the end of the eighteenth century poverty was widespread. It is estimated that over two million people were at near starvation level, and it is on record that destitution was widespread in the country for about thirty out of the fifty-two weeks of the year. There was no legal provision for the poor, the aged and infirm; they could only rely on charity.

The question of relief for the poor of Ireland was therefore a pressing problem that could no longer be ignored by the British Government. However, no practical relief measures were introduced. Instead the Government appointed a Select Committee of the House of Commons in 1804 to make inquiry 'respecting the poor in Ireland'. The Committee considered that 'the adoption of a general system of provision for the poor in Ireland by way of parish rate as in England, or in any similar manner, would be highly injurious to the country and would not produce any real or permanent advantage, even to the lower class of people who must be the objects of such support.'[1] It also felt that the very important matters referred to them required more deliberation than the period of the 1804 session permitted, and they decided that the further investigation of the problem be adjourned and renewed the following session.

This was not done and no recommendations were made by the Committee 'respecting the poor in Ireland'.

The Government continued to be extraordinarily dilatory in taking measures to devise an effective scheme of poor relief for Ireland. As an excuse for action, they proceeded to convene committees of inquiry whose reports and recommendations for relieving the destitution and poverty were not acted upon. Further Select Committees of the House of Commons were appointed in 1819, 1823 and 1830, none of which produced any practical results. In all, 114 Royal Commissions and sixty-one Special Committees of Enquiry were set up and reported on conditions in Ireland in the period 1800–1840.

The 1819 Committee was appointed to inquire into the state of disease, and also into the condition of the labouring poor in Ireland. The Committee considered that the prevalence of fever in Ireland was a calamitous indication of general distress and in order 'to prevent the migration through the country of numerous bodies of mendicant poor who, pressed by want and seeking relief, have fatally contributed to the general diffusion of disease', they made certain recommendations as to the punishment of persons found begging or wandering as vagabonds.

As regards the second head of their inquiry, the condition of the labouring poor, the Committee found themselves 'in a great measure controlled by the unquestionable principle that legislative interference in the operations of human industry is as much as possible to be avoided.' However they did direct their attention specifically to agriculture, reading in the process the report of the Commission on the Bogs of Ireland and the Irish Bogs Act of 1809. These, they considered, 'prove the immense amount of land easily reclaimable and convertible to the production of grain, almost without limit, for exportation.'[2]

Their report was presumably pigeon-holed but, nothing daunted, another Committee set out, in 1823, 'to inquire into the condition of the labouring poor in Ireland, with a view to facilitate the application of funds of private individuals and associations for their employment in useful and productive labour.' That Committee recommended the encouragement of fisheries, the erection of piers, the formation of harbours, the opening of mountain roads and the instruction of the peasantry in agriculture. Government aid in support of local effort was felt to be absolutely necessary.[3]

All this sound advice apparently failed to produce any action, because in 1825 we find Daniel O'Connell giving the following first-hand account of the living conditions of the Irish people to the House of Lords Select Committee on the State of Ireland:

*What is the general state of the habitation of the lower classes?*

It is impossible. I express myself strongly; it would be extremely difficult to have anything worse. The homes are not even called houses; they are called cabins; they are built of mud and covered with thatch partly and partly with a surface called scraws. Any continuance of rain naturally comes in.

*The village of Mienies*

*What sort of furniture?*

Nothing that can deserve the name of furniture. It is a luxury to have a box to put anything into or anything of that kind; they generally have little beyond a cast iron pot, a milk tub they call a keeler, over which they put a wicker basket in order to throw the potatoes, water and all, into the basket so that the water should run into the keeler.

*With regard to their bedding, what does it consist of?*

Nothing but straw and very few blankets. In general without bedsteads. The entire family sleeps in the same compartment; they call it a room; there is some division between it and the part where the fire is. And yet I do believe and indeed I am convinced that that species of promiscuous lying amongst each other does not induce the immorality which one would expect from it.

*With respect of their food, of what does it consist?*

Except on the sea coast, of potatoes and water during the greater part of the year; potatoes and sour milk during another portion; they use salt with their potatoes when they have nothing but water.[4]

In 1830 yet another Committee was appointed by the House of Commons 'to take into consideration the state of the poorer classes in Ireland, and the best means of improving their condition.'

The Committee's elaborate and comprehensive reports were arranged under three principal headings:

1. The state and condition of the poorer classes;
2. The laws which affect the poor and the charitable institutions;
3. The remedial measures suggested.

Amongst the remedies recommended were: emigration, the improvement of bogs and waste lands, the embankment and drainage of marsh lands, the undertaking of public works on a large scale, the education of the people not only in elementary knowledge but in habits of industry, the encouragement of manufactures, the extension of fisheries, and also the introduction of a system of poor laws either on the English or Scottish principles, or so modified as to be adapted to the peculiar circumstances of Ireland. As regards a proposition for extending Houses of Industry or workhouses generally throughout the country, and for rendering their support compulsory, the Committee were of the opinion that 'establishments of this description, combining two distinct purposes of punishment and relief, are not likely to be useful either as prisons or hospitals.'[5]

Once again, the Government took no action, but concerned public opinion, both inside and outside Parliament, continued to press for measures to improve conditions in Ireland.

One of the remedies proposed by the 1830 Committee was already in operation. The growing population and the severity of distress in the country resulted in an outflow of destitute emigrants to Britain. By the 1830s it had reached deluge proportions – not surprisingly, as once they got themselves across the Irish sea they were assured of a modicum of food, clothing and shelter under the English poor law system. The arrival of such vast numbers was a serious problem for the Boards of Guardians in the larger cities and towns in Britain and there was a growing demand for the introduction of poor laws in Ireland. The objective was twofold: to stem the flow of emigrants, thus diminishing the competition with the native labourers; and to ensure that they might, when aged and unfit for work, be sent back to their parishes in Ireland which would be bound to maintain them.

Faced with mounting concern both in Ireland and England, the Government eventually appointed, on 25 September 1833, a Royal Commission to inquire (yet once again) 'into the conditions of the poorer classes in Ireland, and into the various institutions at present established by law for their relief; and also whether any and what further remedial measures appear to be requisite to ameliorate the condition of the Irish poor or any portion of them.'

The Commission, which consisted of ten members presided over by Dr R. Whately, Protestant Archbishop of Dublin, who was also a political economist, sat for three years, from 1833 to 1836, during which time they carried out a very detailed investigation into social conditions and attitudes throughout the entire country and their voluminous reports and appendices contain a vast amount of information of great social and historical value.[6]

While the Commissioners were labouring, horrified travellers were recording the far from passing scene. Alexis de Tocqueville summed up living conditions in 1836:

All the houses in line to my right and my left were made

of sun-dried mud and built with walls the height of a man. The roofs of these dwellings were made of thatch so old that the grass which covered it could be confused with the meadows on the neighbouring hills. In more than one place  I saw that the flimsy timbers supporting these fragile roofs had yielded to the effects of time, giving the whole thing the effect of a mole-hill on which a passer-by had trod. The houses mostly had neither windows nor chimneys; the daylight came in and the smoke came out by the door. If one could see into the houses, it was rare to notice more than bare walls, a ricketty stool and a small peat fire burning slowly and dimly between four flat stones.[7]

*Keillines*

Developments in England were to have a bearing on the situation in Ireland. There outdoor relief had been abolished and under the 1834 Act admission to the workhouse became mandatory for those claiming relief. However, the Commission, which presented its report in 1836, concluded that having regard to the extent of destitution and poverty prevalent in Ireland the English workhouse system, which had been devised to make the lazy and idle seek employment (which was available there) would be unsuitable as a remedy for the situation in Ireland, where the able-bodied and healthy were willing and anxious to work for any wages – even for two pence a day – but were unable to obtain any such employment.

The report draws the clear distinction between the two countries:

> It thus appears that the workhouse system in England is used as a means, not so much of setting the able-bodied directly to work as of putting them upon their own resources . . . The difficulty in Ireland is not to make the able-bodied look for employment, but to find it profitably for the many who seek it. Now if we thought that employment could be had, provided due efforts were made to procure it, the general repugnance to a workhouse would be a reason for recommending the mode of relief, for assistance could be afforded through it to the few that might from time to time fall into distress, and yet no temptation be offered to idleness or improvidence; but we see that the labouring class are eager for work; that work there is not for them, and that they are therefore, and not from any fault of their own, in permanent want. Our conviction is that the able-bodied in general and their families would endure any misery rather than make a workhouse their domicile. As their actual relief is required by the able-bodied in general in Ireland, the workhouse system if applied to them must prove illusory; and if it were established, we

are persuaded that it would be regarded by the bulk of the population as a stratagem for debarring them of that right of employment and support with which the law professed to invest them. We cannot therefore recommend the present workhouse system of England as at all suited to Ireland.[8]

The Commissioners, almost all of them thoroughly acquainted with the condition of the inhabitants of Ireland, then drew up their recommendations. The first report contained a variety of remedial measures for developing the resources of the country so as to make the able-bodied independent and to assist and subsidise those of that class, who might not be able to procure work, to emigrate. They qualified the latter suggestion by stating: 'We do not look to emigration as an object to be permanently pursued upon any extended scale, nor by any means as the main relief of the evils of Ireland, but we do look on it for the present as an auxiliary essential to a commencing course of amelioration.' The second report advised compulsory provision for a system of relief and maintenance for the destitute, sick, infirm, and others incapable of work; a tax was to be levied in each parish for this purpose and the proceeds administered by a voluntary committee. An interesting suggestion was that absentee landlords should be subject to a special tax.

While the Commission did not favour a workhouse system for Ireland, it recommended that for the purpose of carrying out their proposals Ireland should be divided into relief districts with a Board of Guardians for each district and a Poor Law Commission as in England, with Assistant Commissioners to supervise local boards.

Whately's Commission produced, not only a plan for poor relief, but a treatise on the economy of Ireland. It is interesting, after a lapse of a century and a half, to set out the general recommendations made by the Commissioners, and see to what extent events in the intervening years have justified their opinions and suggestions. They included:

1. Reclamation of waste land.
2. The enforcement of drainage and fencing of land.
3. Increasing the funds of the Board of Works.
4. Substitution of healthy houses for unhealthy cabins.
5. Bringing agricultural instruction home to the doors of the peasantry.
6. Enlargement of leasing and land tenure and powers to encourage land improvement.
7. The introduction of direct labour by local authorities for road works (in lieu of the contract system).
8. Authority to Board of Works to undertake useful public works.
9. The development of trade, manufactures, fisheries and mining.
10. The closing of public houses on Sundays and the prevention of the sale of groceries and intoxicating drink in the same house for consumption on the premises.

To implement these proposals it recommended the setting up of a Board of Improvement and Development.

The Commission's plan was not without its defects. It would, however, if well and honestly administered, have had the double advantage of relieving the poverty that actually existed and, by increasing the prosperity and productivity of the country, diminishing the amount of poverty. These blessings, however, were not in store for Ireland.

The Report did not win universal acceptance. Lord John Russell, then Secretary of State for the Home Department and Leader of the House of Commons, observed: 'It appears to me that they have bestowed too great a degree of consideration to the question by what means, by what State resources, you can improve the general welfare of the

# 6

# Proposals for Workhouses in Ireland

*'The standard of their (the Irish) mode of living is unhappily so low that the establishment of one still lower is difficult . . . '*

GEORGE NICHOLLS

The instructions given to Nicholls were precise and restricted. He was advised that 'your attention need not be very specially given to the plans for the general improvement of Ireland contained in the Report of the Irish Commission of Poor Inquiry 1833–1836.' Instead he was to examine how far it would be judicious or practical to offer relief to whole classes; to consider whether such relief might not have the effect of promoting bogus claims without eliminating begging; and whether the condition of the great bulk of the poorer classes in Ireland would be improved by such a measure. It was part of his brief to weigh carefully the important question as to whether a poor rate, limited in its amount rather than its application to particular classes, might be usefully directed to the erection and maintenance of workhouses for all those who sought relief as paupers. In this connection he was to inquire whether a kind of workhouse could be established 'which would not in point of food, clothing and warmth give its inmates a superior degree of comfort to the common lot of the independent labourer.'[1]

Nicholls wrote to Lord John Russell on 15 November 1836. He reported that having consulted with the Lord Lieutenant and having inspected the House of Industry and the Mendicity Institution in Dublin, he had proceeded

country, and have not confined themselves entirely t̠
destitute classes, which was more particularly put into
hands.' Accordingly, these enlightened long-term pr̠
als, though based on the evidence of residents and ̠
persons (including the Commissioners) with first-̠
knowledge of the country, were set aside by the Go̠
ment and only those dealing with poverty and destit̠
were considered.

As a preliminary step, Lord John Russell consider̠
desirable that 'a person well acquainted with the oper̠
of the past and present system of Poor Laws in En̠
should visit Ireland in order to arrive at a practical co̠
sion with respect of any measures to be introduced̠
Parliament in 1837 for the benefit of the poor in Irelar̠

His choice was Mr (subsequently Sir) George Nic̠
one of the English Poor Law Commissioners, who ac̠
ingly proceeded to Ireland in the first week of Septe̠
1836, taking with him the Report of the Royal C̠
mission and armed with the comforting letter of 22 A̠
from Lord John Russell: 'There is no one to whom ̠
entrust such a duty more able to perform it with ju̠
ment and diligence than yourself.'

It is doubtful if he knew exactly what awaited him.̠
world 'the man of judgement' was about to enter̠
described in graphic detail by a French traveller, Gu̠
de Beaumont, in 1839: 'In all countries paupers ma̠
discovered, but an entire nation of paupers is what ̠
was seen until it was shown in Ireland. To explair̠
social conditions of such a country, it would be̠
necessary to recount its miseries and its sufferings̠
history of the poor is the history of Ireland.'[9]

Nicholls could, however, take heart from another ol̠
vation of Beaumont's: 'Despite the widespread poverty̠
deprivation, in no part of the world can a stranger t̠
with more safety than in Ireland.'

to visit Carlow, Thurles, Cashel, Tipperary, Clonmel, Cork, Kilkenny, Galway, Connemara, Westport, Castlebar, Ballina, Sligo, Enniskillen, Armagh and Newry. Everywhere he had examined and inquired in the towns and districts through which he passed, as to the conditions and habits of the people and their character, endeavouring to ascertain whether, and how far, the system established in England under the Poor Law Amendment Act of 1834 would be applicable in Ireland.[2]

It is clear from the opening paragraphs of his report that he was predisposed to the introduction of the English workhouse system to Ireland. Though only in its infancy in England, it appears that it was regarded by the Government with general approval.

George Nicholls had never been in Ireland before. Nevertheless after a stay of some six weeks he produced the report which was to lead to the establishment of the workhouse in Ireland, the institution that was to affect so profoundly the lives of the Irish people.

The report was divided into three sections:

*Part one* outlined the general result of his inquiries into the condition of the country and the habits and feelings of the people.

*Part two* concerned the feasibility of establishing the workhouse system in Ireland, and how far it might be relied upon as a test of destitution and a measure of the relief to be afforded.

*Part three* summarised the administrative arrangements which would be required to frame enactments for establishing a system of poor laws in Ireland based on the English model.

The report is a document of some historical significance. In effect, Nicholls recommended that the proposals for the relief of the poor in Ireland contained in the report of 1833–1836 be set aside in favour of a scheme based on the English system. He ignored or failed to see that the real

objection to the introduction of the English workhouse
system was that the problems of poverty in Ireland were
entirely different in cause and extent, and that millions of
Irish poor who were only just above the low-water mark of
existence – poorly clothed, miserably underfed
and unhealthily housed – would receive no relief or
benefits from such a system. The widespread destitution in
Ireland required the development of the resources of the
country.

Nicholls admits in his report that he entered upon his
inquiry with the feeling that the workhouse system would
be found to be less efficient in Ireland than experience had
proved in England, and that it would probably be applicable to the able-bodied in a limited degree only, if at all.[3] It
seems that before his departure from London he had made
inquiries among workhouse masters and parish officers at
St Giles, Whitechapel, Stepney and Shadwell, in each of
which parishes great numbers of Irish then resided. They
all assured him that in their experience the Irish had a
dislike of the workhouse, even as a last resort, and did not
remain there if they could obtain any means of support
outside it.

However, as a result of his inquiries in Ireland, Nicholls
changed his mind. He concluded that there was no real
ground for apprehension as to the suitability of the workhouse system. He dismissed the possibility of resistance to
the discipline that it would be necessary to impose and
considered that it would be in the interests of the persons
who were admitted or who sought admission to the workhouse to protect the premises and not to destroy them, as
by such destruction they would deprive themselves of the
only aid provided for them by law. He concluded that it
was true that when congregated in large numbers, and
excited by whiskey, the Irish peasantry was prone to
outrage and insubordination, but he concluded that this
was not their invariable nor even their habitual character. 'I
speak,' he said, 'on the testimony of experienced witnesses

when I state that the Irish are easily governed, and easily led, and as in the workhouse they would be free from the influence of ardent spirits and other excitements, I anticipate no difficulty in establishing an efficient system of discipline and classification.'[4]

The governing principle of the workhouse system was that the relief given at public expense should be less than that which could be obtained by exertion outside it. The visionary ideal to which the planners aspired was that the inmates of a workhouse should in all respects be worse situated, worse clothed, worse lodged and worse fed than independent labourers of the district. While, in practice, such standards of perfection were not always easy to achieve, nevertheless the system was meant to ensure that the irksomeness of the labour (which had to be done by all inmates), the discipline, the confinement and the deprivation of the ordinary living standards of the independent outside labourer would produce such a horror of the workhouse that nothing short of absolute destitution and necessity would compel anyone to seek relief there, and ensure that they would quit it again as speedily as possible. The supporters of the system (including Nicholls himself and Russell) were convinced of the efficacy of the 'workhouse test'. It was a means of 'supplying needful relief to the destitute and of testing that destitution so as to detach and repel wilful idleness and thereby afford a new stimulant to exertion.' Outdoor relief was forbidden, so as 'to deter labourers from becoming confirmed paupers, ever after dependent on the parish for their support.'

But even Nicholls, dedicated though he was to the workhouse as a solution to Ireland's problems, was realistic enough to realise that there might be problems:

It would perhaps be in vain, even if it were desirable, to seek to make the lodging, the clothing, and the diet of the inmates of an Irish workhouse inferior to those of the Irish peasantry. The standard of their mode of living is unhappily so low that the establishment of one still lower is difficult and would I think, in the circumstances, be inexpedient. The Irish are naturally, or by habit, a migratory people fond of change, full of hope, eager for experiment. All the opinions which I have collected from persons most conversant with the Irish character confirm this statement. Confinement of any kind is most irksome to an Irishman.[5]

Nicholls recommended that the discipline, mode of employment and general management of the workhouses in Ireland should be as nearly as possible similar to the English model. The one innovation he proposed, no doubt having noted that Ireland was primarily an agricultural country, was the addition of a plot of land varying from six to twelve acres to each workhouse, where labour on the land could be carried out. Other activities to be undertaken included grinding corn in hand-mills and stone breaking. Carried away by a utopian vision of a grand administrative strategy for Ireland, Nicholls even envisaged the workhouse becoming a centre of local government and an 'important engine for effecting improvements in the conditions and habits of the Irish people.'

The British Government accepted the Nicholls' proposals for legislation on the same lines as the English Poor Law Amendment Act of 1834. This entailed, in direct contravention of the proposals of the Commission of 1833–1836, and against the emphatic opinion recorded by the Select Committee of the House of Commons in 1804, the setting up of a workhouse system in Ireland. The Irish Royal Commission had aimed at making Ireland prosperous by providing employment through the judicious development of its resources. Nicholls and the advocates of the workhouse system were, on the contrary, only concerned to relieve the most extreme destitution, and in the process detach the peasant from the soil to facilitate landlordism. The latter objective was clearly enunciated by

George C. Lewis, who was later to join George Nicholls as a Poor Law Commissioner for Ireland: 'The main purpose of a poor law for Ireland is, by offering to the poor man a sure prospect of a maintenance in case of absolute need, to loosen his hold upon the land and thus relieve the landlord from the incubus which now presses upon him and of restoring to the landlords the power of doing what they will with what they own.'[6]

The landlords were to be enabled to evict the tenants of subdivided small holdings by the provision of workhouses into which they could be received. As it turned out, the small tenants (which will not surprise anyone familiar with the Irishman's attachment to the land) did not turn themselves into workhouse day-labourers without a struggle.

The announcement that the Government proposed to submit a Bill to Parliament based on George Nicholls' recommendations led to public agitation and discussions that were remarkable, even in those days of great public excitement, for the ferocity and acrimony with which they were conducted. Groups representing different interests and influenced by different motives united in opposition to the proposals. The drawbacks of the workhouse system were sufficiently obvious; its merits difficult to discover. In spite of the carrot of the possibility of eviction, even landlords were alarmed at the threatened imposition of a poor rate and the enormous expense that would be involved, which they feared should swallow up a large portion of their incomes. But the views of both people and landlords were treated with complete indifference. Even the proposals and suggestions of men in public life, both clerical and lay, who favoured a modified poor law system without institutionalised workhouses, were ignored.

Despite all opposition, the Government went ahead with its legislative proposals. On the 13 February 1837, Lord John Russell introduced the Poor Law (Ireland) Bill in the

*Lord John Russell*

House of Commons as 'a measure of peace, enabling the
country to prohibit vagrancy, the county being overrun by
numbers both of marauders and medicants having no
proper means of subsistence. There is not a want of
industry among the people; it is that the country has been
allowed to be in such a state that industry cannot succeed
in it.'

George Nicholls was the draftsman of the Bill. With his
English experience in mind, he recommended that the
poor law measure, when sanctioned by the legislature,

should be put into operation with as little delay as possible, and that the plan should be implemented as a whole rather than piecemeal and experimentally, so as to avoid the danger of a build-up of hostile local opinion.[7]

The Irish in both Houses of Parliament were solidly opposed to the Bill. In the House of Commons there was a dramatic consensus of opinion between Daniel O'Connell and Lord Castlereagh (then Leader of the House) and their respective followers; and in the House of Lords the Irish peers voted in large numbers against it.

In the course of his speech Daniel O'Connell observed:

> What is now suggested is that a country unable to give employment to its labourers should be made to feed them in idleness within the walls of a poor-house. The workhouse system appears to work well in England, but we have seen upon evidence that the work imposed under the poor law upon the idle population is only a kind of slave labour in order to drive them to seek employment. But see how the principle would act in Ireland. The labouring classes there are anxious to procure employment; they never refused it; they in fact work for twopence or threepence a day rather than be idle. There is no necessity, therefore, for poor-houses in Ireland in order to stimulate its labouring population to look for work; but there will be that necessity once they become the only disposers of Irish charity and turn the sources of Irish benevolence into the public channel.[8]

Other Irish MPs urged that the Bill should be accompanied by measures for the improvement of the country.

Owing to the death of King William IV (in June 1837) the Bill was temporarily suspended. In the interval the British Government considered it desirable that Nicholls should visit Ireland again to report on the applicability of the proposed Bill to the northern counties (on his previous visit he had only been to Enniskillen, Armagh and

Newry).[9] His report, dated 3 November 1837, stated:

> I have now visited most of the northern counties, and
> carefully examined the condition and habits of the
> people with special reference to the contemplated
> measure, and I can, with entire confidence, state it as my
> opinion, not only that a poor law is necessary for the
> north of Ireland, but that the provisions of the Bill are
> even more adapted to the circumstances existing there,
> than those that prevail in the south.[10]

The Bill was reintroduced on 1 December 1837, again by
Lord John Russell, and evoked an immediate response;
eighty-six petitions with 31,221 signatures were presented
against it, and only four petitions with 593 signatures in
favour of it. In the House of Commons, Lord Castlereagh,
reaffirming his opposition to it, stated that at a meeting in
Belfast on the poor law question three cheers were given
for Daniel O'Connell. O'Connell rose and asked the
House to consider that, for the first time, Lord Castlereagh
and he fully concurred in their views, representing the
almost unanimous opinion of the people of Ireland. He
appealed to the English MPs not to force upon Ireland a
measure that the Irish people rejected.[11]

Thus on this historic occasion, north and south,
Protestant and Catholic were united in the common cause
of opposing the Bill. Notwithstanding it was passed with
234 votes for and 59 against – a majority of 175. The
House of Lords also approved it with a large majority,
though some Irish peers criticised its provisions.

Through the Bill was modelled in all its main provisions on
the English Poor Law Amendment Act 1834, there was
one notable omission – the absence of a legal or statutory
right for the Irish poor to be provided with relief, whereas
in England every destitute person had such a right.
Another difference was that in England ministers of
religion of every denomination were eligible to fill the

office of guardian, elected or *ex-officio*; in Ireland no clergy-man of any denomination could be a guardian, 'solely because of the present state of religious opinion in Ireland'. This proviso was intended to obviate religious controversy or sectarianism being introduced into the administration of the poor-law system and the operation of the workhouses.

# 7

# The Act of 1838

*'The Commissioners may, from time to time as they may see fit, build or cause to be built a Workhouse or Workhouses for any Union not having a Workhouse ... and provide any Utensils, Instruments, or Machinery for setting the Poor to work therein.'*

FROM SECTION 35 OF THE ACT OF 1838.

The Act 'for the more effectual Relief of the Destitute Poor in Ireland' passed into law on 31 July 1838.[1] The main ingredients of the mix were:

1.  The establishment of a central authority as a semi-permanent department of state – the Poor Law Commission. It was to consist of the Poor Law Commissioners for England and Wales, who were empowered to appoint Assistant Commissioners to implement the Act in Ireland.
2.  The division of the country into Unions composed of electoral divisions, which in turn were made up of townlands.
3.  The formation of a Board of Guardians for each Union, consisting of two-thirds elected and one-third *ex-officio* members.
4.  The establishment of workhouses in every Union.
5.  The levying of a poor rate to support the system.
6.  The provision of assistance for people wishing to emigrate, such assistance to be limited to the proceeds of one shilling in the pound of the poor rate.

Under the Act the workhouse was to be the central feature of poor law relief, the sole means of providing shelter and food for those seeking it. It was intended both for 'such destitute poor persons as by reason of old age, infirmity or defect may be unable to support themselves', as well as those who 'were unable to support themselves by their own industry or by other lawful means', with the important proviso that no poor person, however destitute, had a statutory right to relief.

Preference was to be given to the aged, the infirm, the defective, and children; only after these had been provided for were the Guardians at liberty to assist other persons in need.

The Act permitted no outdoor relief, which seriously limited its capacity for dealing with the wholesale poverty prevailing in Ireland; all classes, the able-bodied as well as the infirm, the young and the old, male and female, were to be relieved in one manner and in one manner only – in the workhouse.

Whatever the good intentions of the drafters, the 1838 Act did not provide 'effectual relief' for the poor of Ireland. Its terms and conditions ensured that only the utterly destitute would seek admission – or indeed be admitted – to the workhouse. The vast majority were left to struggle on as best they could.

## The Poor Law Commissioners

The Poor Law Commissioners for England and Wales, with the Assistant Commissioners they appointed, were to implement the Act in Ireland. They were empowered to make general rules, constitute Unions and Boards of Guardians as a new form of local government in Ireland, determine the number of Guardians to be elected in the prescribed manner, join townlands to form Unions and cause to be erected in each Union a workhouse. The granting of relief was to be subject to their direction and control. They were, however, prohibited from interfering in individual cases.

Another duty of the Commissioners concerned religion. They were to make orders for the due performance of religious services in workhouses and appoint chaplains, one being of the then Established Church (Protestant), one a Protestant Dissenter, and one a Roman Catholic. No inmate was obliged to be present at any religious service contrary to his or her principles, and no child was to be educated in a creed different from that of his parents.

Though the first Poor Law Commission consisted of the English and Welsh Commissioners and their Irish appointees it was subsequently considered advisable to separate the two systems, so accordingly, under an Amending Act passed in July 1847, the administration of the Irish poor laws was placed under the control of an Irish Commission. Appointed under Royal Warrant, it consisted of a Chief Commissioner, the Chief Secretary and the Assistant Chief Secretary to the Lord Lieutenant of Ireland. An additional Commissioner was appointed in 1851 under the Medical Charities Act.

## The Unions

As the first step towards the introduction of the workhouse system, legal and administrative arrangements were made for selecting and uniting townlands to form 130 Unions throughout Ireland, and for the constitution of Boards of Guardians for each of these Unions.

The intention of the Commissioners was to form the Irish Unions on the same principle as in England, namely, by taking as a centre the chief market town in each part of the country and attaching it to the adjoining rural districts, naturally and by custom belonging to it, within as far as possible a radius of ten miles or thereabouts. In England the Unions were aggregates of parishes, whereas in Ireland the townland was designated as the unit of organisation.

The townland, which became the basic division of the countryside in the mid-seventeenth century, is peculiar to

Ireland (there is no English equivalent) and is generally regarded as corresponding to the old *seisreach* or plowland which was supposed to contain 120 Irish acres, exclusive of wood, moor and mountain, being the quantity of arable land capable of being turned up in the course of a year by a six-horse plough. The townland was adopted by the Commissioners in 1838 under the impression that the entire country consisted of such delineated areas. There was, however, a vast disparity in extent between certain townlands, and in some places there were either no townlands or their boundaries were unknown (in fact, the complete list was not written down definitively until the Census of Ireland in 1861). Consequently it became necessary to rush through Parliament, in March 1839, a short amending Act to remove this difficulty by providing that the Act 'shall be construed to extend and apply to every place in Ireland, whether known as a townland or not.'

The several townlands which constituted each Union having been decided upon they were grouped together to form electoral divisions, which elected a representative Board of Guardians drawn from each division, and were also the areas of collection to fund Union expenditure. The complete total of 130 Unions was declared by the end of 1840 and they were now ready to take over the operation of the workhouses as soon as they had been completed. The number of electoral divisions originally formed was 2,049 but after some years it was found that both Unions and electoral divisions covered areas which were too large for the convenient and effective administration of relief so the number was increased to 3,438 divisions and 163 Unions.

## Boards of Guardians

While the commissioners had the statutory function of seeing that workhouses were provided, the responsibility for their erection, maintenance and running devolved upon the Boards of Guardians of each Union. The number of Guardians to be elected was laid down by the Poor Law Commissioners. It was limited to between sixteen and twenty-four, depending on the size of the area to be administered. These elected Guardians, together with the stipulated one-third *ex-officio* members, gave each Union a board varying in number from twenty-one to thirty-two. Elections took place annually on 25 March. In the course of time, the Unions became centres of local administration for a variety of purposes unconnected with the relief of the poor.

Elections to the Boards of Guardians aroused both religious and political acrimony in many instances. Only ratepayers were eligible for election, thus effectively ruling out the majority of native Irish, who were at the time landless, being mostly tenants-at-will. Furthermore, the number of votes allowed to each ratepayer was made on the basis of the poor law valuation and ranged in a scale set out in Section 81 of the Act from one vote up to six votes for the big property owners. Justices of the Peace, who were in effect Government nominees, were *ex-officio* Guardians. These undemocratic and discriminatory practices for election to the boards, coupled with the disqualification of priests or ministers of religion, added to the general suspicion of and hostility to the workhouse system.

## The Workhouses

The statutory obligation for arranging for the provision of workhouses was covered in Section 35 of the Act:

> The Commissioners may, from time to time as they may see fit, build or cause to be built a Workhouse or Workhouses for any Union not having a Workhouse, or purchase or hire land of any tenure for the Purpose of buildings the same thereon, and may purchase or hire a Workhouse or Workhouses or any Building or Buildings

for the Purpose of being used as or converted into a Workhouse, and according to such Plan and in such manner as the Commissioners shall deem most proper, and may also purchase or hire any Land not exceeding Twelves Acres Imperial Measure, to be occupied with any such Workhouse, and may order and direct the Guardians of any Union to uphold and maintain any Workhouse and to furnish and fit up any Workhouse, and provide any Utensils, Instruments, or Machinery for setting the Poor to work therein.

## Cost of the Workhouses

As part of his report in 1836,[2] George Nicholls furnished an estimate of the cost of the workhouse system, with the qualification that 'there is no data on which such an estimate can be framed with any pretension to minute accuracy.' Working on a population figure of eight millions, he estimated that workhouse accommodation might be required for one per cent, ie, 80,000, which he proposed to house in one hundred workhouses, each capable of taking 800 inmates. (His one per cent was based on workhouse figures in the most highly pauperised counties in England.)

The cost of maintenance in the mendicity institutions which he had visited in Ireland varied from $1^1/_2$d to $2^1/_2$d per head per day, giving a weekly total of $10^1/_2$d to $17^1/_2$d. This funding was provided by Grand Jury and voluntary contributions, which Nicholls obviously thought might have erred on the generous side. With 'good economical management', he was confident of stabilising the figure at one shilling per head per week. Throwing in overheads, he came up with a total outlay of one shilling and sixpence per head weekly. From these assumptions he made the follow‑ing estimates of annual costs:

1. One hundred workhouses, each capable of holding 800 persons and fully occupied throughout the year, the total charge, in-

cluding maintenance, salaries, clothing,
wear and tear etc, would be . . . . . . . . . . . . £312,000

2.  If three-quarters full throughout the year, the
establishment and other charges continuing
the same, the total charge would be . . . . . . . .  £260,000

3.  If half occupied throughout the year, the
establishment and other charges contin-
uing the same, the total would be . . . . . . . £208,000

The estimate prepared during the progress of the Bill
through Parliament in 1838 and printed by order of the
House of Lords added the cost of staff:

Assuming that there will be a hundred Unions, each
with a workhouse capable of accommodating 800
persons, the paid officers, with their respective salaries in
each workhouse, may be stated as follows:

| | |
|---|---:|
| Clerk of the Union | £60–£80 |
| Master and Mistress of the Workhouse | £50–£80 |
| Chaplain | £50–£80 |
| Medical officer and medicines | £100–£150 |
| Auditor | £20–£30 |
| Returning Officer | £10–£20 |
| Collector | £50–£70 |
| Schoolmaster and Schoolmistress | £50–£80 |
| Porter and Assistant Porter | £20–£30 |
| Other assistants in the workhouse, say, | £30–£30 |
| | £450–£650 |

It may be further assumed that, on average throughout
the year, the workhouses will be three parts full and that
the total cost of maintenance, clothing, bedding, wear
and tear etc. will amount to 1s/6d per head per week
which is equal to £3.18 or, say, £4 per head per annum
– this will give an expenditure of £240,000 per annum
for running the hundred workhouses which, added to
the £55,000 for salaries, will make a total charge of

£295,000 annually for the relief of the destitute under the provisions of the Bill.

## The Poor Rate

As up to this time there had been no provision for the relief of the poor in Ireland there existed no recognised or legal procedure for such a purpose. Now there loomed on the horizon the prospect of a hundred workhouses, each requiring to be built, funded, managed and maintained. How would the money be raised and who would be liable to pay it?

The solution introduced by the Act of 1838 was the introduction of the poor rate. Section 35 authorised the guardians to 'assess, raise and levy such Sum or Sums of Money as the Commissioners from time to time shall direct, as a Poor Rate, or to borrow Money for such purposes under the Provisions of this Act and to charge the same, with interest, on the future Poor Rate of such Union.'

Realising that this ideal state of things was unlikely to happen overnight, and that in the interim the workhouses had to be built, the Commissioners promised: 'The money for the building of the workhouses is to be advanced by the Government, free of interest for ten years; and is to be repaid thereafter by annual instalments of five per cent.'

The poor rate was a new administrative and financial arrangement in Ireland. The only previous general valuation in the country was made under an Act of 1826 for the purposes of levying the Grand Jury cess (an old word for rate or tax), which was a charge levied on land or premises. The proceeds of the cess were applied towards the construction and repair of roads and to meet expenses in connection with courthouses, lunatic asylums, county infirmaries, and county fever hospitals. It was also used to make contributions to industrial and reformatory schools and for some other purposes -- but not specifically the relief of the poor or destitute.

As the 1826 Act valuation system did not meet the requirements of the 1838 Act, a new system had to be devised. Accordingly the Boards of Guardians were empowered to have surveys carried out for the valuation of lands and buildings in order to levy the new poor rate. In many instances the job was assigned to incompetent and dishonest people. As a result the valuations were often either above or below the standard value and were by no means uniform as between the various Unions. These discrepancies gave rise to widespread complaints, and dissatisfaction with the system was reinforced by the fact that there were now two different sets of valuations in operation in the country – one for county cess levied by the Grand Juries and the other for the poor rate levied by the Boards of Guardians. This anomaly was eventually brought to an end by the Valuation Act of 1852 which provided for one valuation to be used for all assessments and enabled the boards to proceed on a unified basis in assessing and levying the poor rate. This valuation became known as 'Griffith's Valuation' as it was carried out under the direction of Richard Griffith, then in charge of the Board of Works Relief Department.

# 8

# The Building of the Workhouses

*'The style of the building is intended to be of the cheapest description compatible with durability; and effect is aimed at by harmony of proportion and simplicity of arrangement, all mere decoration being studiously excluded.'*

REPORT OF THE POOR LAW COMMISSIONERS, 1839

George Nicholls returned to Ireland in September 1838 to set up the organisation for the implementation of the 1838 Act, under the general direction of the English Poor Law Commissioners. In this large-scale and challenging assignment he was assisted by four Assistant Commissioners. Having been legally advised that the building of the workhouses could not be assigned to the Office of Public Works or delegated to any other body, he and his Assistant Commissioners had to set up their own technical and administrative offices in Dublin. After extensive enquiries, in England as well as in Ireland, it was decided to engage an architect experienced in the construction of English workhouses, and to instruct him, in conjunction with the Assistant Commissioners, to draw up plans, prepare specifications and contract documents, and check estimates.

George Wilkinson, who had been practising in Oxford and who had worked for the Commissioners on workhouse projects in England, was the architect chosen and an excellent choice he proved to be. He agreed to take on the work of preparing the plans for a salary of £500 per annum, and asked for an assistant, 'an experienced person of active habits, familiar with drawing, and possessing a good practical knowledge of building,' whom he thought

*The Cork workhouse*

could be obtained for £150 per annum. He also wanted an
office clerk or draftsman at a salary of £100 per annum.
Thus the cost of the architect's office in Dublin was £750
per annum. When the building of the workhouses started,
a clerk of works would be added for each building, at a
salary of two guineas per week.

Hugh Dixon of the Historic Buildings Council of
Northern Ireland, referring to the architectural style of the
workhouse, describes Wilkinson thus:

A man of his period; and in the early Victorian era
architects chose styles for their association with the past.
As an Englishman he was choosing a style which he
particularly associated with alms-houses and local
charities – the sort of places which had been built in

Tudor and Jacobean periods in England. So we have got in workhouses, a building which has lots of gables and some decorative barge-boards on those gables in the main block in front. We have towers which look as though they have come from Hardwicke Hall or Longleat, which are presumably converted for water towers. We have windows with mullions and transomes in them, large stone cross pieces actually in the window and with diamond glazing in them, as though they are leaded lights. In actual fact they are made of cast iron but they are meant to look like leaded lights, as though they come from an original type.[1]

Wilkinson arrived in Ireland in January 1839 to begin his formidable job; it had been decided to establish 130 workhouses (nineteen in Connaught, thirty-six in Leinster, thirty-two in Munster, and forty-three in Ulster). He was not exactly given a free hand. The criteria laid down by the Commissioners decreed: 'The style of building is intended to be of the cheapest description compatible with durability; and effect is aimed at by harmony of proportion and simplicity of arrangement, all mere decoration being studiously excluded.'[2] It is hard to avoid hearing the echo of Mr Brocklehurst's admonition to the young ladies of Lowood about eschewing the frivolity of curls.

Wilkinson lost no time in preparing plans, carrying out necessary revisions with the aid of the best local information available and following consultations with the Office of Public Works. He had to inspect and report on the sites offered for workhouses, and a great many old buildings had to be seen – and rejected – before new buildings were approved. In all this work he had the benefit of his English experience but it is obvious he must have worked with great energy and zeal because he submitted his plans and specifications for approval in February 1839. By the time the Commissioners made their report, on 1 May 1839, standard plans had been prepared and approved for suitable types of workhouses, specifications prepared, and public advertisements and posters inviting tenders for contracts issued. (Standard contract at Appendix 1.)

The estimated costs having been approved and the contracts finalised, the Boards of Guardians proceeded with the building of the workhouses. Almost all were built to Wilkinson's standard plans and there were three types, depending on the size required – small ones for 200-300 inmates, medium-sized ones for between 400-600, and some very large ones for 1,000 or more; all were capable of expansion to accommodate a further 100-200 people.

The cost of each of the Irish workhouses was only two-thirds that of similar workhouses in England and Wales, the reduction being achieved by a rigid economy in their

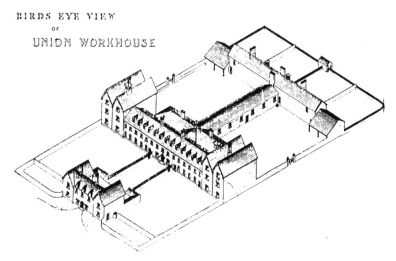

BIRDS EYE VIEW
OF
UNION WORKHOUSE

construction and fitting-up. The walls were of limestone masonry, the insides unplastered but heavily whitewashed. The floors at ground level were of mortar or clay, being as Wilkinson said in his report 'less cold than stone and less liable to decay than wooden floors'. In general, conditions in the workhouses were designed to be such that only dire necessity could drive a poor person to seek admission for himself or his family. Only the bare essentials were provided, with very few refinements; the atmosphere was one of penury.

The layouts of typical workhouse buildings are shown in the illustrations. There was a small entrance block, known as the workhouse administration unit, which housed the board-room and offices. Passing through this block one came to the main institution, usually a transverse three-storey building of stone. This block contained the workhouse master's office and several wards, usually for ambulant inmates. At the rere were the kitchens, wash-houses and store rooms.

The wards were large and commonly had unplastered walls, no ceilings other than bare rafters, and rough bare floors. A number had a central valley or depression which

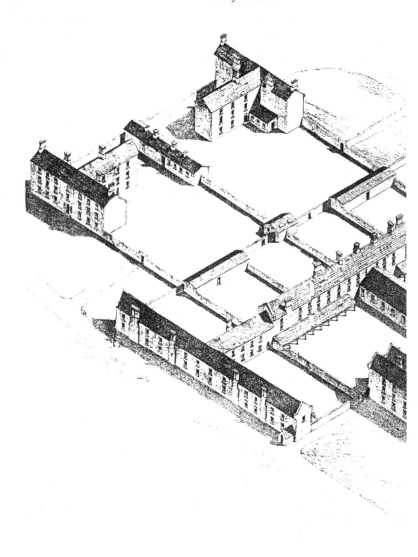

*Birds Eye View
of
Union Workhouse*

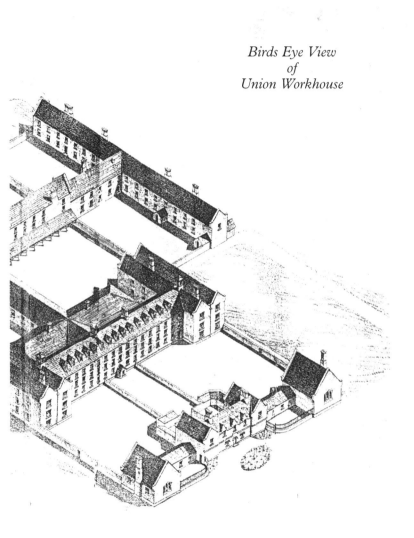

served as a gangway. The inmates slept, not on beds, but on straw mattresses spread on sleeping platforms on a raised portion of the floor on either side of the gangway; this arrangement meant a great saving in space.

The stairways were of stone, steep and narrow, and could hardly have been less suited to the needs of the old, the frail and the infirm for whom the buildings were for the most part designed. Windows were small, with diamond panes, and in general they were ineffective for the purposes of ventilation or light. Heating was usually by means of open turf fires, one to a large room or ward. Invariably they were incapable of supplying sufficient heat and quite often they smoked, thus adding to the prevailing gloom.

The low standards of comfort and amenities evident in the wards were even more striking in the day-rooms. The eating areas consisted of long wooden forms and bare, crudely constructed tables, all in a dark depressing setting.

Behind the main block, about a hundred feet away, there was a second somewhat similar transverse building which housed the infirmary and 'idiot' wards. Joining the two blocks and at right angles to both was a central nave section which usually contained the chapel and the hall. The latter was used for a variety of purposes including eating. Quite often the hall, being large, was cold and draughty. A plan for an altar, for Roman Catholic worship, was designed and distributed to the Unions, and such altars were in fact placed in nearly all the workhouses, usually in the hall.

The exercise and work yards between the blocks were generally bare and frequently used for the storage of fuel and other commodities. A privy, positioned near the cesspools, which were underground and vaulted over with large stones, was provided in each of the various yards. An unpleasant effluvium often arose and it was necessary to have the cesspools cleaned out in a proper manner; it was not considered good practice to employ the paupers of the house to do this.

The workhouses were usually well sited, but the grounds, though spacious, were not too carefully tended or well planted. They were bounded by high grey stone walls which conveyed a rather dismal prison-life impression. Wilkinson endeavoured to minimise this impact by the use of local stone, in the hope that the buildings would blend in with the background to create a not unpleasing architectural presence.

In order to qualify for relief the whole family had to enter the workhouse together (the only exception to this rule being orphans and deserted children who were admitted unaccompanied). On entry the families were classified and segregated, fathers and sons going into the male quarters, mothers and daughters into the female section; children over two years were separated from their parents and sent to the children's wards. One tragic aspect of this separation was that during the famine times, parents often did not know that their children had died, husbands their wives, mothers their sons, daughters their fathers.

The workhouse divisions were:

1. The admission or receiving wards
2. The male wards
3. The female wards
4. The school and children's wards
5. The infirmary
6. The idiot wards.

In addition, there was, on the female side, a nursery and maternity ward.

It is of interest to note that the one category of persons for which provision was not made at that time in Ireland was the unmarried mother. George Nicholls noted in his report:

As far as I had opportunities of observing and inquiring, the Irish females are generally correct in their conduct.

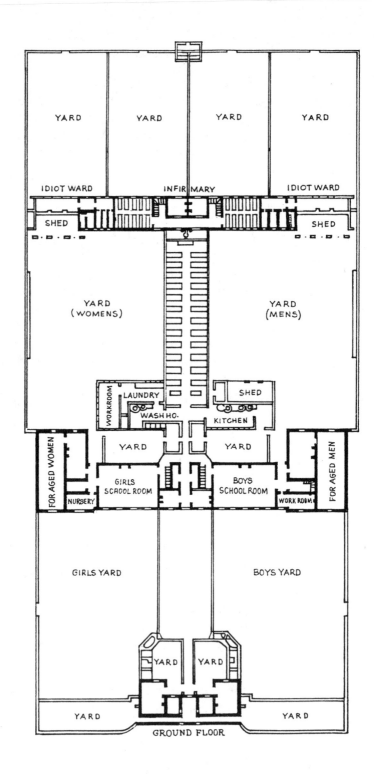

GROUND FLOOR

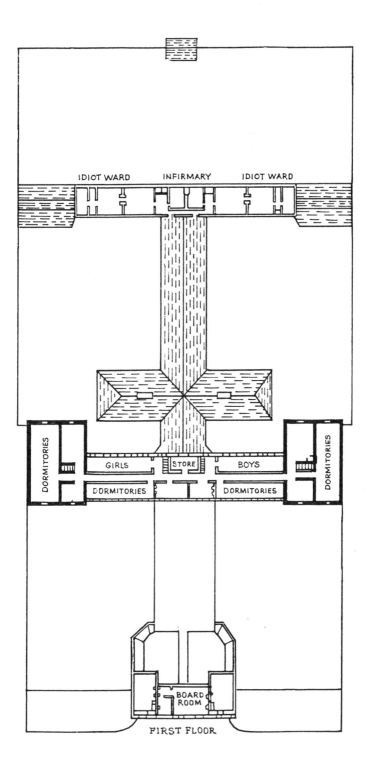

IDIOT WARD     INFIRMARY     IDIOT WARD

DORMITORIES

DORMITORIES

GIRLS     STORE     BOYS

DORMITORIES     DORMITORIES

BOARD ROOM

FIRST FLOOR

Our impressions of the moral conduct of the Irish females are highly favourable. Their duties appear to be much more laborious than those of the same class of females in England. Their dress, too, is very inferior, and so likewise seems their general position in society; yet they universally appear modest, industrious and sober. I state this as a result of my own observations, and I do so here because, if the Irish females have preserved their moral character untainted, under the very trying circumstances in which they are placed, it affords a powerful argument for 'letting well alone'. If it had been otherwise, however, and if the extent of bastardy, and its demoralising influence on public manners had been much greater, I should still have recommended that the Irish females should be left, as now, the guardians of their honour.[3]

In practice it was found that provision had to be made in the workhouse for women and their illegitimate children, as it became the custom for unmarried mothers to go into the workhouses to have their babies. Section 54 laid down that 'the mother of every bastard child shall be liable to maintain such bastard child until such child shall attain the age of fifteen years.' Nevertheless it can be concluded that despite degrading conditions the majority of Irish women at the time preserved their virtue.

It will be readily appreciated that the gathering together under one roof of so many different classes, of all ages and the most diverse character, was not conducive either to good management or the comfort and improvement of the inmates. Children, in particular, were a special problem.

Wilkinson reported, on 25 March 1840, that eighty-four workhouses were under construction and a further ten ready for tender. These were all new buildings except in north and south Dublin, Clonmel and Fermoy, where major reconstruction work was carried out to existing buildings. The good progress continued and by April 1843 Wilkinson was able to report that of the 130 workhouses decided upon, 112 were finished and eighteen others nearing completion.

The fitting out of the workhouses was also proceeding and on 2 May the Commissioners were able to state: 'Eighty-one of the workhouses have been declared fit for the reception of the destitute poor. By the end of the approaching summer we expect that at least a hundred of the workhouses will be completed and opened.'

It was not all plain sailing as can be gathered from the following inclusion in the report:

> The weather in Ireland has been extremely unfavourable for building operations during the past three years, there having been an unusual quantity of rain; and this prevalence of wet weather has necessarily impeded the progress of the buildings and greatly increased the difficulty of superintendence. Even with favourable seasons, it is by no means a light task to superintend and direct extensive buildings, proceeding simultaneously in every part of the country; but with such weather as that of the last three years and with not less than a hundred of these buildings in progress at one time, and all requiring frequent inspection and constant super-intendence, the difficulty has been proportionately increased ... The sites, although generally good, have not always been the most favourable for building; and the difficulties attending the transport of materials, and of finding suitable work people in some localities, have likewise in several instances served to impede the operations of the contractors.

Wilkinson's work did not involve only the buildings; he was called upon to arrange for the supply of fixtures, fittings and furnishing such as boilers, grates, stores, dressers, kitchen equipment, bedsteads, tables and seating forms.

Some idea of the extent of the operation can be gauged
from the fact that for most of the building programme a
hundred workhouses were being built simultaneously,
employing directly, at any one time, over 11,000 workmen
and over 10,000 horses and carts. It appears from
information supplied by the Poor Law Commissioners for
the Census of 1841 that the number of artificers and
labourers employed was as follows:[4]

| | |
|---|---:|
| Masons, bricklayers and paviors | 2,614 |
| Carpenters | 962 |
| Plumbers, painters, glaziers and smiths | 216 |
| Slaters and plasterers | 263 |
| Labourers | 6,759 |

Notwithstanding the vigour and dedication with which the
Commissioners and the architect tackled and accomplished their task, difficulties were bound to arise,
particularly having regard to the centralised standard
planning, the unprecedented number of major buildings to
be erected and the rapidity with which the projects proceeded. Boards of Guardians had little or no effective say
in regard to the planning and design of the workhouses,
and this led to a feeling of frustration among some of
them. Among the difficulties encountered by the architect
was the anomaly created by the Poor Law Act in making
the Commissioners responsible for the building operations,
but requiring the Boards of Guardians to provide the
money. Accordingly any Boards of Guardians with complaints in regard to the construction of their workhouses,
such as usually are associated with building operations,
were not slow in bringing these forcefully to the notice of
the Commissioners. Such complaints related mainly to the
choice of site, standard of workmanship, the amount of
extra costs, and the expenses incurred on decoration and
fittings.

The Government decided that these matters should be
properly investigated by an outside expert and appointed

James Pennethorne, a well-known English architect, for this purpose. Pennethorne came to Ireland in 1843 and carried out an independent investigation. He visited and inspected fifty-eight workhouses, although there were only complaints about twenty-four, and interviewed Boards of Guardians but did not consult with Nicholls or Wilkinson. He submitted a long report in which he detailed instances of careless workmanship and faulty design, resulting in the Boards of Guardians concerned being obliged to incur additional expenditure on remedial measures. Though he had also some critical comments to make, Pennethorne's main conclusion was that most of the defects and difficulties that had arisen might be traced to the mistaken economy of having only one architect to superintend and conduct the erection of the workhouses. George Nicholls reacted very strongly to these criticisms and in a series of detailed replies challenged Pennethorne's conclusions and pungently added: 'It is always easy to find fault and, after a thing has been done, to point out ways in which it might have been better done; but such after-wisdom is practically of little value.'

The satisfactory completion of the construction of the workhouses in Ireland was regarded as a matter of importance, so a select committee of the House of Commons decided that a further inquiry was necessary in view of the conflict of the expert opinions. The Treasury accordingly commissioned George Barney of the Royal Engineers to inquire into the execution of the contracts for certain workhouses in Ireland. After visiting and carefully examining each workhouse in Ireland, Barney reported, in 1845, that the results of his inquiries were that the probable extent of repairs attributable to defects on the original contracts amounted to £21,932, and that extra charges for fixtures and fittings amounted to £24,744, making a total of £46,676. The Treasury authorised on 21 February 1845 that the several Boards of Guardians concerned should be relieved of liability for this excess expenditure. (Barney's Report is at Appendix 2).

Although it means a slight leap forward in time, George Wilkinson's general report to the Commissioners in April 1847 is perhaps best included here as a summary of the first phase of the building operations:[5]

> I have the honour to submit the following general account of the building operations connected with the Union poor-houses in Ireland since the period of their completion up to the present. First, however, I will briefly exhibit the general result of the building operations with reference to the original buildings.
>
> All the 130 Union workhouses have been completed agreeably to the contract arrangements outset into with the respective parties employed to build them. Of the 130 workhouses, 125 of them have been new buildings and the five others have been old buildings repaired and enlarged. The total accommodation afforded in the workhouses as originally built may be estimated at 93,860 persons, divided into four principal classes of adults, children, infirmary patients, and idiots or lunatics not dangerous, each of these classes having distinct wards and yards attached, in addition to which are wards and yards for probationary paupers of each sex.
>
> The total cost of the building sites, buildings, and fixtures, including bedsteads, tables etc, clerk of works, and law expenses for title and conveyances of land was £1,145,800, being at the rate of about £12 per head for each inmate provided with accommodation.
>
> I may also add, with regard to the construction of the workhouses, that I feel much satisfaction in being able to state that the construction design of the original buildings has been universally followed in all the various buildings which have since been erected.
>
> I can also state that up to this time I am not aware of any failure in the works that deserves even mention or,

from first to last, of even a settlement in the walls of any of the main buildings of the 130 workhouses and the best proof of the substantive character of the buildings is the way in which they have been used by raising new walls on others never intended for them, adding new floors, and greatly increasing the weight on the new walls, and even suspending new floors to roofs originally designed to carry their own weight only. *(Wilkinson had tested all the different building stones used in Ireland in order, in various ways, to test the proportionated quantities of the different kinds of materials requested.)* Many of the buildings, however, require much more attention from the Guardians than has yet been given to them; for the painting of the wood and iron work, the repairs of the roofs, machinery of pumps, cleansing of drains etc, is much neglected at some of the workhouses.

I entertain the belief that, when the present calamitous period (the famine) has passed, the Irish poor-houses will, at no distant time, be found, with regard to their general building arrangements, a very superior class of public institutions of the kind.

This brought the original programme for the building of the workhouses to a conclusion. In a remarkably short space of time, an elaborate workhouse relief system covering the whole country, involving large-scale administrative planning and organisation had been implemented – in effect, the first network of administration, however inadequate, on a nationwide basis.

# 9

# The Management of the Workhouse

*'No individual capable of exertion must ever be permitted to be idle in a workhouse.'*

THE ACT OF 1838

While architect George Wilkinson was arranging for the erection of the workhouses, George Nicholls and the Poor Law Commissioners were laying down the framework for their administration and operation.

The Commissioners issued directions and orders relating to all aspects of workhouse life – the admission and classification of paupers, the framing of dietaries, discipline and punishments for misbehaviour. The staffing of the workhouses was also their responsibility; they prescribed qualifications for the paid officers, defined duties and laid down regulations for their appointment and control (also their suspension and removal from office if found unfit).

The management of the workhouses was under the control of the Boards of Guardians who acted in accordance with the guidelines laid down by the Commissioners.

## Admission to the Workhouse

Paupers could only be admitted to the workhouse in one of the following ways:

1. By a written order of the Board of Guardians
2. By a written order of a relieving officer
3. By the Master of the workhouse (or during his absence by the Matron) in case of any sudden or urgent necessity, or on the receipt of a written recommendation (the red ticket) from a local warden.

94

The Commissioners were prohibited from interfering in individual cases; admittance was solely at the discretion of the Boards of Guardians.

## *Officers*

One of the first tasks of the Boards of Guardians was the appointment of the  following staff to each workhouse:

1. Clerk to the Board of Guardians.
2. Treasurer of the Union.
3. Medical Officer of the workhouse.
4. Master of the workhouse
5. Matron (who deputised for the Master)
6. Porter of the workhouse
7. Schoolmaster of the workhouse
8. Schoolmistress of the workhouse
9. Chaplain

As whole families entered the workhouse together and as they were invariably large, children formed a sizeable proportion of the workhouse population. So schools of a kind were provided.

Rate collectors and relieving officers were also employed, with the approval of the Commissioners. In addition the boards could add such extra staff – nurses, attendants and servants – as they deemed necessary.

The workhouse rules permitted the employment of the inmates, so the number of paid staff was kept at an inadequately low level – the average number was twelve to fifteen in each workhouse.

## *Appointment of Staff*

The appointment of officers and staff was made by majority vote of the board of Guardians. It was stipulated that an advertisement giving notice of vacant positions be inserted in some public paper at least seven days before an appointment was made but this safeguard could be, and frequently

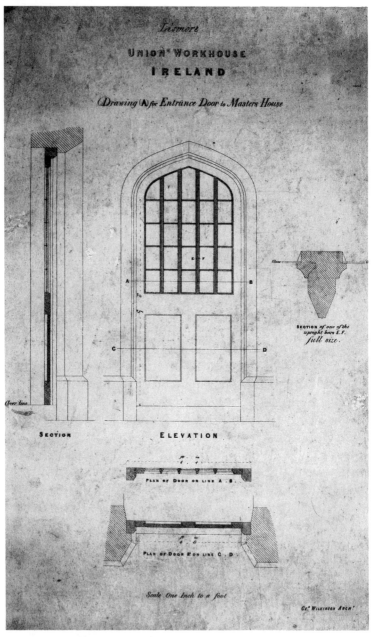

*Entrance door to Master's house*

was, circumvented by employing a person temporarily in the first instance. The lower age limit for officers was twenty-one years of age. There was, however, machinery which allowed the Guardians to dispense with this requirement, with the result that very junior and inexperienced people were sometimes appointed to responsible posts. This laxity in appointment procedures encouraged favouritism and indeed blatant nepotism, and the employment of unsuitable people inevitably resulted in mismanagement and maladministration.

As a general principle, officers were mainly selected for their ability to discipline and regiment the inmates rather than for their humanitarian qualities. The high dismissal rate of workhouse masters and officers, and the frequent reports of gross neglect and incompetency of officers, reflect the poor quality and performance of the staff. Quarrelsomeness, drunkenness and immorality were not uncommon.

## Duties of Staff

The duties of the various members of the staff were laid down in the general rules, those of the Master being set out in great detail (see Appendix 3). As well as the duty of admitting paupers in accordance with the prescribed procedure, he was required, *inter alia,* to (a) enforce industry, order, punctuality; cleanliness and the observance of the several rules; (b) to read prayers to the paupers before breakfast and after supper every day, or cause prayers to be read, at which all the inmates had to attend; (c) to cause the paupers to be inspected and their names called over, immediately after morning prayers every day, in order that it could be seen that each individual was clean, in a proper state, and accounted for; (d) to provide for and enforce the employment of the able-bodied adult paupers during the whole of the hours of labour, and to allow none who were capable of employment to be idle at any time; (e) to say, or cause to be said, grace before and after meals.

Not all the jobs came with such elaborate blueprints. No particular qualifications were prescribed at that time for nurses, and unqualified and inexperienced persons were often employed.

## Wardens

Section 50 of the Act required the Board of Guardians to appoint 'a fit person in each parish or townland to be styled the warden for such parish or townland'.

Parish wardens held office for one year, and were eligible for reappointment after the annual election of Guardians. They were not paid officers, but the appointments were eagerly sought as a means of enhancing the standing and influence of the holder in the local community. They were required to:

1. Attend meetings of the Boards of Guardians as requested and report to them on the state of the poor within their parish.
2. Receive all applications for admission into the workhouses which might be made to them by or on behalf of any destitute persons within their parish; they had power to issue tickets, known as red tickets, authorising admission into the workhouse.
3. To arrange, if necessary, the conveyance of any destitute poor person who might be unable to walk or otherwise travel to the workhouse.

## Diet

The guiding principle of the 1838 Act was that which had inspired the English Act of 1834, namely that the workhouse inmates should 'be worse fed, worse clothed and worse lodged than the independent labourers of the district'. This was to prove a major problem, particularly as regards diet.

In the Ireland of the 1840s, labourer and small tenant-farmer lived in subhuman conditions. Edmund Burke gives a graphic description in *The Reformer*, a newspaper which he edited as an undergraduate at Trinity College:

As for their food, it is notorious they seldom taste bread or meat; their diet in summer is potatoes and sour milk; in winter they are still worse – living on the same root, only made palatable by a little salt accompanied with water. Their clothing so ragged that they rather publish than conceal the wretchedness it is meant to hide. Nay, it is no uncommon sight to see half a dozen children run quite naked out of a cabin scarcely distinguishable from a dunghill. You enter one of these cabins, or rather creep into it, at a door of hurdles plastered with dirt; within you see (if the smoke will permit you) the men, women, children, dogs and swine lying. Their furniture is much fitter to be lamented than described, such as a pot, a

*Interior in Schull*

stool, a few wooden vessels, and broken bottles. *In this manner all the peasantry to a man live.*[1]

The Devon commission paints an even bleaker picture. Composed entirely of landlords it visited every part of the country and examined 1,100 witnesses. Its report was made in 1845, just before the commencement of the famine period:

> It would be impossible to describe adequately the privation which labourers, cottiers, small landholders and their families habitually and patiently endure. It will be seen in the evidence that in many districts their only food in the potato, and their only beverage water; that their cabins are seldom a protection against the weather; that a bed or blanket is a rare luxury, and that nearly in all cases a pig and manure heap constitute their only property.

So, as regards diet, Nicholls was faced with a real problem. Was it possible to devise one which would 'not be equal to the ordinary mode of subsistence of those outside the system'?

The only logical approach seemed to be to find out just what this 'mode of subsistence' was, so he arranged for his officials to tour the country and carry out a survey of the eating habits of the Irish people. This confirmed that the poor ate potatoes and milk for breakfast and potatoes and milk for dinner; if things were good they had supper, and on a red-letter day they might have a herring or an egg. The menu of the poor was enshrined in the Irish verse:

> *Pratai i maidin,*
> *Pratai san lo,*
> *Agus ma eirighim san oiche,*
> *Pratai a geobhainn*

(potatoes in the morning, potatoes in the day, and if I got up at night, potatoes I would get.)

The Poor Law Commissioners, having considered the matter on the basis devised by George Nicholls, finally decided that for adults the workhouse diet should consist of two meals a day as follows:

*Breakfast:* Eight ounces of stirabout and half a pint of milk;

*Dinner:* Three and a half pounds of potatoes and one pint of skimmed milk.

It was generally accepted that the children should have three meals a day. In January 1842, the Commission recommended that children from nine to fourteen years of age should have the following:

*Breakfast:* Three ounces of oatmeal and half a pint of new milk;

*Dinner:* Two ounces of potatoes and half a pint of new milk;

*Supper:* Six ounces of bread.

Younger children were to receive smaller amounts at the discretion of the Guardians and, in the case of very young children, rice or bread could be substituted for oatmeal or potatoes. The Commissioners were not insistent on the adoption of these dietaries and their recommendations were intended only as guidance to the various Boards of Guardians.[2]

It is on record that some Boards of Guardians, to their credit, wanted to give the inmates meat on special occasions but, as this was not provided for in the approved dietary scale, the Commissioners informed the boards that they should desist from this practice.

## Clothing

The prescribed clothing for adult males was a coat and trousers 'of barragon', cap, shirt, brogues and stockings, and for females a striped jerkin, a petticoat of 'linsey-woolsey' and another of stout cotton, a cap, a shift, shoes and stockings. Children were not provided with shoes and stockings on the grounds that they were not accustomed to footwear. This standard of clothing was, however, seldom supplied in the famine years because of lack of funds. This applied particularly in the distressed Unions in the south and west. The shoddiest clothing was considered good enough for the paupers, many of whom during the famine period came in to the workhouse half naked as well as half starving.

## Work

It was a fundamental rule of the workhouse system that 'no individual capable of exertion must ever be permitted to be idle in a workhouse and to allow none who are capable of employment to be idle at any time'. So the inmates were set to work, the men breaking stones, grinding corn, working on the land attached to the workhouse or at other manual work about the house; the women at house duties, mending clothes, washing, attending the children and the sick, as well as manual work, including stone breaking. Even children were required to occupy themselves. It was work without incentive or motivation; the rules decreed that 'no pauper shall work on his own account; and no pauper shall receive any compensation for his labour'.

An infernal contraption for grinding corn, designed by a Richard Perrott of Cork, was accepted by the Commissioners for use in the workhouse as a means of keeping large numbers occupied simultaneously. This involved groups of over a hundred inmates, including children, manually rotating a large wheel which kept them walking in a circle without respite for hours on end, adding exhaustion to their rarely relieved lives of harshness and monotony. As well as grinding the corn this mill-wheel was seen as a ready instrument for enforcing discipline. The forced labour involved in its operation was regarded as so

*The Perrott wheel*

objectionable and inhumane that its use was discontinued after about five years. It was all rather reminiscent of the cruel mistreatments at Bethlehem Royal Hospital, London, which became known as Bedlam, where the more troublesome patients were strapped on a tranquillising wheel which could be spun around until they lost consciousness.[3]

# 10

# Life in the Workhouse

*'I still have vivid and harrowing memories of the prison-like interior ... the dark wards ... the appalling "uniforms" ... the great witch's cauldron in which one inmate cooked a watery Indian meal stirabout ... the rancid butter and stale bread ...*

THOMAS HARRINGTON

What was life like in the workhouses? One thing was sure; it was well-regulated and disciplined. Rules abounded, 'thick as autumnal leaves that strow the brooks in Vallembrosa', while the staff were strictly enjoined to enforce 'regularity, orderliness, strict application of discipline and cleanliness, constant occupation, the preservation of decency and decorum, and the exclusion of all irregular habits and tempting excitements, and the observance of the several rules ...[1]

The bell rang about seven am when the inmates had to rise. They dressed in their rough workhouse clothes and brogues and went to the central dining hall where (in accordance with regulations) they waited for prayers to be read. The roll was called (paupers were Government property and had to be accounted for) and then they were inspected for cleanliness. The routine having been completed, they took their pannies and tin mugs and lined up for their stirabout and milk. They sat down on wooden forms, grace was said collectively, and the first meal of another day in their poor lives was eaten in silence; one of the regulations stipulated that 'any pauper who shall make any noise when silence is ordered to be kept shall be deemed DISORDERLY and shall be punished accordingly.'[2]

After breakfast, the inmates were set to their work, with only the thought of the next meal to cheer their spirits. Dinner, which consisted either of potatoes or brown bread and soup, was usually in late afternoon. The potatoes for each person were weighed and put in a net, then they were boiled, put on trays, still in their nets, and carried to the dining hall. In some workhouses the inmates had wooden or tin platters for their potatoes, in others they ate them off the table. The nets were collected, grace was said and the meal was eaten in silence.[3]

Leisure time was strictly circumscribed. The inmates could not go to the dormitories until bedtime at eight o'clock, nor were they allowed to play cards or any game of chance, smoke, or have or consume 'any spirituous or fermented drink'. They could see visitors only in the presence

*Sleeping quarters of a typical workhouse*

*Accommodation at the Belfast City Hospital*

of the Master of the workhouse, the Matron or other duly authorised officer.

The beds on which the inmates slept were forms six foot long, resting on a deal trestle at the head of a ledge formed in an economic manner by the construction arrangement of the framework on each of the side walls (see Appendix 4). The floor sloped on either side from the walls to the centre of the dormitory and the central valley or depression served as a gangway for the inmates, who slept on straw mattresses spread on the raised portion of the floor which served as the 'economical bed'. The dormitories were often overcrowded and segregation of the sexes not always possible, which added to the low reputation of the workhouses. There was a lack of water and no toilet facilities except for two large tubs for urination in each ward, which, not unnaturally in view of the large number of inmates, usually overflowed on to the gangway and created a foul atmosphere, made worse by inadequate ventilation. It is scarcely surprising that in these conditions disease spread rapidly and that the mortality rate was extremely high amongst both patients and staff.

As well as living in primitive conditions, the inmates were, in many instances, half starved and half clothed. Bed coverings consisted mainly of rough rags, and it was not uncommon to find the living and the dying stretched side by side on filthy straw, under the same miserable coverings, on the 'sleeping' platforms. Thomas Harrington who was born in an Irish workhouse, recalled in later years:

I still have vivid and harrowing memories of the prison-like interior; the dark wards that were locked summer and winter from 8 am to 8 pm; the straw beds spread on the floor; the appalling 'uniforms' that the inmates were forced to wear; the great witch's cauldron in which one inmate cooked a watery Indian meal stirabout for the other inmates breakfast, a cauldron which was used again without being half scrubbed to provide watery soup for the midday meal; the rancid butter and stale bread; the grim stone-breaking yards; the primitive sanitary arrangements.[4]

A punishment book 'for misbehaviour of paupers' was kept by the Master of the workhouse who was empowered to punish any pauper for any of the following 'misbehaviours':

Making any noise when silence is ordered.
Using obscene or profane language.
By word or deed insulting any person.
Threatening to strike or assault any person.
Not duly cleansing his person.
Refusing or neglecting to work.
Pretending sickness.
Playing at cards or any game of chance.
Attempting to introduce any drink or tobacco.
Disturbing the other inmates during prayers.
Entering or attempting to enter other wards.
Climbing over any wall or fence, or attempting to quit the workhouse premises.
Endeavouring to excite other paupers to acts of insubordination.
Wilfully disobeying any order of any officer of the workhouse.[5]

As a set of rules for a crowd of noisy, boisterous youngsters (with the prospect of being home again in a few months), they might not have seemed unduly hard. Adults who had lost any sense of dignity that they possessed when they entered the workhouse could only see them as harsh and unfeeling, a grim reminder that they were no longer people; they were paupers, serving a life sentence for the crime of poverty.

The fact that rules for discipline were laid down and enforced by the staff did not mean that the inmates always accepted or abided by them; there is abundant evidence to show that there was often widespread resentment, amounting on occasions to open revolt. There were also incidents at time over religious matters, an inevitable extension of the wider tensions amongst the various religious orders and sects operating in Ireland during the famine years and mainly associated with 'souperism', the dispensing of soup to the starving people as a means of proselytising them, a practice that was bitterly resented by the Catholics.

Among the various contemporary records of the Irish workhouse is that of English novelist W.M. Thackeray, who recorded a visit to one in 1843:

> Near Stoneybatter lies a group of huge gloomy edifices – a hospital, a penitentiary, a madhouse and a poorhouse. I visited the latter of these, the North Dublin Union Workhouse, an enormous establishment which accommodates two thousand beggars. Among the men there are very few able-bodied, most of them, the Keeper said, having gone out for the harvest time or as soon as the

*The needle room in an English House of Correction*

potatoes came in. The old men were assembled in considerable numbers in the long dayroom. Some of them were picking oakum by way of employment, but most of them were past work, all such inmates of the workhouse as are able-bodied being occupied on the premises. We were led with a sort of satisfaction by the Guardian to the kitchen. It was Friday, and rice-milk is the food on that day, each man being served with a pint-canful, of which cans a great number stood smoking upon stretchers – the platters were laid each with its portion of salt. The old women's room was crowded with, I should think, at least four hundred old ladies, sitting demurely on benches, doing nothing for the most part. There was a separate room for the able-bodied females; and the place was full of stout, red-cheeked, bouncing women. If the old ladies looked respectable, I cannot say the young ones were particularly good-looking – sly, leering and hideous. But this chapter must be made as short as possible. So I will not say how much prouder the Keeper was of his fat pigs than of his paupers – how he pointed out the burial ground of the families of the poor; their coffins were quite visible through the niggardly mound – and children might peep at their fathers over the playground wall.[6]

# 11

# Pre-Famine Ireland

*'No vegetable ever affected the same amount of influence upon the physical, moral, social and political condition of a country, as the potato exercised over Ireland.'*

CENSUS OF IRELAND 1851

Potatoes, introduced into Ireland in the mid 1700s, are rooted not only in the soil of Ireland but in her history. It was because of the potato that the Irish population expanded so rapidly and dramatically between the eighteenth and nineteenth centuries. An acre of land could produce enough potatoes to feed a family for the year and leave a surplus to be sold. So the practice arose of tenants dividing their land among their children, erecting a mud cabin for each newly married couple. The sons in turn subdivided. Though the figure recorded in the census of 1841 was 8,175,124, some believe it may well have been over nine million.[1]

The vast majority of the poor of Ireland depended on one resource – the land. French traveller; Gustave de Beaumont, observed in 1837: 'The Irish Catholic finds only one profession within his reach – and when he has not the capital necessary to become a farmer he digs the ground as a labourer ... He who has not a spot of ground to cultivate dies of famine.'[2] And as the population grew, the competition for land increased and in many areas rents rose dramatically.

The Halls, who visited Ireland several times before 1845 were startled at the degree of dependence of the Irish peasant on the potato:

For above a century and a half, the potato has been almost the only food of the peasantry of Ireland. They raise corn, indeed – wheat, barley and oats, in abundance – but it is for export; and we have no hesitation in saying there are hundreds in the less civilised districts of the country who have never tasted bread. Some (of the Irish) side with Cobbett in execrating 'the lazy root', 'the accursed root', as, if not the originator, the sustainer of Irish poverty and wretchedness; others contend that its introduction is an ample set-off against the wars and confiscations of Elizabeth, her counsellors and her armies.

There can be little doubt that the ease with which the means of existence are procured has been the cause of evil. A very limited portion of land, a few days of labour, and a small amount of manure, will create a stock upon which a family may exist for twelve months; too generally, indeed, the periods between exhausting the old stock and digging the new are seasons of great want, if not of absolute famine; but if the season is propitious the peasant digs day after day the produce of his plot of ground, and, before the winter sets in, places the residue in a pit to which he has access when his wants demand a supply. Nearly every soil will produce potatoes; they may be seen growing almost from a barren rock, on the side of a mountain, and in the bog where the foot would sink many inches in the soil. Every cottage has its garden

– its acre or half acre of land, attached; and the culture requires but a very small portion of the peasant's time ... He can live, at all events – if his crop do not fail; and he can pay his rent if his pig, fed like himself out of his garden, do not die. To decency of clothing, and to any of the luxuries that make life something more than mere animal existence, he is too often a stranger.[3]

The key phrase in the above excerpt is – *'if the crop do not fail'*. But fail it often did. Twenty-four failures in various parts of the country are recorded between 1728 and 1851. But failures or not, the population kept on rising inexorably.

The land system which supported this exploding population was built on shifting sands. With few exceptions Irish landowners were not noted for the careful management of their estates. Many, only interested in hunting, drinking and building large houses, let their land in parcels of from 100 to 1,000 acres to middlemen on long-term leases. Some were for ninety-nine years; some for 'two, three or four' lives (the lives of young people named in the lease). Having thus disposed of their immediate interest in their estates, the landlords usually proceeded to borrow, and often mortgaged their property beyond its value, aided by antiquated laws and laxity in registrations; indeed in some cases it proved impossible to sell an estate because of the difficulty of proving title. (All this would eventually be sorted out by the Encumbered Estates Act of 1849).

In theory the middleman was supposed to manage the land he had leased, though this rarely happened in practice. In the case of one estate in County Cork, after a ninety-nine-year tenure, it was found that 'the entire property was precisely in the same condition (as) a century ago, without roads, drains, plantations, fences or other works to adapt it for cultivation.'[4] The middleman's main interest was profit so he put as many tenants as possible on

the land. And given the desperate land hunger of the Irish
– no land, no livelihood – this was not difficult.

Ireland was in the main not a cash economy. Landlords
(or their agents) and farmers hired labourers in return for
certain concessions – a cabin, a portion of bog for fuel, the
keeping of some sheep or a pig, and, most importantly, an
acre or half an acre on which to grow the potatoes to feed
his family. In return the labourer 'bound' himself to the
farmer for work. Theoretically he was supposed to be paid
wages whenever he worked, out of which he paid rent for
his cabin and land; in practice he was lucky if he came out
at the end of the year with a few pounds. Labourers who
were not bound to a landlord or farmer had to hire a patch
of land on which to grow their potatoes and rely on casual
labour at low wages, and maybe a surplus of crop which
they could sell, to pay the rent. This was the 'conacre'
system and those living under it eked out a precarious
existence in which everything depended on the abundance
of the potato crop.

The rapacity of the middlemen combined with the very
long leases meant that estates became hopelessly
congested. Holdings were sublet and subdivided. Cabins
were thrown up for members of the family, 'A nuisance to
the property,' according to Charles Bailey, agent to
Viscount Midleton in County Cork, 'and a nursery for
increasing the population ... mouths sufficient to swallow
up the whole of the produce, leaving nothing for rent.'[5]
One landowner, Peter Fitzgerald, who owned most of
Valentia Island off the Kerry coast, described how he had
let his estate on thirteen leases of three lives and found (in
1847) that the fruit of all this was the 'augmentation (of
the population) from something like 400 to above 3,000
persons'.[6]

This was not an isolated incident. In *Realities of Irish
Life*, W.S. Trench, Lord Lansdowne's agent, paints what
must have been a familiar picture on all but the few well-
managed estates:

The estate of the Marquis in the Union of Kenmare had at this time been much neglected by its local manager. It consists of about sixty thousand acres, and comprises nearly one-third of the whole Union. No restraint whatever had been put upon the system of subdivision of land. Boys and girls intermarried unchecked, each at the age of seventeen or eighteen, without thinking it necessary to make any provision whatever for their future subsistence, beyond a shed to lie down in, and a small plot of land whereon to grow potatoes. Innumerable squatters had settled themselves, unquestioned, in huts on the mountain sides and in the valleys, without any sufficient provision for their maintenance during the year. They sowed their patches of potatoes early in spring, using seaweed alone as a manure. Then as the scarce seasons of spring and summer came on, they nailed up the doors of their huts, took all their children along with them, together with a few tin cans, and started on a migratory and piratical expedition over the counties of Kerry and Cork, trusting to 'their adroitness and good luck in begging to keep the family alive till the potato crop again came in. And thus, in consequence of the neglect or supineness of the (previous) agent, who – in direct violation of this lordship's instructions, and without his knowledge – allowed numbers of strangers and young married couples to settle on his estate, paying no rent, and almost without any visible means of subsistence, not only the finances, but the character and condition of the property, were at a very low ebb indeed. The estate, in fact, was swamped with paupers.[7]

The profusion of beggars was noted by the Halls:

The first peculiarity that strikes a stranger on landing here, or indeed in any part of Ireland, is the multiplicity of beggars. Age, decrepitude, imbecility and disease surround the car the moment it stops, or block up the shop-doors, so as, for a time, effectually to prevent either

entrance or exit. In the small town of Macroom ... it
cost us exactly three shillings and tenpence to redeem
the pledge we had given (of a halfpenny each upon all
who might ask it), no fewer than ninety-two having
assembled at the inn gate. We encountered them, nearly
in the same proportion, in every town through which we
passed.[8]

The first serious outbreak of blight (caused by the fungus
*Phytophthora infestans*) was recorded on the north-east
coast of North America in 1842. It came to Ireland in
1845, resulting in a partial though fairly extensive failure of
the potato crop. Though not the country-wide calamity of
the following year, it was serious enough to force the
British government to take action. The failure of the potato
would mean that substitute food would have to be found.
But what? The Corn Laws, which protected the interests of
English grain growers by imposing duties on imports,
meant that grain prices were artificially high. But the Tory
Prime Minister, Sir Robert Peel, had come around to the
idea that free trade should replace protectionism and the
threat of famine in Ireland jogged him into action. To the
fury of his party and after a series of government crises he
forced through the repeal of the Corn Laws. Meanwhile he
authorised the import of a small quantity of Indian meal
into Ireland, intending to throw supplies on the market in
case grain prices rose unacceptably due to increased
demand.

The main plank of Peel's plans for Ireland was the Relief
Commission for Ireland which first met in November
1845. The members were to organise local committees to
raise money for food and encourage landlords to set up
employment schemes, for which the Government would
bear fifty per cent of the cost. On a national scale, the
Board of Works was authorised to construct new roads and
piers to give employment.

It was originally envisaged that the Boards of Guardians

could be used for the distribution of food but as relief
could not be granted outside the workhouse (unless the
workhouse was full) this idea had to be abandoned. Nevertheless the workhouses were to be an important element in
the relief plans. As fever inevitably followed famine, the
Poor Law Commissioners issued orders for the building of
fever hospitals in workhouse grounds. The Boards of
Guardians were advised that they had to provide medical
care and nursing for all fever patients.

The results of all this activity were not exactly im-
pressive. The Indian corn presented several problems. It
had to be dried and ground and there were few mills
throughout the country, while efforts to get other food to
the more impoverished areas (principally in the west) were
hampered by lack of ships and suitable harbours. The
road-building programme also ran into difficulties, and the
local landlords, having done nothing in previous famines,
turned a deaf ear to exhortations to provide money; this
naturally led to local unrest.

The trials of 1845, ironically described as a 'probationary season of distress'[9], did however produce one

concrete result. Early in 1946, four Bills to provide for public works in Ireland, under the control of the Board of Works, were passed.

The repeal of the Corn Laws proved to be Peel's downfall and his government fell in late June 1846, to be replaced by the Whigs led by Lord John Russell. On his agenda was Ireland, that 'cloud in the west', as Gladstone had described it the previous year, and in August he advised the House of Commons of the impending failure of the potato crop and the need for 'extraordinary measures for relief'. This did not include, as Peel's plan had, the supplying of food; effort was to be concentrated on employment schemes but this time, unlike the previous year, the Government would not bear fifty per cent of the cost. A new Bill was introduced, the Labour Rate Act, designed to 'facilitate the employment of the "Labouring Poor" for a limited period in distressed districts in Ireland.' The object was to force Irish landlords to pay for the relief of their afflicted tenantry. Money for the works would be advanced by the Treasury and would be repayable within ten years – through a rate levied on all persons possessed of property in a distressed area. The property of Ireland was to pay for the poverty in Ireland, and as the appeals of previous years had fallen on stony ground now there would be compulsion by law.

The Act was rushed through without opposition before Parliament rose in August, much to the anger of Irish landlords. Foreign Secretary, Lord Palmerston, who had estates in Ireland, voiced the general concern when he said that if the Act remained law for any length of time 'landlords will be as well qualified as their cottiers to demand admission to the Union House (the workhouse)'.[10]

It is charitable to suppose that Russell (a son of the sixth Duke of Bedford) and his cabinet, familiar with the riches (derived from progressive farming on rich agricultural land, supplemented by profitable mining and industry) of the British aristocracy, concluded that Irish landlords, with estates of thousands of bog and mountain acres, must be equally wealthy and well able to support the teeming multitudes of the destitute on their doorsteps. It would prove to be a pious hope.

The downfall of Peel was disastrous for Ireland. Russell was less sympathetic to Irish affairs and another even less sympathetic figure was waiting in the wings – Charles Edward Trevelyan, the man who held the Treasury strings and who would exercise control over all aspects of relief to Ireland.

# 12

# The Workhouse
# in the Famine Years

*'It is hard upon the poor people that they should be deprived of knowing that they are suffering from an affliction of God's providence.'*

CHARLES EDWARD TREVELYAN, 6 JANUARY, 1847.

In his investigations into the workhouse system in England George Nicholls had found that the Irish immigrants were unwilling inmates. This was also true in their land of birth. In Ireland they clung to their patches of land, preferring to endure misery and near starvation rather than leave their cabins for the dreaded workhouse. The first had been opened in 1840 – Cork in March, Dublin in April and Londonderry in November – yet by August 1846, in spite of widespread distress and poverty, the workhouses were only half full.

Then there occurred 'the most terrible of all terrible disasters in Irish history'. This was the Great Famine, the worse of its kind in European history, which was to have such appalling consequences for Ireland and its people.

The partial failure of the potato crop in 1845 meant that the summer months of 1846 were lean and hungry ones but there were high hopes that the new crop would be a bumper one. But in late July and early August disaster struck with lightning and unbelievable rapidity. Frances Power Cobbe of Newbridge in County Dublin noted the onset in one part of the country:

I happen to recall precisely the day, almost the hour,

when the blight fell on the potatoes. A party of us were driving to a seven o'clock dinner at the house of our neighbour, Mrs Evans of Portrane. As we passed a remarkably fine field of potatoes in blossom, the scent came through the open windows of the carriage and we remarked to each other how splendid the crop. Three or four hours later, as we returned home, in the dark, a dreadful smell came from the same field, and we exclaimed, 'Something has happened to those potatoes; they did not smell at all as they did when we passed them on our way out.'

The Annual Report for 1846 of the English Poor Law Commissioners records:

In the early part of the month of August 1846 it became known that the potato crop in Ireland had suddenly, and to a very wide extent, been injured by a blight, of which the effects became visible during the last two or three days of July and the first six or seven days of August in almost every part of the country ... Early in September we had received replies from nearly every Union showing the state of things in more than 2,000 localities in Ireland. The fearful prospect held out by these returns was such as led us to consider with great anxiety in what manner the laws in force for the relief of the poor in Ireland could be made to operate as beneficially and effectually as possible. The power of affording relief from the poor rates being limited by law to accommodation in workhouses, it was manifest that in a widespread and overwhelming state of distress like that anticipated, such power could be relied on only to a small extent for relieving the destitution of the people.[1]

The chilling answers to the queries sent out to the Boards of Guardians that August show how complete was the devastation: equally pessimistic were the forecasts as to the probable yield of the healthy crop (see Appendix 5). It was clear that relief on a large scale would be required.

From the start, the financial arrangements for the operation of the workhouse system were unsatisfactory and
inadequate. The principle of poor law relief – that the
property of Ireland should relieve the poverty in Ireland
– was fine in theory, problematic in practice. In many
instances the Boards of Guardians found it difficult to
collect enough money to meet the running costs of the
workhouses and any increase in rates led to determined
resistance by the ratepayers. In 1844 it was necessary to
send in 700 troops as well as police to collect the poor rate
in Galway, while in Mayo the authorities took the British
Empire route of sending in a warship, plus two cruisers,
two companies of the 69th Regiment, a troop of the 10th
Hussars, fifty police, two inspectors and two magistrates.
In spite of all this the operations only brought in a quarter
of the rates and the Catholic Dean of Mayo estimated it
cost a pound to collect every shilling.[2]

Certainly there were grave anomalies and injustices in
the levying of rates. It was estimated that in 1846 the Duke
of Devonshire paid only about 7 per cent of his rental
income in rates, while at the same time a Mallow landowner with 1,000 acres claimed he was paying 40 per cent
of his income.[3] The Commissioners were less than understanding, insisting, in spite of all the evidence, that any
difficulties in levying and collecting the rates were due to a
want of energy on the part of the boards.

Some Boards in the poorer western regions took the
extreme step of refusing to open the workhouses or co-
operate with the Commissioners in their operation unless
compelled to do so by writs of mandamus. The Westport
workhouse was pronounced 'fit for the reception of the
destitute poor' in 1842. But in such a poverty-stricken
area, the Guardians were unable to collect the poor rate, in
spite of enlisting the aid of the constabulary and even
troops in their efforts, so the workhouse remained shut

until the issue of a writ of mandamus compelled its opening in November 1845. It was the same story at Tuam and Castlerea.

Many which did open soon found themselves in difficulties. James H. Tuke, a Quaker who visited various workhouses in November and December 1846, records one such example:

> I have already stated that owing to the want of funds, great difficulty exists in many Unions in providing for the inmates. The worst which I visited was that of Carrick-on-Shannon (which opened in 1842); it is in a miserable state and the doors were closed against further admissions; and although built for 700 had but 280 inmates; gates were besieged by seventy or eighty wretched beings who in vain implored for admission. Numbers of them were in various stages of fever, which was terribly prevalent in the neighbourhood, and the fever-shed overcrowded. Two months before my visit, the doors of the workhouse were opened and the inmates expelled, entailing upon them the most dire misery.[4]

So though the workhouse system was in operation from 1840 onwards, it was a makeshift affair, least efficient in the areas in which it was most needed, and utterly and absolutely incapable of dealing with the complete breakdown of the social fabric of Ireland which resulted from the famine of 1846.

By autumn 1846, the full disaster of the failure of the potato crop became apparent. Having endured the partial failure of 1845 and the hungry summer months of 1846, people looked at their blackened and rotting crops and realised that starvation stared them in the face:

> The desolation which a sudden failure of the staple food of the people, in a remote valley like this (Kenmare) must necessarily bring along with it, may be imagined.

As the potato melted away before the eyes of the people, they looked on in dismay and terror; but there was no one with energy enough to import corn to supply its place. Half Ireland was stunned by the suddenness of the calamity, and Kenmare was completely paralysed. Begging, as of old, was now out of the question, as all were equally poor; and many of the wretched people succumbed to their fate almost without a struggle.[5]

But this time, unlike 1845, there would be no Government-subsidised food; the theory of *laissez faire* was to prevail and any officials who distributed food were severely rebuked. The public works of 1845 had been closed down and those envisaged by the new Labour Rate Act would not start until November. Food was available but, in the main, cottiers who grew crops had to sell their grain to pay the rent; and although some landlords did reduce or forego rents, in most cases non-payment of rent meant eviction. The relationship between farmer and tenant-labourer collapsed. The labourers who were bound to the farmers wanted cash payment which was not forthcoming. The farmer in turn wanted cash in advance for renting land to the unbound tenants. Crowds of starving labourers, with no money to buy food, swarmed the streets, often trying to prevent ships from loading grain for export. It was one of the images of the famine that became indelibly printed on the Irish consciousness.

As autumn lengthened into winter (and a harsh and bitter winter it was to be, with snow coming unseasonally early in November), when the last of the gleanings, the hedgerow fruits, the nettles and cabbages had been eaten, the few spare rags pawned, the position become desperate. Though relief committees were set up as soon as the extent of the famine became known (the Quakers as early as November) for the vast majority there were only two alternatives – public works or the workhouse. But the public works programme was beset by delays and difficulties and

*Attacking a potato store*

it could not benefit anything like the number clamouring for work. In September the number on the rolls was 30,135, in October 150,259, in November 285,817. There were neither plans nor overseers to cope with such huge numbers, even though they were only a fraction of the starving population.

So labourers in their hundreds of thousands deserted their cabins and patches of land and turned their faces towards the workhouse. It had taken the horror of famine, accompanied by the twin spectres of starvation and fever, to make the Irish poor overcome their natural reluctance to seek admission to the workhouse. As J.H. Tuke records:

'Stern necessity, to a considerable degree, overcame the strong prejudices of the poor people to enter these workhouses and they are now generally full. In the Swinford Union the prejudices of the population to a workhouse were so deep and inveterate that the workhouse was a long time before one pauper could be induced to enter it. Famine, however, came on with such unrelenting severity that in a short time the workhouse was filled with the number (700) it was intended for.'[6]

At first it was a trickle, then a steady stream, then a torrent which finally overwhelmed the system. In August 1846 the 128 workhouses then completed were only half full, with 43,000 inmates. By March 1847, when all 130 workhouses were open, they were crammed to capacity with 115,000 occupants. By 1851 the numbers would reach 217,000. Workhouses capable of holding only some hundreds were forced to cater for thousands. In Fermoy (to give just one example) a workhouse designed for 800 contained over 1,800.

Standards of accommodation, minimal to begin with, sank even lower. Workhouse dietaries were scaled down to the barest subsistence levels. In several instances the Poor Law Commissioners were compelled to supply workhouses with bedding and clothing and with the means of procuring food for the immediate wants of the inmates. It was all only a drop in the ocean. In a letter, 'Distress in Ireland', Joseph Crosfield described conditions in several country workhouses in December 1846:

> The workhouse in Athlone is a large building containing upwards of 700 persons. Here a miserable state of things presented itself; the Union being very much in debt and their credit exhausted; and the poor inmates have scarcely clothes to cover them and little if any bedding at night. In a large room were more than 200 boys, collected round a turf fire which afforded the only light in the apartment, and though three windows were open, the close and oppressive smell indicated the want of a proper attention to cleanliness. There were about 100 girls assembled in another apartment, the state of which was still more offensive.
>
> At the Castlerea workhouse a shocking state of things

existed, the poor inmates lying upon straw and their dormitories being in such a state of dirt that we were unable to venture into them. In this workhouse there are at present 1,080 paupers, but the last 434 were admitted in so hurried a manner that there is neither bedding nor clothes for them; it is probable that there will be frightful mortality among the inmates. In the children's room was collected a miserable crowd of wretched objects, the charm of infancy having entirely disappeared and in its place were to be seen wan and haggard faces, prematurely old from the effects of hunger and cold, rags and dirt. In the schoolroom they spend some hours every day in hopeless listless idleness; though there are both a schoolmaster and schoolmistress there are no books nor slates, nor any of the apparatus of a school.

We visited the workhouse in Glenties, which is a dreadful state; the people were in fact half starved and only half clothed. Bedding consisted of dirty straw in which the inmates were laid in rows on the floor – even as many as six persons being crowded under the rug. The living and the dying were stretched side by side beneath the same miserable covering.[7]

The Poor Law Commissioners must have been aware of the desperate situation in the workhouses. On Christmas Eve, 1846, one of their officers, Captain Wynne, District Inspector for Clare, wrote to Lt. Colonel Harry Jones, Chairman of the Board of Works:

There is no doubt that the Famine advances upon us with giant strides. The effects of the Famine are discernible everywhere; not a domestic animal to be seen. It is an alarming fact that, this day, in the town of Ennis, there was not a stone of breadstuff of any description to be had on any terms, nor a loaf of bread ... I ventured through the parishes to ascertain the condition of the inhabitants. Although a man not easily moved, I confess myself unmanned by the extent and

intensity of suffering I witnessed, more especially the
women and little children, crowds of whom were to be
seen scattered over the turnip fields, like a flock of
famished crows, devouring the raw turnips, mothers
half naked, shivering in the snow and sleet, uttering
exclamations of despair whilst their children were
screaming with hunger. I am a match for anything else I
may meet here but this I cannot stand. I have traversed a

considerable extent of my district this week and I find
distress everywhere on the increase. Without food we
cannot last many days longer; the Public Works must fail
in keeping the population alive. The workhouse is full,
and police are stationed at the doors to keep the
numerous applicants out; therefore no relief can be
expected from that quarter.[8]

Extra accommodation was hurriedly provided by way of
additions to existing workhouses (they were usually of
wood and became known as 'the sheds'). And 'buildings of
all kinds, including store houses, old factories and dis-
tilleries, mansions, farm-buildings and long rows of
dwelling houses in streets of towns' were requisitioned and
fitted up.[9] (Details are given in Appendix 6).

But the flood of people soon swallowed up those extra
facilities and it became impossible to admit any more.
Thus in the time of greatest distress, the Guardians had to
set harsh conditions for the granting of relief, including
refusal of admission to thousands. It became a common
sight to see masses of men, women and children before the
workhouse doors, clamouring for admission. Tuke gives a
description of the scene at Swinford:

On the dreadful 10th November 120 were admitted
beyond the regulated number. Hundreds were refused
admission for want of room, some unhappy being
pushed on the high roads and in the fields. Influenced by
terror and dismay – leaving entire districts almost
deserted – the better class of farmers, in numbers, sold
their property, at any sacrifice, and took flight to
America. And the humbler classes left the country in
masses, hoping to find a happier doom in any other
region. In this Union 367 persons died in the workhouse; the Master of the workhouse also died. In the
adjoining Union, Ballina, 200 were admitted to the
workhouse beyond the number it was built for (1,200).
Hundreds were refused admission for want of room and

1,138 died in the workhouse; the medical officer of the workhouse was also carried off. In another adjoining Union, Ballinasloe, all the officers of the workhouse were swept away, and 254 inmates of the workhouse perished.[10]

It was the same story at Castlebar according to a local newspaper report:

We saw hundreds of people crawling in from the countryside, with asses carrying in baskets starved children and crippled old men and women. They numbered at that time about 3,000 people. It is surprising that so many asses have survived. A gloom hangs over the town. And this hunger outside the workhouse is only a drop in the ocean. Many never made it to the workhouse. The many thousands brought to the workhouse screaming for food couldn't be relieved. Many were buried where they fell.

In many places the pathway to the workhouse became known as *casan na marbh* (pathway of death) because so many died when turned away from the workhouses.

The workhouse system had failed. Inadequate though it was, this avenue of escape from famine and fever was now cut off. And with chilling inexorability the Poor Law Commissioners (though well aware of the extent of the problem – see Appendix 7) insisted on honouring the intentions of the Irish Poor Relief Act of 1838. Relief would be granted in the workhouse and in the workhouse only. Hearing that the Boards of Guardians of several Unions had, on their own initiative, introduced a system of outdoor relief in 1846 by giving food daily on the workhouse premises to persons not admitted as inmates they had this to say in their report for the year:

We felt bound to oppose the introduction of the new system, and in adopting this course we were influenced by the following considerations: Firstly it appeared to us certain that the system was contrary to the intention of the Legislature in passing the Irish Poor Relief Act 1838, and we were desirous of reserving for the Legislature alone the question of whether it was or was not desirable to alter the existing law. Secondly, we entertained no doubt that the Unions of Ireland (with a few exceptions) were not in such a financial position as would enable them to defray from their own resources the expenses which the new system would involve. Thirdly, if the system were to be introduced at all, we knew that it would lead to great abuse and confusion, unless accompanied by checks and precautions, which the existing state of the law did not enable us to adopt. The Guardians of the Unions, partly moved by our requests to discontinue the practice, and still more by the abuses and tendency to confusion (involving danger even to the public peace), which a short trial of the system showed to be practically inseparable from it, one by one abandoned it and reverted to the legal course of administering relief only in the workhouse.[11]

With the workhouse gates closed against them, the only hope of the starving was the public works. But once again, the system collapsed under the sheer weight of numbers. Though by March 1847, 734,000 were employed, at an average wage of 9d a day, countless thousands were turned away. Those who got work found that the wages were insufficient to buy enough Indian meal to satisfy the hunger of a family, and in many cases it was impossible to buy meal or other food due to the inadequate distribution network. So people sometimes died though they had the money for food, while others, half starved and in rags, fell victim to the harsh winter of 1846-47 and collapsed as they worked. 'It is difficult,' wrote Isaac Butt, 'to trace this history without indignation, when one thinks of those who while toiling at the public works fell dead of exhaustion with the implements of labour in their hands.'[12]

The fate of those barred from the workhouse and unable

to get work was predictable. The *Southern Reporter* gives a piteous account of west Cork in January 1847: 'Every village I entered exhibited the same characteristics – no clothing, no food, starvation in the looks of young and old. Hundreds are daily expiring in the cabins in the three parishes of this neighbourhood (Ballydehob).'

In the north-eastern region, which included Belfast, the standard of living, assisted by the growth of the linen industry, was somewhat higher than in the south and west of the country. Better conditions, however, were by no means universal in the northern counties and in many districts there was, and had long been, as much poverty as anywhere in the country. One landed proprietor wrote in January 1847:

> The moment I open my halldoor in the morning until dark, I have a crowd of women and children crying out for something to save them from starving. The men, except the old and infirm, stay away and show the greatest patience and resignation. The only reply to my question of 'What do you want?' is: 'I want something to eat.' We are also visited by hordes of wandering poor who come from the mountains, or other districts less favoured by a resident gentry; and worst of all, Death is dealing severely and consigning many to an untimely tomb.[13]

Given the level of British Government interest in Ireland it is hardly surprising that during the first terrible winter aid for the famine victims came mainly from voluntary bodies. The Society of Friends (Quakers), supported by a sister committee in London, set up a Central Relief Committee in November 1846 in Dublin. Their outstanding contribution in setting up a model system of kitchens for feeding the starving, and the response of the citizens of the United States to appeals for monetary help, are rightly recorded in history. The transactions of the Society record:

*A soup kitchen in Cork*

'The chief source whence the means at our disposal were derived was the munificent bounty of the citizens of the United States. The supplies sent from America to Ireland were on a scale unparalleled in history.'[14]

Somewhat less well known is the British Association for the Relief of the Extreme Distress in the Remote Parishes of Ireland, which was set up on 1 January 1847 by the merchant princes in London, headed by Baron Rothschild. It was an influential organisation in securing substantial funds for the relief committees. It succeeded to raising by voluntary subscriptions throughout Britain the then considerable sum of £500,000, including a contribution of £2,000 from Queen Victoria. And there were many other relief agencies at home and abroad which were involved in the raising of additional money to fund the relief committees.[15]

The standard form of relief was the soup kitchen; in

Cork Father Theobald Mathew organised the feeding of three to four thousand poor a day and had in fact pioneered the setting up of kitchens before the British Government came up with a similar idea. It was mainly through the organising efforts of clergymen of all denominations that the soup kitchens were kept operating, with the voluntary assistance of the community at large and under the overall control of a Dublin-based Irish Relief Association.

At the first session of Parliament, in early January 1847, the Irish famine policy of the Government was attacked in the House of Commons by Lord George Bentinck: 'Never before was there an instance of a Christian government allowing so many people to perish without interfering ... The time will come when we shall know what the amount of mortality has been; when the public and the world will be able to estimate, at its proper value, your management of the affairs of Ireland.' And in his last appearance in the House of Commons, in February 1847, a few months before his death, Daniel O'Connell made a desperate appeal to the Government in these words: 'Ireland is in your hands, in your power. If you do not save her, she cannot save herself. I solemnly call on you to recollect that I predict with the sincerest conviction that a quarter of her population will perish unless you come to her relief.'[16]

The famine pinpointed the fatal weakness of the workhouse system: the principle that relief for the poor should only be provided within the workhouse was unrealistic and could only fail in an emergency. Of a population of over eight million, one million were to die during the famine years (1846–51), but the workhouses were only designed to cater for approximately 110,000. They were already full when famine policy was discussed by the House of Commons.

By then, the *Illustrated London News* the *Illustrated Times* and the *Penny Post* were bringing home to the English

444     THE ILLUSTRATED LONDON NEWS.     [Dec. 29, 1849.

DRIVING CATTLE FOR RENT BETWEEN OUGHTERARD AND GALWAY.

JUDY O'DONNEL'S HABITATION (NEAR THE BRIDGE AT DOONARD.)

SCALP AT CAHERMORE.

(*To be continued next week.*)

people the full extent of the catastrophe, sending artists to Ireland to record the scenes there. There was such widespread public concern that the British Government was obliged to change its policy and rush through special legislation in February 1947 – the Temporary Relief Destitute Persons Ireland Act (known as the 'Soup Kitchen' Act) for the setting up of relief committees, under the auspices of a new Relief Commission, throughout the country to provide food for those unable to gain admission to the workhouse. The relief was to be confined to those attending in person (excepting only the sick and children) and there was to be no preference on religious ground. Recommended portions were: one and a half pounds of bread *or* one pound of flour or meal *or* one quart of soup per day per person *or* similar rations, usually cooked in a boiler (the Board of Health in Ireland had laid down that the amount of cereal food necessary to supply daily sustenance for an adult was one pound of meal).

The quality of the soup was generally lacking in nourishment, not so much soup for the poor as poor soup. As literally millions had to be fed, various economical recipes (see Appendix 8) were used to minimise the cost, the most infamous being that concocted by Alexis Soyer, chef of the Reform Club in London, for 'the destitute poor of Ireland'. He claimed it could be produced for three-farthings a quart. It was made of peas, whole-ground barley, pepper, salt and water in the proportion of one pound each of peas and barley to one gallon of water. In each quart were placed small cuttings of wheaten bread or biscuit on which the boiling soup was poured. The English medical journal, *The Lancet*, called it a 'quackery'. Nevertheless, at the invitation of the Lord Lieutenant, Soyer came to Dublin where he set up a model kitchen with a three-hundred-gallon soup boiler in front of the Royal (later Collins) barracks, near the main entrance to the Phoenix Park, which opened on 5 April 1847. Hundreds of bowls, with spoons attached on chains, were provided and the time for partaking of the soup by the starving multitudes was controlled on a rota basis by a bell.

*The Dublin Evening Packet* wrote, tongue in cheek:

> His Excellency the Lord Lieutenant was there; the ladies and many fair and delicate creatures assembled; there were earls and countesses, and lords and generals, and colonels and commissioners, and clergymen and doctors. For reader, it was a gala, a grand gala ... For the privilege of watching the hungry eat, the gentry were expected to donate five shillings each, which was to be distributed by the Lord Mayor in charity. Five shillings each to see paupers feed! Five shillings! When the animals in the Zoological Gardens can be inspected at feeding time for sixpence.

The native Irish were quick to bestow on Soyer the accolade 'Head Cook to the People of Ireland', and called him a 'broth of a boy'. And he did not escape the shafts of ridicule; a writer in the *Nation* lumped him with the witches in Macbeth:

> *Round about the boiler go,*
> *In twice fifty gallons throw*
> *Water in the noisome tank.*
> *In the boiler then you'll throw*
> *Onion slice and turnip top,*
> *Crust of bread and cabbage chop,*
> *Tomtits' gizzards, head and lungs*
> *Of a famished French-fed frog,*
> *Root of pratee digged in bog.*

Though it was claimed that at the peak of their operations in July 1847, the Government soup kitchens (about 2,000 in all countrywide) were feeding over three million a day, they gave at best only minimal relief and were merely a haphazard, rough and ready response to the famine.[17] The scheme was not adequately funded, the Government advancing only a modest sum of £50,000 as a start-up clined to 104,455, while the rate of mortality had continued to increase notwithstanding that reduction.

4. The returns subsequent to the return of the 10th April, 1847, show a gradual decline in the rate of mortality in the workhouses through the months of May and June, at the end of which latter month it had descended to half the rate prevailing on the 10th April. It is observable however that during the same period the total numbers in the workhouses had undergone no material decrease, and that the number of fever patients, which on the 1st May reached its maximum of 10,226, continued to fluctuate between 10,000 and 9,000 until the 3rd July.

5. Through the months of July and August the still rapidly declining rate of mortality in the workhouses was accompanied by a decrease of the total numbers of inmates and the number of fever patients and other sick. In the last week of August the total number of inmates was 76,319; the number of fever patients, 5,782; total sick, 15,240; and the total number of deaths, 646, giving a rate of 8 per 1,000 inmates weekly. The number of inmates was at its minimum, 75,376, on the 4th September, and in the week ended on the 2nd October, there were 433 deaths among 83,719 inmates, giving a ratio of 5 per 1,000 weekly.

6. The above fluctuations indicate at a glance the fearful state of the pressure on the workhouses in the spring of 1847; and also the alleviation of that pressure finally effected by the progress of the operations under the Temporary Relief Act, 10 Vict., cap. 7, and the Fever Act, 10 Vict., cap. 22. The progress of those operations may be briefly traced in the following results derived from the reports of the Relief Commissioners.

The first return of the amount of daily rations relates to the 8th May, 1847, on which day the total rations issued appear to have been 826,325. The return of the 5th June shows that rations were issued on that day equivalent to the support of 2,729,684 persons; on the 3rd July, to 3,020,712 persons; on the 1st August, to 2,520,376 persons; on the 29th August, to 1,105,800 persons; and on the 12th September, to 505,984 persons. At the end of September all issues of rations under the Temporary Relief Act finally ceased.

The temporary fever hospitals established under the Acts above cited, are shown in the Seventh Report of the Relief Commissioners to have provided for the treatment of 26,378 persons in the month of September, showing an average daily number in hospital of about 13,000 patients. Comparing these results with those stated in paragraphs 4 and 5, it appears that the alleviation of the pressure on the workhouses proceeded, as might have been expected, *pari passu* with the progress of the operations under the Temporary Relief and Fever Acts.

*A page from the Poor Law Commissioners report*

grant-in-aid. The Boards of Guardians, many already in serious debt, were assigned the next to impossible task of meeting the shortfall from the already overburdened rates, supplemented by voluntary subscriptions.

A.M. Sullivan, who was a boy during these times, described in *New Ireland* the operation of a soup kitchen in Cork: 'Around the boilers on the roadside there daily moaned and shrieked and fought and scuffled crowds of gaunt cadaverous creatures that once had been men and women made in the image of God. The feeding of dogs in a kennel was much more decent and orderly.'[18]

The Soup Kitchen Act was limited to six months' duration. It was superseded by an Act of June 1847 which authorised the Guardians 'to relieve such poor persons being destitute as aforesaid, either in the workhouse or out of the workhouse, as to them shall appear fitting and expedient in each individual case', the cost to be met from the Irish poor rates. It was the first time that what became known as 'outdoor' relief was authorised for Ireland and was a fundamental change of direction from that enshrined in the Poor Law Relief Act of 1838. The 1847 Act also provided for the appointment of relieving officers who were empowered to grant provisional and emergency relief to the poor.

What were the qualifications for being classed among the 'destitute poor'? The June 1847 Act enacted that: 'No person who shall be in occupation of any land of greater extent than the quarter of a statute acre shall be deemed to be a destitute poor person, and it shall not be lawful for any Board of Guardians to grant relief within or out of the workhouse, to any such person.' This infamous addition became known as the Gregory Clause (it was included on the proposition of Sir William Gregory, who was later to become the husband of Augusta Persse, the Lady Gregory of Abbey Theatre fame). Henceforth, any person who occupied more than a quarter of a statute acre who applied for a place in the workhouse or for food for his family had to give up his patch of land to the landlord or face starvation. Desperate to hold on to their small patches, men tried to transfer their property to better-off relations or to send their wives and children to the workhouse, where they were usually rejected. It was not until the following year, after thousands of deaths from starvation, that the Poor Law Commissioners advised that families of the 'quarter acre' men could be helped.

Meanwhile, the Government, while giving with one hand was taking away with the other. Instead of keeping the public relief works in operation, even on a scaled down basis, it terminated them with callous haste when the soup kitchens were introduced By June 1847, upwards of 700,000 people had been discharged from the works; only about 20,000 were kept on to complete unfinished works. This was a savage blow and left hundreds of thousands in a desperate and pitiable state.

The saga of distress continued. On 5 November 1847 a crowd of destitute people marched on the workhouse at Tralee carrying a black flag marked 'flag of distress', declaring they would enter the workhouse by force. They had been deprived of outdoor relief of a 'halfpenny a day' by the Guardians, 'because the Board's finances could not bear even so small an allowance.'[19] They succeeded in breaking down the main gate. Police and troops were called out and the people were forced, after a struggle, to depart.

The Poor Law Commissioners had not been entirely idle during the famine years. The failure of the potato crop in 1846 spurred them into rethinking the workhouse dietary and on 5 February, 1849, a General Order was issued authorising the substitution of other food for potatoes – bread or Indian meal, as well as oatmeal, peas, turnips, carrots, parsnips, onions, cabbage, with milk and buttermilk; Boards of Guardians were given limited discretion in regard to the new diets (see Appendix 9). But the introduction of the new diets did not mean that workhouse difficulties were at an end. In March, a month after the General Order was issued, more than 200 men, women and children were refused admission to the workhouse or relief of any kind in Louisburgh, County Mayo. On their trek homeward, over the barren Delphi mountains, many of them died from starvation and exposure in bitter weather conditions – their sad journey is now remembered in local folklore as 'the trail of tears'.[20]

The famine multiplied the problems of the workhouses a hundredfold. Boards of Guardians, particularly in the acutely distressed areas of the west and south, soon found themselves unable to cope with the vast accumulation of human misery and suffering. Despite strong representations by the Guardians no financial contributions were forthcoming from the Government towards running costs, other than the provision of repayable loans and a grant-in-aid scheme; the latter proposed a levy on the richer Unions to help the poor Unions and was resisted as unfair.

Not surprisingly, many Boards, pressed with heavy debts to contractors, in arrears with their treasurers, and without adequate credit or resources, fell into a state of the most ruinous financial embarrassment approaching bankruptcy. In January 1847, Ballina workhouse had a debt of £2,000, Castlebar of £3,000, Scariff was about to close and Galway had already closed, its inmates driven out into the wilds. Westport, in perpetual financial crisis since its forced opening the previous year, would have had to turn out its 600 inmates but for the intervention, first of one of the Guardians, George Hildebrand, and later of the Marquess of Sligo.

Overwhelmed by the impossibility of bringing order out of chaos some workhouses requested the central authority to relieve them of their responsibilities. The Commissioners were still inclined to blame the Boards of Guardians for the situation and temporarily dissolved thirty-nine of them as inefficient and incapable of satisfactorily carrying out their functions; the administration of these workhouses was assigned to vice-guardians and inspectors appointed by the Commissioners.

As the poor rates were entirely inadequate to meet the emergency situation that had arisen in the years 1847–49, funds were supplemented under the Rates-in-Aid Act of 1849, when the Government made available to the Boards of Guardians a sum of £421,990, which, together with fines and penalties collected of £12,375, made a total of £434,365.

The workhouses were not the only body to suffer the financial effects of the famine. The cost of providing relief on such a vast scale by way of the poor rate proved disastrous for many landowners. As a consequence it became necessary to introduce the Encumbered Estates Act in 1849 to make the sale and transfer of estates of impoverished and ruined landlords easier. Some five million acres – about a quarter of all the arable land in the country – changed hands in the years following the famine. Many of the new landowners were Catholics who shrewdly acquired parcels of the insolvent estates at depressed prices. These new propertied classes were in the main of an acquisitive and conservative disposition, not overmuch concerned with the social and economic conditions of their poorer fellow-countrymen. The day of the strong farmer had dawned.

The most ironic footnote to the famine is the abortive rising of 1848. When Daniel O'Connell died in March 1847 the mantle of nationalism passed to the Young Irelanders, the most prominent of whom were James Fintan Lalor, John Mitchel, Gavan Duffy, Thomas Francis Meagher and William Smith O'Brien. The militants in the party took over and as historian F.S.L. Lyons puts it, 'They stumbled, or were pushed, into insurrection.' William Smith O'Brien attempted to raise the country without success and he himself was captured in Tipperary, complaining that 'the people prefer to die of starvation or flee as voluntary exiles to other lands, rather than fight for their lives and liberties.'

One wonders whether he noted the crowded workhouses in the towns through he passed on his recruiting campaigns – Enniscorthy, Carrick-on-Suir, Kilkenny, Cashel, Clonmel, Roscrea? Was he never passed on the road by small groups of desperate people making their way to ports for emigration east and west? At this remove we can only wonder at the extraordinary detachment of the Young Irelanders.

# 13

# Death in the Workhouse

*'Rattle my bones over the stones,*
*I'm a poor pauper that nobody owns.'*

AN OLD SAYING FROM THE WORKHOUSE DAYS

In *The Great Famine,* O'Rourke wrote: 'The year 1846 closed in gloom. It left the Irish people sinking in thousands into their graves under the influence of a famine as general as it was intense, and which trampled down every barrier set up to stay its desolating progress. But the worst was yet to come. It was in 1847 that the highest point in misery and death was reached ... in the deadly effects of a new scourge – fever.'[1]

Part of Sir Robert Peel's plan to deal with the anticipated famine of 1845 concerned the fever which inevitably followed famine. If no fever hospital was available locally (and there were only twenty-eight in the whole country, mostly in the cities and towns, with none at all in the most deprived areas) the workhouses were to provide one within the grounds. Only about fifty workhouses had acted on these instructions.

In March 1846, under imminent threat of even worse famine conditions, the Government passed an Act to make temporary provision for 'the relief of the destitute poor persons afflicted with fever in Ireland.' Under the Act, which expired on 31 August of the same year, a Central Board of Health was established in Dublin with powers to require Boards of Guardians to set up fever hospitals and to provide dispensaries and appoint extra medical officers.

The board was headed by Dr Dominick Corrigan. But there were complaints about 'useless expenditure of so much money' and the board was quietly allowed to disappear. It was not until spring 1847, when the epidemic was becoming increasingly serious, that it was reappointed. The intentions were excellent. Temporary fever sheds were to be erected, there was to be a bed for every patient and clothing was to be changed frequently. The only question was: where were the Boards of Guardians to find the money? In the meanwhile, until these utopian conditions came into being, the fever-stricken had, in most cases, only the workhouse to rely on.

It had never been envisaged that the workhouses would have to deal with large numbers of sick people. The Commissioners Report for 1846 reminded its readers that the hospital wards in the workhouse proper 'were provided to meet the casual sickness arising in a number of inmates generally presumed to be healthy'. But these were not normal times, and the Commissioners had to face an appalling truth: 'In the present state of things, nearly every person admitted is a patient.'[2]

In his 'Medical History of the Famine', Sir William MacArthur wrote:

The advent and extension of famine and the consequent deterioration in the sanitary standards of the afflicted people provided a fertile soil ready to receive the seeds of fever. Those exhausted by hunger and struggling to keep body and soul together by what they could find of dock leaves and nettles or an odd handful of raw meal were not likely to trouble greatly about personal cleanliness, even had they the strength to fetch water or firing to heat it. Such of their clothing as had any market value had been sold to passing peddlers, and the rags that were left they wore night and day, huddling together for warmth. The lack of cleanliness, the unchanged clothing and the crowding together provided ideal conditions for disease

to spread rapidly. In general the worse the famine in any
part the more intense the fever, and crowds of starving
people forsook their homes and took to the road,
carrying the disease with them wherever they went.

The famine fever was made up of two distinct species
of disease – typhus and relapsing fever. The widespread
and fatal dysentery which prevailed during the famine
was generally attributed to bad food: in most parts hard
hit by famine, dysentery was rampant before fever began
to spread. The extent and degree of scurvy in any
locality indicated the severity of famine there. It might
be of assistance to state the order in which the diseases
made their appearance: 1) scurvy, mouth signs first, later
purpura and haemorrhages; 2) extensive dysentery; 3)
famine dropsy; 4) very fatal typhus; 5) relapsing fever,
fast propagated by contagion but not so fatal.[3]

Though the British House of Commons was told in
January 1847 that fever had not yet appeared in Ireland,
outbreaks has occurred the previous year, in Galway in
April, in Carrick-on-Shannon in June, in Waterford in
October and in Mitchelstown in November. James Tuke
reported sickness almost everywhere he went:

> We left Ballyshannon late in the evening and passing
> through a miserably poor district we arrived at Sligo.
> The following day we visited the workhouse, which
> contained 1,162 inmates. It was in a bad condition as
> regards fever and dysentery, no less than 200 being
> reported sick. The deaths here were frightful, nearly
> twenty per week. The admissions during the past week
> were fifty, and as many as 200 had been admitted during
> one week. The crowding of the poor Irish into these sad
> refuges is but another confirming proof of the famine
> which exists; hunger has overcome even the Irishman's
> dread of infection and disease. We saw an open cart
> hastily traversing the streets of Sligo, without any other
> attendant than a driver, containing not less than six

coffins with bodies from the workhouse, thus passing without ceremony to the silent grave.[4]

By early 1847, fever had reached epidemic proportions all over the country. It is scarcely surprising that it spread so rapidly. Due to the lack of accommodation new admissions, whether sick or healthy, were crowded into already full wards, sometimes as many as four or five to a bed. The Board of Guardians in Fermoy reported in March, 'Every room is so crowded that it is impossible to separate the sick from the healthy ... fifty patients are crowded into a room too small for twenty ... bedding is so short as to render it necessary to place four or five in many of the beds ... thirty children labouring under disease were found in three beds.'[5]

Conditions were equally bad almost everywhere. Inspectors sent around to assess the situation gave horrifying reports: Dunmanway was 'dirty and disorderly'.[6] Bantry, where the inmates were down to one meal a day due to lack of funds, was even worse – 'The filth of the wards ... is past endurance'.[7] Lurgan buried its fever dead not far from the hospital, around the well which supplied the workhouse water.[8]

Mortality was high, not only due to the appalling conditions but also to the fact that many of those admitted were already on the point of death from starvation and fever. At least half the workhouse population was sick and thousands died each week. Medical and nursing facilities were minimal. The mortality rate among the staff was also severe; in 1847 alone fifty-four officers, including seven clerks, nine masters, seven medical officers and six chaplains died. This pattern was repeated throughout the period 1847–1850.

One of the most tragic aspects of the workhouse system in those years was the splitting up of families. Children over two years of age were put into children's wards. Mothers and daughters under two went into the female

*Funeral at Skibbereen*

quarters; fathers and sons into the male quarters. Many
families never saw each other alive again; sometimes, as
described by Charles Kickham in *Sally Kavanagh*, they
never knew if members were alive or dead.

Death became a way of life in the workhouse and the Irish
Poor Relief Extension Act of June 1847 empowered the
Guardians to acquire land adjacent to the workhouse for
use as burial ground for deceased inmates of the workhouse, as the ordinary graveyards were unable to cope with
the vast numbers of workhouse dead. These workhouse
graves, the loneliest few patches of soil in Ireland, 'to bury

strangers amid the friendless poor', became known as the 'Paupers' Plot' or the 'Potter's Field'. Deaths were so numerous that corpses were carried on special carts day after day to be thrown into mass pauper graves or pits in the workhouse grounds and covered with lime. Many were buried without coffins. In some instances a special mobile coffin with a sliding bottom was used, from which the corpse was dropped into the grave. The mobile coffin was mounted on wheels and was also used to collect the bodies of the poor who had not gained admission to the workhouse and who had died of starvation or fever by the roadside. Though the Guardians had power to arrange for the burial of poor persons, corpses were often left in the cabins, which were then knocked down on them as a sort of tomb, because of the danger of fever. As one account put it: 'Parishes all over the country being exhausted by rates refused to provide coffins for the dead paupers, and they were thrown coffinless into holes.'

W.S. Trench has left an eye-witness account of conditions in one part of the country in 1849:

> When I first reached Kenmare in the winter of 1849–50, the form of destitution had changed in some degree; but it was still very great. It was true that people no longer died of starvation; but they were dying nearly as fast of fever, dysentery, and scurvy within the walls of the workhouse. Food there was now in abundance; but to entitle the people to obtain it, they were compelled to go into the workhouse and 'auxiliary sheds', until these were crowded almost to suffocation. And although out-door relief had also been resorted to in consequence of the impossibility of finding room for the paupers in the workhouses, yet the quantity of food given was so small, and the previous destitution through which they had passed was so severe, that nearly as many died now under the hands of Guardians, as had perished before by actual starvation.
>
> I spent six weeks in Kerry; and having completed an elaborate report describing the past and present condition, and probable future of the estate, I forwarded it to Lord Lansdowne. The district of Kenmare at that period – January 1850 – was not in a desirable condition. 'The famine', in the strict acceptation of the term, was then nearly over, but it had left a train behind it, almost as formidable as its presence.[9]

When conditions in the country improved somewhat, the relatives and friends were able to afford to claim the bodies of inmates dying in the workhouse and arrange for decent and dignified burials. In this way the workhouse burials and 'Paupers' Graves' were gradually discontinued. Eventually the local sanitary authority became the main burial board for the provision of graveyards and decent burials under the Burial Grounds (Ireland) Act 1856 and the Public Health Acts 1878 and 1879. These Acts also helped to counter some of the abuses under the Anatomy Act of 1832 which decreed that the unclaimed bodies of paupers who had died in the workhouses should be made available to medical schools where they could be used for dissection in anatomy classes; Jeremy Bentham's disciples were instrumental in having this undesirable provision included.

However not everyone chose to die in the workhouse. Spencer T. Hall in *Life and Death in Ireland* (1849) recalled an incident which particularly struck him:

We found by the side of the green lane a man named Connor McInerney in a state of disease from which it seemed almost impossible that he could recover. His body and legs were so much swollen and so inert that at any point of pressure the indenture remained, almost as though it has been made of dead clay; and everything about him betokened a near dissolution. How happened he to be there? was one of our first enquiries when he informed us that he had crawled from the workhouse in Limerick. But why in that wretched state had he done so? Because, said he, his wife had died there already, and his two children would soon be gone too, and he had so longed once more to breathe the fresh air and to die, if he must die, near his home and among his people, that he had come away as best he could and had thus far accomplished his object. If ever a wild Irishman was seen in the world, sure enough he had his fellow in Connor. Yet notwithstanding all his roughness, there was a touch of nature in his soul that pleased me. He loved the sunshine and flowers and his boyhood home, and comfort according to the poor law was not half so precious to him.[10]

And what of the fate of those who either did not seek admission to the workhouse or were turned away. Sir William MacArthur gives one account:

> Neighbours and friends began avoiding all contact with a cabin where typhus fever was suspected. In some instances, brothers and sisters, and even mothers and fathers, would leave a stricken loved one alone in a cabin they believed to be infested with the disease. It was not desertion so much as quarantine, for once or twice a day these people would feed the ailing one inside by tying a can of water and a bit of hot gruel to the end of a long pole. The person inside would remove the food, tie an empty spare can to the end of the pole, and give the pole a tug as a signal that it should be withdrawn. It was only when there were no more tugs on the pole, when the food was left tied to the end of it, when shouted queries and entreaties were unanswered, that the whole cabin was pulled down on the dead person and set afire.'[11]

The Blasket Island writer, Peig Sayers, remembered getting a stern warning from her mother about going into cabins where people had died of famine fever: 'Stay away from the place or you will come to no good.'

It seems strange to us now that people who lived in such close proximity to one another should then have sought to isolate themselves from fever victims. But in those days nothing would have been known of incubation periods. People were presumed healthy until the first signs of fever appeared. Then all the inherited fear of infectious diseases such as cholera, typhus, typhoid, dysentery and smallpox, which killed in terrifying numbers and for which there was no apparent cure, would surface and the still healthy would distance themselves from those they knew must die.

Those who were refused admission to the workhouse, often having travelled a long distance to get there, had the alternative of dying by the roadside or seeking shelter elsewhere. One such refuge was sketched for the *Illustrated*

*London News* by James Mahony of Cork who had been commissioned to do some drawings in Skibbereen, where 'the scenes of starvation, horror and death were such as no tongue or pen could convey the slightest idea of'. There was an accompanying report by the local doctor:

On my return home, I remembered that I had yet a visit to pay, having in the morning received a ticket to see six members of one family named Barrett. They had struggled to the burying-ground, and literally entombed themselves in a small watch-house that was built for the shelter of those who engaged in guarding against exhumation by the doctors when more respect was paid to the dead than is at present the case. The shed is exactly seven feet long by about six in breadth. By the side of the western wall is a long newly made grave; by either gable are two of shorter dimensions, which have been recently tenanted, and near the hole that serves as a doorway is the last resting-place of two other children.

*The watch-house in Skibbereen*

In fact, this hut is surrounded by a rampart of human bones, which have accumulated to such a height that the threshold, which was originally on a level with the ground, is now two feet beneath it. In this horrible den, in the midst of a mass of human putrefaction, six individuals, males and females, labouring under the most malignant fever, were huddled together as closely as were the dead in the graves around.[12]

The final summing up comes from the Census of Ireland 1851:

No person has recorded the number of forlorn and starving who perished by the wayside or in the ditches, or of the mournful groups, sometimes of whole families who lay down and died, one after another, upon the floor of their miserable cabins, and so remained un-coffined and unburied till chance unveiled the appalling scene. No such amount of suffering amid misery has been chronicled in Irish history and yet, through all, the forbearance of the Irish peasantry and the calm submission with which they bore the deadliest ills that can fall on man, can scarcely be paralleled in the annals of any people.[13]

# 14

# The Workhouse and Emigration

*'Weep sore for him that goeth away; for he shall return to more, nor see his native country.'*

EPISTLES TO THE CORINTHIANS, ST. PAUL.

The massive explosion in population that occurred between 1779 and 1841 could not continue indefinitely. Even before the famine, efforts were being made to control the situation.

In his excellent study, *The Land and the People of Nineteenth-Century Cork,* James Donnelly refers to the more vigorous management of Irish estates that became clearly visible in the 1830s and 1840s:

> In order to increase their rents, or at least to make the payment of them more certain, landowners began to show a strong desire to eliminate middlemen, consolidate small and scattered farms, stop subdivision and sublettings and execute badly needed permanent improvement.[1]

Their aim was to increase the size of farms and turn from tillage to more profitable pasture.

But how could they rid themselves of unwanted tenants? Eviction was the answer, often by force, sometimes by inducement. When rents fell behind, tenants could have their arrears cancelled and be permitted to take away the materials of their cabins and re-erect them in another place – if they could find one. This worked to some extent in ridding certain estates of surplus population but neither forced nor induced evictions solved the problem; one landowner's cleared estate meant more congestion on another.

The Irish Poor Relief Act of 1838 had one important side effect. Landowners could now evict unwanted tenants with a clear conscience. The old question, 'Where am I to go?' could now be answered by, 'Go to the Union if you have no other resource for a maintenance.' But Irish labourers and cottiers did not take kindly to the workhouse. Thrown out of their cabins they found refuge in 'scalps', holes in the ground roofed over with sticks, or 'scalpeens', made within the ruins of the tumbled cabin.

In *A German in Ireland* (1842) J.H. Kohl warns:

Let the traveller look where he is going or he may make a false step, the earth may give way under his feet or he

*A 'scalp'*

*A 'scalpeen'*

may fall into – what? Into an abyss, a cavern, a bog? No, into a hut, a human dwelling-place, whose existence he has overlooked, because the roof on one side was level with the ground and nearly of the same consistency; if he draws back his foot in time, and looks around, he will find the place filled with a multitude of similar huts, all swarming with life. Of what is this human dwelling place composed? The wall of the bog often forms two or three sides of it, whilst sods taken from the adjoining surface form the remainder and cover the roof. Window there is none, chimneys are not known; an aperture in front, some three or four feet in height, serves as a door, window, chimney – light, smoke, pigs and children, all pass in and out of this aperture.[2]

The presence of these evicted tenants was a constant threat to the landowner who lived in fear of having his buildings burned and his cattle maimed. Scalps and scalpeens were declared illegal and if discovered the occupants were remorselessly hunted out, often with no other choice of refuge but the workhouse.

But the workhouse solution was not ideal for the landlord either. As Charles Bailey, Viscount Midleton's agent, pointed out, with 'an overpopulation and no means of sufficient and profitable employment at the union house, a burthen is at once created in another (though less objectionable) shape.' He was referring to the poor rate. So, as the 'most reasonable mode of lessening the redundant population by which alone the small holdings may be consolidated and made to form properly sized farms to command respectable and safe tenants,' he recommended assisted emigration.[3]

Emigration on a permanent basis had never been popular with the Irish and if one excludes the migration of the Presbyterians of Ulster who went to America at the end of the eighteenth century the numbers would have been very small indeed. Emigration was expensive and only relatively few could afford it. All this was to change in the the first quarter of the nineteenth century. During the Napoleonic wars, Great Britain could no longer get timber from Europe. She turned to Canada for supplies, and even when the war was over duties imposed on European timber ensured that the trade continued to flourish. There was only one drawback to this thriving traffic; exports to Canada were negligible so shipowners had the problem of empty ships going over. The solution was to find human 'ballast' and very soon shipping companies were sending agents around Ireland offering very low fares to would-be emigrants.

It was a development that was not lost on the landowners of Ireland. In *The Martins of Cro'Martin,* set in the 1830s, Charles Lever mentions the subject. On being advised that some of her tenants were displaying a 'wealthy independence', or turning to crime to combat want and destitution, Lady Dorothea called upon the superior on-the-ground knowledge of her agent:

> I don't see why we are to nurse pauperism either into fever or rebellion. To feed people that they may live to infect you, or, perhaps shoot you, is sorry policy. You showed me a plan for getting rid of them, Henderson – something about throwing down their filthy hovels or unroofing them or something of the kind, and then they were to emigrate – I forget where – to America, I believe – and become excellent people, hard-working and quiet. I know it all sounded plausible and nice ... [4]

In County Cork the Earl of Kingston sent two hundred families to Canada in 1835 at a cost of between £20 and £30 per family, and Lord Midleton is recorded as incurring 'a very great expense in sending to America all such as were disposed to emigrate'.[5]

The Government gave wholehearted support to assisted emigration schemes. It viewed such measures as a means of reducing the numbers of destitute persons, lessening the burden of the crippling poor rate on the landowners, and promoting better estate management. Thus, the interest of the Government and the landlords coincided, the only pawns in the *laissez-faire* game of the time being the people. The Poor Relief Acts of 1838, 1843, 1847 and 1849 empowered the Boards of Guardians to raise such sums 'not exceeding the proceeds of one shilling in the pound' of the annual poor rate to 'assist poor persons who would otherwise have to be accommodated in the work-house' to emigrate, preferably to the British colonies.

The Colonial Land and Emigration Commission was set up in England in 1840, under the control of the British Colonial Office, to organise and supervise emigration from both Britain and Ireland to the colonies. The objective was not only to reduce the numbers on poor law relief; it was regarded as a form of colonisation of countries then under British rule – Australia, Canada and New Zealand. But the favoured country of Irish emigrants was the United States of America which, no longer being a colony, was independent of the Emigration Commission (it was not until 1848, in the aftermath of the famine, that the scheme was extended to foreign countries other than the British colonies).

The availability of emigration was constantly brought to the attention of the Boards of Guardians in circular letters issued by the Poor Law Commissioners. Both those who were already supported from the poor rates in the work-houses or whose poverty-stricken state rendered them eligible for admission were covered by the scheme. The representatives of the Emigration Commission visited every workhouse in Ireland to inspect and select persons for emigration and those chosen were offered a free passage and supplied before departure with clothing and a little money to support themselves on arrival.

Emigration was thus established in Ireland during the 1830s and 1840s but it was not until the famine that it was institutionalised as a permanent feature of Irish life. In the years between 1845 and 1854 an average of 200,000 persons a year emigrated from Ireland to the United States, Canada, Australia and Britain, a total of two million people. Some of this emigration was officially assisted. Some of it was paid for by the people themselves in one way or another, by borrowing, selling their small holdings or by remittances from emigrant relatives. And during the worst years of the famine more and more landowners took advantage of the situation to accelerate land clearance by paying the passage of the emigrants or by chartering ships specially for this purpose.

The emigration schemes undertaken by the landowners were known as 'shovelling out' the tenants, because of the practice of demolishing their little cabins as they emigrated. In *Gleanings in the West of Ireland,* the Rev S.C. Osborne recorded in 1850 that a good gang of 'destructives' could pull down thirty cabins in a morning.[6] Even if a tenant refused the landlord's offer of emigration his cabin would be pulled down anyway. On the estate of Earl Fitzwilliam at Coollattin, County Wicklow, where his agents arranged in 1847 for the emigration of three hundred families comprising over 1,600 people, 'cabin to be thrown down' was the order, irrespective of acceptance or not. While the majority were glad of the offer, not all the tenants agreed to go and were prepared to accept the prospect of the workhouse or the scalpeen rather than leave Ireland, as the Coollattin Emigration papers show:

> Matt Doyle, wife and three children. Declines going. Cabin to be thrown down.
>
> William Byrne, aged fifty-six, with wife and eleven children. Declines going to America. Cabin to be thrown down.
>
> Simon Byrne, aged sixty-four and seven dependants. Won't go. Cabin to be thrown down.[7]

Sir William Butler describes in his autobiography an eviction and 'tumbling' he witnessed as boy in Tipperary:

> It dwells in my memory as one long night of sorrow. The sheriff, a strong force of police, and above all the crowbar brigade, a body composed of the lowest and most debauched ruffians, were present. At a signal from the sheriff the work began. The miserable inmates of the cabin were dragged out upon the road; the thatched

roofs were torn down and the earthen walls battered by crowbars (practice had made these scoundrels adepts at their trade); the screaming women, the half-naked children, the paralysed grandmother and the tottering grandfather were hauled out. It was a sight I have never forgotten. I was twelve years old at the time, but I think if a loaded gun had been put into my hands I would have fired into the crowd of villains as they plied their horrible trade.[8]

It is estimated that during the period 1846–49 thousands of tenants were evicted. The dispossessed wandered about the country, wretched, homeless, helpless, destitute and suffering. No neighbour was allowed to take them in; there was only the workhouse.

These evictions brought the accumulated evils of centuries to a crisis and resulted in a succession of assassinations of landlords. The most notorious was that of Major Denis Mahon of Strokestown, County Roscommon, who had evicted over three thousand persons, including eighty widows. He was shot on 2 November 1847 on his way back from a meeting of the Board of Guardians, which he had attended in connection with the underfunding of the workhouse. Many resident landlords, fearful for their lives, fled to London.

It was a sad chapter in Irish social history and many landowners paid dearly for their neglect of their estates. On well-managed estates evictions were rare and innumerable landlords such as the Rosses of Ross House in Connemara and the Brownes of Westport House did all they could to help famine and fever victims; indeed many were bankrupted because of the crippling poor rates. The dilemma facing the landlords is neatly summarised in one of the most detailed accounts of assisted emigration (that from Lord Landowne's Kenmare estate – see Appendix 10). Paupers from the estate who had gone into the workhouse numbered 3,000. Poor rates payable, at £5 a head, would amount to £15,000 a year – while rents brought in less than £10,000. If emigration were offered to all tenants in the workhouse, the cost would be from £13,000 to £14,000 – a once-off payment.[9]

It must be borne in mind that many destitute people were glad to emigrate; they saw no future for themselves or their families in the Ireland of that time. This was particularly true along the western seaboard. Population changes in Cork poor law Unions between 1841 and 1851 show reductions of between twenty and thirty-six per cent. So many people wanted to uproot themselves from the Earl of Bandon's estates in west Cork that inducements had to be offered to persuade some of them to stay and prevent 'whole tracts from being left desolate'.[10]

Chartering of ships by landlords for the transport of emigrants was not unusual. The Gore Booth Estate in Sligo transported over 1,300 emigrants in three chartered ships to Quebec, Canada, in the course of the year 1847. The master of one of these vessels wrote in June 1847 to Sir Robert Gore Booth as follows (sic): 'Sir: Your Kind acts at hoam to privint famine and to Elivate the Condition of the Poor is as well here as in the Town of Sligow. Your

Thankful Tennants were Highley Respected on being landed.'[11] However, the emigrants from Sligo carried in the third ship, in September 1847, were described on landing as a 'freight of paupers ... they did not have enough clothes for decency and the master had bought a quantity of red flannel shirts and blue trousers so that they could land without exposure.'[12]

As the demand for passages grew the emigrants were often the unsuspecting victims of heartless and fraudulent emigration agents, ship-brokers, speculators and touts. Many of the ships in which they were forced to travel were old, inadequate and totally unsuitable for the numbers carried. In the overcrowded conditions, fever and dysentery were rampant, and there was a lack of food and water. An official report, 'Papers Relative to Emigration', had this to say:

> The ships used were of the cheapest and worst kind. However, more responsible landlords were concerned by alarming reports of the dreadful deprivations and terrible suffering endured by the emigrants during the voyages, which took ten to twelve weeks, and indeed after their arrival. One such landlord, Sir Stephen de Vere of Limerick, travelled steerage on an emigrant ship in order 'that he might speak as a witness respecting the sufferings of emigrants'. He reported that 'hundreds of poor people, men, women, and children of all ages, were huddled together without light, without air, wallowing in filth and breathing a foetid atmosphere, sick in body, dispirited in heart; fever patients lying in sleeping places so narrow as almost to deny a change of position – their agonized ravings disturbing those around them, living without food or medicine, dying without spiritual consolation and buried in the deep without the rites of the Church.'[13]

Because of the number of deaths during the voyages, these emigrant ships became known as 'coffin ships' and it is estimated that in the year 1847 alone about 40,000 of the 215,000 emigrants died at sea. Nor did all ships reach their destinations; some of them were so unseaworthy that they sank with great loss of life. But the terrors of the journey could not deter the flight from a doomed land where there was only the prospect of the workhouse (if they were among the lucky admissions) or starvation (if they were not).

The Poor Law Commissioners, in recommending emigration to workhouse inmates, had Canada in mind primarily. The passage was cheaper than to the United States and the British Government provided help in taking emigrants into the interior. But the low fares also meant that the standards both of safety and of health were inferior to those on United States ships. Emigrants to Canada sailed up the St Lawrence waterway to destinations in Quebec and Montreal but before they were allowed to land they had to stop at Grosse Ile, the quarantine station about thirty miles from Quebec. One of the most tragic stories of the westward flood of Irish emigrants was to take place in this pleasant, flowering island.

Through 1846 and early 1847 the Canadian authorities were aware, through ships' manifests, of the numbers of passengers sailing to Quebec. They knew by April 1847 that more than 28,000 Irish had left Liverpool and Irish ports. They were also aware that the United States had doubled the cost of passage and was instituting strict health controls on passengers.

It was a late spring and the St Lawrence river did not open until mid-May. One of the first ships to arrive, either the *Urania* from Cork or the *Syria* from Liverpool, carried the first cases of typhus, or ship's fever as it was known. The hospitals at Grosse Ile could care for 200 sick and there was shelter for 800 healthy people. On 23 May the hospitals already held 530 sick and forty to fifty deaths a day were being recorded. Soon Grosse Ile was swamped by the waves of immigrants – 12,000 by 1 June, 14,000 by 8 June. They were discharged in their thousands, ragged and bewildered, weak from hunger, exhaustion and often fever.[14] The death toll was savage; of the 100,000 Irish who left for Canada in 1847, over 42,000 perished – 17,000 during the voyages, over 5,000 in quarantine at Grosse Ile and a further 20,000 at the landing points upstream in Quebec and Montreal.

The authorities at Grosse Ile and Quebec did their best but there were simply not enough facilities to stem the tide of disease and death. The sick were nursed in the overcrowded hospitals, in tents and hastily erected sheds, the dead buried, the orphans consigned to relatives or Canadian families who adopted them. The authorities could not but be struck by the contrast between German immigrants arriving, 'all healthy, robust and cheerful', and the Irish who resembled emaciated spectres as they tottered and crawled off the Irish ships.[15] The Canadians made their views known. The Mayor of Montreal signed a petition to Queen Victoria:

> That your petitioners have learned with equal surprise and pain that some Irish landlords, among whom is said to be one of your Majesty's ministers, have resorted to the expedient of transporting the refuse population of their estates to Canada. We cannot turn these people away famished, like the Eastern United States and Liverpool did . . .'[16]

The emigration agent at Quebec sought the reason behind the mass Irish exodus and a series of sworn depositions disclosed the tragedies and heartbreak that lay behind some of the 'assisted' emigration. The deposition of Bryan Prior, labourer, of the parish of Drumreilly, County Leitrim, read:

> He has a wife and four children under twelve. He farmed five acres on the estate of Collins. For six weeks

before leaving he had nothing. Collins' agent Benson promised to give him relief if he gave up his land. The minute he did this his house was pulled down. Then Benson said the land was of insufficient value, therefore he could give them nothing. Benson refused to send wife and children to America, it was expensive enough to send him, 'and be thankful for it'. The wife and children are now in Ireland without a house or a home, as far as this deponent has any knowledge of their condition and he now declares that he is in a most distressed state of mind, without money, clothing or food. Signed at Grosse Ile, 12 September 1847. Robert Symes, JP.[17]

Other Priors from the same parish appear on the list of orphans in the Catholic orphanage of Quebec as being admitted on 20 September 1847. They were adopted by 'Person in Rimouski'.

The *Quebec Mercury* was sufficiently interested to reprint from an article from *The Whig*, in October:

There is a large British force in Ireland; larger than the whole army and navy of the United States, including the armies of Mexico. At the beginning of September there were in Ireland ten regiments of cavalry; thirty battalions of infantry; two troops of horse artillery; nine companies of artillery, two companies of marines, making a total of 28,000 rank and file; plus 21,182 enrolled pensioners, militia staffs and recruiting parties. Add 11,000 constabulary and you get 60,000 men.[18]

The British remained unmoved. Two officials of the Colonial Land and Emigration Office adopted the Trevelyan line:

We confess that after reflecting on these difficulties, we are led to think that when it has pleased Providence to afflict Ireland with a famine, and consequent fever, which could not be subdued, even on the land, it was little likely that any human contrivance could have averted the same evil from the multitudes who had made arrangements for a long passage by sea.[19]

An extraordinary footnote to the Grosse Ile story concerns the fate of nearly 1,000 immigrant orphans. There still exist lists made by Catholic and Protestant church authorities for Quebec and Montreal. That preserved by the Grey Nuns of Quebec gives the names of the orphans, their age, their mother and father, parish and county of origin, the ship in which they sailed and the name of their adoptor (an excerpt is given at Appendix 11). Some notations, made up to the 1860s, record marriages or ordinations of charges of the orphanage. At the unveiling of the memorial to 'les immigrants Irlandais' in 1909, many French-speaking people could say, 'I was taken as a nameless child from this island and given to a family who did not let me forget that I was Irish.'[20]

A memorial in the shape of a Celtic cross, with inscriptions in Irish, England and French, was unveiled on 15 August 1909. It stands on Telegraph Hill, the highest point of Grosse Ile.

> Sacred to the memory of thousands of Irish emigrants, who, to preserve the faith, suffered hunger and exile in 1847–48, and stricken with fever, ended here their sorrowful pilgrimage. Erected by the Ancient Order of Hibernians in America.[21]

Another memorial was erected on the site of the emigrant cemetery:

> In this secluded spot lie the mortal remains of 5,294 persons who fleeing pestilence and famine in Ireland in the year 1847 found here a grave. Sacred to the memory of thousands of Irish emigrants who suffered hunger and exile and stricken with fever ended here their sorrowful pilgrimage.[22]

One of the 5,294 was the wife of a John Ford of Cork. He

survived, made his way to Detroit, and became the grandfather of Henry Ford.

The Irish emigration to the United States was not accompanied by the tragedy of the Canadian landings. There was
such massive emigration to the States, via New York and
Boston, that Passenger Acts were passed by the US Congress as an emergency measure in 1847 providing for stringent controls on arrivals at Americans ports. The result
was that the destitute and fever-stricken were almost invariably landed in Canada. Also, because of the unprecedented influx a Commission of Emigration was set up in
New York in 1847, headed by the Mayor and comprised of
voluntary members, to look after the welfare of emigrants,
to arrange for care of the sick, and to provide advice and
assistance in getting jobs. These measures meant that
although there were hardships, nothing like the decimation
and death experienced at Grosse Ile occurred in New York.

The United States, not Canada, was the mecca for Irish
emigrants. Even those who landed or were forced to land
in Canada tried, despite police patrols, to make their way
across the border to the States on the other side of the St
Lawrence waterway. It is estimated that the numbers of
Irish emigrants entering the United States directly (and
indirectly through Canada) were:

| | | |
|------|---------|---------|
| 1846 | 105,000 | |
| 1847 | 216,000 | |
| 1848 | 174,000 | |
| 1849 | 213,000 | |
| 1850 | 209,000 | 917,000 |
| 1851 | 250,000 | |
| 1852 | 218,000 | |
| 1853 | 179,000 | |
| 1854 | 135,000 | |
| 1855 | 73,000 | 855,000 |

Thereafter numbers began to decline.[23]

There was some emigration to Australia during the famine years but the total of 19,000 was not significant. Among that number were 4,000 girl orphans from the work-houses.[24]

Labour had become extremely scarce in Australia around the time of the famine in Ireland and the colonists in New South Wales and Western Australia begged the Colonial Office in London (which was responsible for developing the colonies) to secure more settlers. Arrangements were made with the Colonial Land and Emigration Commissioners for a scheme of assisted emigration under which the first 5,000 adults were sent in 1847 to Australia. The Emigration Commissioners, who had promised to send as many young unmarried women as possible to meet the acute shortage there, reported in 1848 that they had great difficulty in securing single females of suitable character for Australia. This was an old difficulty. So the Colonial Secretary, aware of the large numbers of orphan girls in workhouses, suggested to the Emigration Commissioners that the scheme be extended to Irish workhouse orphan girls 'with an industrial and domestic education suitable for colonial life'. The Commissioners seized upon the idea, as did the Irish Poor Law Commissioners.

The project was no sooner suggested than it was put into operation, with a quota of 2,500 for the first year. In March 1848 the Poor Law Commissioners sent a circular memorandum to all the Boards of Guardians advising them of the scheme and requesting a list of suitable oprhan girls, between fourteen and eighteen years of age. All the expense the Guardians had to bear was the cost of getting the girls to Plymouth, where a depot had been long estab-lished, and of supplying their clothes for the voyage – the recommended 'trousseau' was six shifts, two flannel petticoats, six pairs of stockings, two pairs of shoes and two gowns (one of which must be made of warm material). Spiritual needs were catered for by the provision of a prayer-book and a bible for each girl – the authorised bible for the Protestants and the Douai version for the Catholics. The workhouses contributed from £3 to £5 per girl, the balance of the cost of the scheme being funded by the Colonial Office. The response of the Boards of Guardians was very positive, for they had found it impossible to place the hordes of orphan children which the famine had left on their hands in their workhouses. A list of orphans was proposed and the girls were inspected by the Dublin agent of the Emigration Commissioners. Those selected were sent to Plymouth as soon as possible and the first vessel managed to get away in May 1848. Others followed later. Both the diet and accommodation at sea and the facilities on board were said to be vastly superior to those on ordinary vessels. The voyage to Australia took about a hundred days.

On the whole the workhouse emigration was regarded as tolerably successful, both from the standpoint of the colonies and the girls themselves. As for the Boards of Guardians, when the scheme came to an end in July 1849 they had been relieved of more than 2,000 orphans who could not have been provided for at home. Indeed the Guardians were now complaining that their quotas had been insufficient, while those Guardians who had sent none felt a sense of grievance. In the circumstances, the Poor Law Commissioners authorised the selection of a further 2,000 orphan girls. The second emigration followed closely the pattern of the first.

But at this stage a general feeling amongst the colonists in Australia against the Irish children seems to have developed. The main cause of dissatisfaction was apparently the increasing difficulty in finding work for girls who were inadequately trained, and also some reluctance to colonisation on the part of the girls themselves (some of whom had been taken from gaols). As a result the scheme was abandoned entirely, after having been in operation for two years, 1848/49 and 1849/50. In all, 4,175 orphan girls were sent out from workhouses in Ireland – 4,114 to

Australia and 61 to the Cape of Good Hope (see Appendix 12).[25]

Meanwhile, the assisted workhouse emigration of adults had proceeded steadily since 1847. It was negligible in comparison with the great exodus to the USA and Canada but at least 15,000 who could not otherwise have reached Australia benefitted before such assisted emigration also ceased.

Emigrants to America, Canada and Australia knew that in all probability they would never see Ireland again. For those who were left behind the moment of parting was like a death in the family:

> A deafening wail resounds as the station bell gives the signal for starting. I have seen grey-haired peasants to clutch and cling to the departing child at the last moment that only the utmost force of three or four friends could tear them asunder. The porters have to use some violence before the train moves off, the crowd so presses against door and window. When at length it moves away, amidst a scene of passionate grief, hundreds run along the fields beside the railway line to catch yet another glimpse of the friends they shall see no more.

The Halls recorded the departure of an emigrant ship from Cork:

> We stood, in the month of June, on the quay at Cork to see some passengers embark in one of the steamers for Falmouth, on their way to Australia. The band of exiles amounted to two hundred and an immense crowd had assembled to bid them a long and last adieu. The scene was very touching ... It is impossible to describe the final parting. Shrieks and prayers, blessings and lamentations mingled in one great cry from those on the quays and those on shipboard, until a band stationed in the forecastle struck up 'Patrick's Day'. The communicating plank was withdrawn, the steamer moved

forward majestically on its way. Some, overcome with emotion, fell down on the deck. Others waved hats, handkerchiefs, and hands to their friends; the band played louder; and the crowds on shore rushed forward simultaneously, determined to see the last of those they loved.[26]

Not all emigration was westward or 'down under'; there was also emigration of immense proportions eastwards. It was not assisted and was vigorously discouraged by the British authorities, but as it only cost a few shillings to cross the Irish sea, with the possibility of being accepted free as ballast on board boats returning to England from Irish ports, England was within reach of even the poorest. The English Poor Law Commissioners reported to the Government in 1847:

> The severity of the distress in Ireland has produced an influx of Irish, in a state of extreme destitution into several towns on the western coast of England. Liverpool, as being the port nearest to Dublin, and with which the principal steam communication is carried on, received the largest number of this class of immigrants.
>
> The numbers, having begun to increase in December, advanced rapidly in January and February and still more rapidly in March and April. From the 13th of January to the 20th April, 1847, during which period an accurate account of Irish immigrants was kept, there arrived at Liverpool 133,069 persons from Ireland. Some have remained chargeable on the rates of Liverpool, others have proceeded further into the interior of the country, but several thousands have emigrated to Canada and the United States.
>
> Many have reached Manchester and other manu-facturing towns of Lancashire: and we have received statements from several Boards of Guardians on the subject of provision for the increased number of Irish

vagrants. Large numbers of Irish have also landed at Newport and Chepstow, and have thence moved on to Cheltenham and other towns in the midland counties. A considerable number of Irish poor (estimated at about 1,000 within a week) have recently been landed in London by steamers from Cork and Dublin. In addition, to these some Irish have reached London from Bristol and Newport.

The numbers of Irish emigrants arriving in England has reached deluge proportions. It is recorded that by June 1, 1847, 300,000 Irish had landed in Liverpool in five months, descending on a town with a native population of only 250,000.

Similarly great numbers of Irish landed in other ports in England, Scotland and Wales during 1847. Once the emigrants got themselves across the Irish sea they were assured of a modicum of food, clothing and shelter under the Poor Law Relief Act, which had been passed in 1834, setting up the workhouses in England.[27]

It was primarily because of their desire to minimise this uncontrolled emigration to Britain that the Government and its agencies so actively promoted the schemes for emigration to America and the colonies. Even when colonial-assisted emigration ceased, in 1850, the Poor Law Commissioners were still very active in encouraging Boards of Guardians to continue with poor rate assisted emigration from the workhouses, especially in the case of those having friends or relatives in America, Canada and Australia, who had sent portion of the sum necessary to defray the cost of emigration, as well as in the case of inmates dependent on free passages borne by the rates. Proposals to assist inmates of workhouses to emigrate had to be approved by the Poor Law Commissioners, who had received assurances from their emigration agents that there was a growing demand for labour in these countries. In accordance with usual procedure the Guardians made arrangements to see the emigrants on board the vessels at the various Irish ports and ensure that the shipowners provided bedding and provisions for the voyage as laid down in the Passenger Acts, ie, seven pounds of provisions to be given out weekly and three quarts of water per person daily.

The total number of workhouse inmates – men, women and children – assisted to emigrate from 1851 to 1907 was 44,800, and the amount advanced from the rates was £161,550, plus a grant of £10,000 from the remaining balance of the Rate-in-Aid fund for assisting emigration from the worst circumstanced workhouses in the west and south-west of the country. There was a change of policy for the provision of relief under the Local Government (Ireland) Act of 1898, and assisted emigration was gradually phased out.[28]

The latter half of the nineteenth century saw the diaspora – the scattering of the Irish across the Atlantic ocean, that 'bowl of bitter tears'. It was these emigrants, leaving their homeland with sadness and bitterness in their hearts, who built up communities in America and other lands, and whose descendants, preserving memories of the sufferings and injustices borne by their forefathers, were to have a significant influence in helping the cause of national independence at home. It has truly been said that 'the Irish connection is an essential ingredient to the understanding of America and vice-versa.'

It is estimated that between 1841 and 1925 gross overseas emigration included 4$\frac{1}{2}$ million going to the USA, 70,000 to Canada and over 370,000 to Australia.[29] As a consequence of this mass emigration Ireland is a mother country with large overseas populations who still have ties of affection with and racial pride in their ancestral homeland. The descendants and children of Ireland's emigrants from those days gave Ireland what has been described as a 'spiritual empire'. In recognition of this, and as a bond of unity with the greater Ireland beyond the seas, the Government and people of Ireland ensured, with the Irish Nationality and Citizenship Act of 1956, that anyone with an Irish-born parent or grandparent, ie, first, second or even third generation Irish descendants of emigrants in the United States, Great Britain, Canada, Australia, New Zealand or elsewhere is entitled as a right to claim Irish citizenship and heritage and the same privileges as a native-born citizen.

# 15

# Later History of the Workhouses

*'The exclusion of meat, cheese, tea and butter (which are used in the workhouses in England) from the workhouse dietary in Ireland was due to the fact that meat was not an ordinary article of food for the Irish labourer or peasant . . . '*

REPORT OF THE POOR LAW COMMISSIONERS FOR 1860

The average number of inmates in the workhouses in the period 1845-1855 was:[1]

| | |
|---|---|
| 1845 | 38,497 |
| 1846 | 42,089 |
| 1847 | 83,283 |
| 1848 | 128,020 |
| 1849 | 193,650 |
| 1850 | 211,047 |
| 1851 | 217,388 |
| 1852 | 166,855 |
| 1853 | 129,390 |
| 1854 | 95,197 |
| 1855 | 75,599 |

The workhouse population reached its peak of 217,000 in 1851 – the system, it may be remembered, was designed to cater for 80,000 people. From then on it began to decline. The use of the 'sheds' was gradually discontinued and the situation was further eased by the provision of another thirty-three workhouses in the following Unions:

1849: Dingle.
1852: Ballymahon, Ballyvaughan, Bawnboy, Belmullet,

> Castletownbere, Claremorris, Clonakilty, Corofin, Croom, Dromore West, Glin, Glenamaddy, Kildysart, Killala, Millstreet, Mitchelstown, Mount Bellew, Newport, Oughterard, Portumna, Schull, Strokestown, Tulla, Tubbercurry.
>
> 1853: Borrisokane, Castlecomer, Castletowndevlin, Donaghmore, Kilmacthomas, Thomastown, Urlingford, Youghal.

These additional workhouses were built to an improved design to meet criticism of the planning and structural shortcomings in the original plans. A statement showing the complete list of the 163 workhouses provided in the thirty-two counties of Ireland is given at Appendix 13, together with details of the cost, the area of the workhouse site and lands, numbers intended to be accommodated, and the opening date. In every case the workhouses were provided under the central authority at that time – the Poor Law Commissioners.

In 1857, when the workhouse population was 50,688, the Poor Law Commissioners were able to report that 'the state of administration of relief of the destitute in Ireland may be looked upon as nearly identical to that contemplated on the passing of the 1838 Act.'[2] With the population now reduced, by famine, disease and emigration, to about five million, workhouse accommodation was at one per cent of the population, the figure on which the financing estimates for the workhouses were originally based.

The achievement of George Wilkinson and his small staff in arranging for the erection of 163 major buildings and ancillary accommodation, in the space of about ten years, received an ironic reward; in 1854 the Poor Law Commissioners were able to order the closing down of the architect's department in Dublin, as part of an economy campaign. George Wilkinson's contract was terminated.[3]

The decrease in numbers after the famine years and the changeover to the more humane system of outdoor relief, restricted though it was, led to better conditions within the workhouse, but it was many years before any improvements were made in the dietary scale, which continued to be monotonous and at subsistance level. The Irish Poor Law Commissioners in their annual report for 1860 stated: 'The exclusion of meat, cheese, tea and butter (which are used in the workhouses in England) from the workhouse dietary in Ireland was due to the fact that meat was not an ordinary article of food for the Irish labourer or peasant, all diets being fixed in conformity with the character of the diet used generally by the peasantry of Ireland.'[4]

However, by the end of the nineteenth century, inmates of delicate health and the aged were allowed tea and bread for breakfast instead of the stirabout and milk which continued to be the fare of the majority. A meat-soup dinner was gradually introduced on a few days a week in most workhouses, the Commissioners specifying that it 'consist of three oxheads to one hundred inmates or an equivalent quantity of other description of meat ingredients.'

Potatoes were allowed for dinner 'one or more days in the week – three and a half pounds with half a pint of milk'. Tea, where given in the workhouse dietary, 'may be propared according to the standard in Article 13, No 14, of the Workhouse Regulations, viz., in the proportion of half a pound of tea and two pounds of sugar to eight gallons of water and two quarts of New Milk.' Eventually the inmates were given an allowance of tobacco and snuff.

Care for the sick was also improved. The Poor Relief (Ireland) Act 1862, provided for the admission to the hospital wards of the workhouse, people requiring medical or surgical aid. Admissions were at the discretion of the Guardians and a charge was made. The Act also authorised the Guardians to send any inmates of workhouses who required treatment to any hospital (including voluntary hospitals) willing to receive them, and to pay the cost of treatment and conveyance. In addition, it also repealed the section of the 1847 Act which prohibited the giving of relief in a workhouse to a person who had over a quarter of an acre of land (the prohibition on granting outdoor relief to such persons remained in force until 1921).

In the original job specifications of the workhouse, no particular qualifications were prescribed for nurses, so unqualified and inexperienced persons were often employed. This changed in 1861 with the appointment of Sisters of Mercy, who were dedicated to the relief of the sick poor as qualified nurses (in addition to the three traditional vows, the Sisters took a vow of service to human needs). This development was not altogether welcomed by the Poor Law Commissioners, who were at first reluctant to give their approval on the ground of the 'impolicy' of appointing, as officers of a workhouse in Ireland, persons bound by religious vows.

The first appointment of Sisters of Mercy, to Limerick workhouse in 1861, followed prolonged correspondence by the Board of Guardians and the Commissioners, who had originally opposed the appointments. The Guardians pointed out that out of over 1,300 paupers in the workhouse, there were 400 in the hospital section, that there was no hospital matron to exercise direction and control, that the sick were cared for by only three nurses and thirty-six pauper attendants, and that there appeared to be an entire absence of moral control over either nurses or patients. At one stage, the three Sisters of Mercy proposed for appointment even offered to donate their salaries of £20 per annum each to improve the condition of the patients. Eventually the Commissioners yielded to the insistence of the Guardians and conveyed their approval to the appointments in January 1861.[5]

This resulted in the single most important reform in workhouse administration as regards nursing. The arrangement whereby any female inmate of the workhouse could be employed in the sick wards was phased out. From then on no inmate could be employed in the sick or lying-in wards except by special permission of the medical officer.

In due course, the Sisters became matrons and were an active force in improving conditions in the workhouses. The authorities were not slow to react. Eleven years later there was a glowing reference to them in an official report:

> Their devotion to their work, care of the patients and the whole tone of the wards left a most favourable impression. With the full sanction and approval of the highest ecclesiastical authorities, the nuns have been allowed to adopt, in lieu of their black dress of the Mercy order, a suitable washing habit of white drill with a plain white coif. This change is most welcome.[6]

A circular was issued to all Boards of Guardians in 1881 recommending that Sisters of Mercy be engaged as nurses in all workhouses.

That appointment of the first Sisters of Mercy in 1861 established an important precedent and the Sisters were appointed in other workhouses. The tradition survives into the present time; in the Limerick Regional Hospital, under the Mid-Western Health Board, the matron is a Sister of Mercy, as are some of the staff. Other hospitals and institutions are also under the care of the Sisters of Mercy.

In time, as social and economic conditions throughout the country began to improve and the workhouse population reached manageable proportions, there was a gradual easement of discipline and rather more tolerable conditions eventually prevailed. Over the years the role and function of the workhouse changed. It became more and more an institution for the old, the sick, and vagrants, and less and less a semi-prison for able-bodied men and women. But the dreadful conditions which pertained during the famine years remained in the memory of the people for generations. The stigma of the workhouse would never be eradicated. It is an extraordinary comment on the depth of this folk consciousness that very few people in subsequent generations would admit to having had family members or relatives in the workhouse.

## Children in the Workhouse

Up to the passing of the Irish Poor Relief Act of 1838 children were taken into charge by the Dublin Foundling Hospital, which became a gigantic depository for abandoned and illegitimate children from all over the country. The mismanagement of the hospital was so notorious that it was phased out by Section 34 of the 1838 Act. W. D. Wodsworth, a one-time secretary of the Irish Local Government Board, in his history of that establishment observed that 'it took one hundred and thirty years to convince people of the error of founding such an institution.' Unfortunately, the alternative, under Section 41 of the 1838 Act, was to entrust the care of destitute children to Boards of Guardians, who were generally slow to adopt boarding-out arrangements except for very young children. The majority were set to work in the workhouses, where they were generally treated in an indifferent and heartless manner and brought up in appalling conditions. In the earlier years of the workhouses the number of children under fifteen years of age was over fifty per cent of the total number of workhouse inmates.

In their report for 1853 the Poor Law Commissioners made a special survey of the number of young people in the workhouse on 2 April, under the headings of age, state of education, whether they had been in gaol and whether illegitimate or not (see Appendix 14). They conceded that the continued residence of children in the workhouse had harmful effects, both physically and mentally.[7]

The Poor Relief (Ireland) Act of 1862, though mainly devoted to the provision of hospital care, was important in that it gave more effective powers to Boards of Guardians for the boarding-out of orphans and deserted children, raising the age limit from five to eight years of age.

Gradually the proportion of children in the workhouses dropped and by 1870 it was down to twenty-five per cent. The powers to board out were greatly extended by the Orphans and Deserted Children Act of 1872 and the Pauper Children (Ireland) Acts of 1898 and 1902. As a result great numbers of children were removed from the unsuitable workhouse environment and by the early nineteen hundreds the percentage of children in the workhouses had dropped to thirteen per cent.[8]

But the workhouses remained pathetically unsuitable for children, posing problems in regard to their education, occupational training and discipline. Being institutionalised from an early age they were neither equipped nor trained to make their way in the outside world. Many girls, disowned because they became pregnant, had to enter the workhouse as a last resort to have their babies and this gave rise to special difficulties. Those who survived into adulthood drifted mainly into menial jobs on farms or in domestic service or emigrated (over 4,000 of them to Australia, as we have seen).

From the 1850s onwards, with the encouragement of Cardinal Cullen, Archbishop of Dublin, religious orders became active in caring for orphans and homeless children and opened several orphanages and industrial schools. The Society of St Vincent de Paul opened an orphanage for boys in 1858 (in Glasnevin, Dublin), which was taken over in 1861 by the Irish Christian Brothers. The Protestant and Presbyterian churches were also active in this work and provided for their homeless children through boarding-out and day-centres rather than in institutions.

When the workhouses were adapted as County Homes in the early 1920s the number of children in institutional care was reduced further. On 31 March 1925, the number of children in County Homes (out of an overall total of 18,100) was returned as 1,528, the number in extern institutions as 768, and the number boarded out as 1,907, a total of 4,257.[8]

# 16

# The Irish Workhouse in Writings

*'There was no room in the workhouse for half of them. Those who could not get in just went and lay down on the bank of the river below the bridge. They were to be seen there every morning after spending the night there, stretched in rows, some stirring, and some who were quiet enough and stirring no longer. Presently people came and lifted those who were still, put them into carts and carried them up to a place near Carrigastyra where a big, wide, deep pit gaped open for them, and threw them all into the pit together.'*

MO SCEAL FÉIN.

In Ireland, as in other countries, literature is the mirror in which the events of a nation's history are reflected, so the study of literature may in many respects be regarded as the study of a country and its people. But such was the deep and abiding abhorrence of the workhouse that, not surprisingly, it makes only a muted appearance in our creative writing. And so the lost and secret voices of the nineteenth century destitute are mainly unrecorded in Irish literature. Nevertheless the workhouse and its miseries are part of the history of our land and our race, both at home and beyond the seas. As such they deserve to be recalled and remembered. Our roots are in the past, and the past, both the good and the bad, belongs to us.

Charles J. Kickham (1828-1882) was an Irish writer on whom the workhouse made a deep impression:-

> *My father died; I closed his eyes*
> *Outside our cabin door.*

*The landlord and the sheriff too*
*Were there the day before!*
*And then my loving mother,*
*And sisters three also,*
*Were forced to go with broken hearts*
*From the Glen of Aherlow.*

*For three long months, in search of work,*
*I wandered far and near.*
*I went then to the workhouse*
*For to see my mother dear:*
*The news I heard nigh broke my heart,*
*But still in all my woe,*
*I bless the friends who made their graves*
*In the Glen of Aherlow.*

In his novel *Knocknagow*, set in Ireland at the mid-nineteenth century, he gives this account, in the form of a letter from one of the characters, of the feelings of the people about the workhouse:

Poor Father McMahon is heartbroken at the sufferings of the people. The workhouse is crowded, and the number of deaths is fearful. Last Sunday, when requesting the prayers of the congregation in the usual way for the repose of the souls of those who died during the week, the list was so long that he stopped in the middle of it, exclaiming with a heart-piercing cry, 'O my poor people! my poor people!' and then turned round and prostrated himself at the foot of the altar convulsed with grief, and could not go on reading the list of deaths for a long time. Then he got into a rage and denounced the government as a 'damnable government'.

I was quite frightened at the excitement of the people. Some faces were quite white, and others almost black. But a very effecting incident turned their anger into pity, though one would think it ought only incense them all the more against their rulers. When Father McMahon resumed the reading of the list, a woman shrieked out and fell senseless upon the floor. She was one of the paupers in the auxiliary workhouse, who are marched to the parish chapel every Sunday, as the chapel in the regular workhouse is too small even to accommodate the inmates of that house. This poor woman was only admitted the week before with her husband and children from whom, according to the infamous rules of the workhouse, she was at once separated. She now heard her husband's name read from the altar-list of the dead, and with a wild shriek fell down, and was borne senseless out of the chapel. The workhouse had not even taken the trouble to inform her that her husband was dead! Were human beings ever treated before as our poor people are treated? I often wondered at the almost wild looks of the paupers while the list of deaths was being read. But I understand it now. Oh! I must drive away the thought of such barbarous cruelty, and not distress you with such pictures of human suffering. But perhaps it is well to think of these things sometimes and pray to God to alleviate the misery around us. I do my best to keep up my spirits.[1]

In another novel, *Sally Cavanagh*, Kickham describes a scene that must have happened over and over again in the annals of workhouse admissions:

'The youngest little boy, Sir!' exclaimed Sally Cavanagh as she clasped her treasure to her bosom – as if to hide it there – and looked imploringly into the face of the workhouse official. But it was no use; she had to comply with the rules.

The children followed the official into a long corridor. Before the door closed behind them, they turned around to take a last look at their mother, and as they did so their little hearts died within them. Surely something horrible was going to happen to them! For their mother stretched out her hands towards them with a look of despair, as if she saw a bottomless pit yawn and swallow them up before her eyes. Poor terror-stricken children! Miserable heartbroken mother!

'This way, good woman,' said the matron. And Sally followed her mechanically.

She is stretched upon a pallet in the crowded dormitory. She knows not whether she is asleep or awake; she has such horrid, horrid visions. Poor Sally was delirious, raving of her husband and her children and the youngest little boy.

Another day and night wore on. But when tomorrow and tomorrow passed, and a week passed, and they were still putting her off, a terrible dread took possession of her.

Having heard that the children in the workhouse were all marched out daily at a certain hour for air and exercise, Sally Cavanagh stole out and hid herself in a clump of evergreens which the children were to pass. Not a face in that long line of pauper boys escapes her scrutiny. But Corney is not there, nor Tommy, nor Nickey. Sally Cavanagh feels an almost irrepressible impulse to scream aloud. The pauper girls are coming now. But poor Norah is not there, and Sally Cavanagh appears turned to stone as the procession moves past.

The priest, who was coming from the hospital, approached and spoke soothingly to the poor distracted mother.

'Where are they?' she asked.

'In Heaven – with the saints in Heaven,' replied the priest. 'Yes, they're all dead.'

She looked distractedly about her and then, uttering a wild shriek that rang through every corner of 'the place of poverty', the brokenhearted woman rushed through the gate – her hands stretched towards the mountains.

Sally Cavanagh was a maniac. When she escaped from the workhouse, her reason was entirely gone – she remembered nobody.[2]

*Illustration from 'The Martins of Cro' Martin'*

In his *Recollections* O'Donovan Rossa (1838-1898) recalled the bad times in the Skibbereen workhouse:

Morty Downing of Skibbereen was a Poor Law Guardian; and, in connection with his business, I got acquainted with everyone connected with the Skibbereen Poor Law Union. Neddie Hegarty, the porter at the main gate, was the man I skurreechted (sic) most with. He had most to tell me about the starvation times of the years that had just passed by. The Chairman of the Board, during most of those times, was Lioney Fleming, of Oldcourt, a small landlord magistrate. He was a pretty fair specimen of the English planter in Ireland, who considers that Ireland was made for England, and that all the people to whose fathers Ireland belonged are better out of it than in it. Sheep and oxen were tenants more welcome to Lioney's estate than Irish men, women and children; and the faster the men, women and children in the workhouse would die, the oftener would Lioney thank the lord. 'When we were burying them in hundreds every week,' said Neddie to me one day, 'the first salute I'd get from Lioney, when he'd be coming in every board-day would be: "Well, Hegarty, how many this week?" and if I told him the number this week was less than the number last week his remark would be: "Too bad, too bad; last week was a better week than this." '

An inmate of the workhouse named Johnnie Collins was Neddie Hegarty's messenger boy He was lame, he had been dead and buried, but had been brought back to life by a stroke of Rackateen's shovel – Rackateen was the name by which the workhouse undertaker was known. The dead were buried coffinless those times. Rackateen took the bodies to the Abbey graveyard in a kind of trapdoor wagon. He took Johnnie Collins in it one day, and after dumping him with others into the grave-pit, one of his knees protruded up from the heap of corpses. Rackateen gave it a stroke of his shovel to level it down even; the corpse gave a cry of pain, and the boy was raised from the pit. That lame man – whose leg had been broken by the stroke of the shovel – used to come into my shop every week, and we used to speak of him as the man who was raised from the dead.[3]

As social records, the writings of Kickham and O'Donovan Rossa have the ring of truth. The workhouse was part of their heritage, tales told at the hearth, memories that would never be erased and would descend from generation to generation.

Lady Gregory's *The Workhouse Ward*, on the other hand, strikes an oddly false note.[4] Supposed to be set in the Gort workhouse in County Galway the two feuding and fighting characters talk boastfully about their families, their little land-holdings, their Champion potatoes, gooseberries, and cabbage, young ducks and donkeys, pigs and goats, sounding more like retainers in the gate-house of an estate like the Persses' Roxborough House than two paupers ending their days in an institution because they have no families to protect their old age, nowhere to go. And the final decision of Mike who, offered escape by a long-lost sister, prefers to stay in the workhouse, deepens the sense of disbelief. The feeling that it is not really about work-houses at all is reinforced by Lady Gregory's own com-ment: 'I sometimes think the two scolding paupers are a symbol of ourselves in Ireland.'[5] And Micheál Mac Liammóir described it as 'that most subtly national and topical of one-act plays.'

The poet Padraic Colum (1881-1972) was born in the workhouse at Longford, where his father was Master.[6] In his poetry he recalls the circumstances that drove the people to the workhouse:

> *They carved the name above the gate, 1839,*
> *When they built the workhouse on the hill*
> *Of limestone tall and fine.*
> *A plague wind blew across the land,*
> *Fever was in the air.*
> *Fields were black that once were green*
> *And death was everywhere.*
> *People came to drink the soup*
> *Ladled from greasy bowls;*
> *They died in whitewashed wards that*
> *Held a thousand Irish souls.*

Ireland writes in two languages, Irish and English; though in Irish in the mid-nineteenth century the oral tradition predominated. An t-Athair Peadar O'Laoghaire (1839-1920) in his *Mo Sceal Féin* (My Own Story) recounts a family's experience of the workhouse which, as he says, was typical of the fate of many thousands of families. This is a translation:-

The Famine came, and Sheila, her father and mother and little Diarmuid had to go down to Macroom and go into the workhouse. As soon as they were inside they were separated. The father was put with the men and the mother with the women. Sheila was put with the little girls and little Diarmuid with the younger children. The workhouse was full and all the poor people in it were sunk in every kind of dangerous sickness. The people were falling with the sickness as fast as they came in, God save the hearers, and dying as soon as it came on them. There was not room in the workhouse for half of them. Those who could not get in just went and lay down on the bank of the river below the bridge. They were to be seen there every morning after spending the night there, stretched in rows, some stirring, and some who were quiet enough and stirring no longer. Presently people came and lifted those who were still, put them into carts and carried them up to a place near Carrigastyra where a big, wide, deep pit gaped open for them, and threw them all into the pit together. The same was done with those who were dead in the workhouse after the night.

Not long after they went in and he was separated from his mother, little Diarmuid died. The small corpse was heaved into the cart, carried up to the big pit, and thrown into it with the other corpses. But it did not matter to the child. His soul was happy above in the presence of God long before his body was thrown into the pit. Soon Sheila followed little Diarmuid. Her young body went into the pit, but her soul ascended to where Diarmuid was, in the presence of God, and in the joy of Heaven, where she had solace and the company of the saints and angels, and the Virgin Mary.

The father and mother were enquiring as much as they could for Sheila and Diarmuid. The children were not long dead when they heard of it. All the poor people knew Irish, but those in charge did not know it, or knew it but badly, so that the poor people could often get information secretly about one another. When the parents found out that the two children were dead, they grew so heartbroken that they could not stay in the place. They were separated, but they managed to get some word to each other. They agreed to steal away. Kate was the wife's name. Patrick slipped out of the workhouse first. He stood up at the top of Sop Road waiting for Kate. After a while he saw her coming, but she was walking very slowly. She had the sickness. They went on up Sop Road towards Carrigastyra, and reached the place where the big pit was. They knew that their children were below in the pit among all the other corpses. They stood by the pit and cried their fill. Above at Derryleight, east of Cahireen, was the cabin where they had lived before they went into the workhouse. They left the big pit and faced north west towards Derryleight, where the cabin was. It was six miles away, and night was falling, but they kept on. They were hungry and Kate had the sickness. They had to walk very slowly. When they had covered a couple of miles Kate had to stop. She could travel no further. They met neighbours. They were given a drink and some scraps of food, but everyone was afraid to let them in because they had come straight from the workhouse, and the wife had the bad sickness. So Patrick took his wife up on his back and continued north-west towards the cabin.

The poor man himself was very weak. He would have found it hard to do the journey, even without a burden. Laden as he was he had to stop often and rest his burden behind him on the ditch for a while. But however tired he was, he continued the journey and did not part with his burden. He reached the cabin. It was cold and empty before him, without fire or heat.

The next day some neighbour came to the cabin and went in. He saw the two of them lying dead, with his wife's feet held to Patrick's breast, as if he were trying to warm them. It would seem that he had noticed the death weakness coming on Kate and her feet growing cold, and he drew them to his breast to take the chill off them.

'That was a fine, a faithful and noble man,' someone will say perhaps, 'and he did a noble deed.'

'That is true. But I tell you this. Thousands of deeds of the same kind were done throughout Ireland during that time, and no one wondered at them very much. Everyone thought that Patrick Buckley did only what any man would do who was worthy of the name of Christian.'[7]

Though this book is primarily concerned with the Irish workhouse, it is perhaps not inappropriate to mention Charles Dickens. In January 1837 he wrote to a friend that he had hit on a 'capital notion' for a new book. This 'capital notion' was *Oliver Twist* and the book was to ridicule the English Poor Law Act of 1834 under which the workhouse system was set up. This new law cut back on outdoor relief, and, as in Ireland, the poor were driven into the workhouses, soon to become known as 'bastilles', where families were broken up and virtually imprisoned under near-penal conditions. 'Since the new system of feeding has come in,' he wrote in the opening chapters, with a sarcasm worthy of Dean Swift, 'the coffins are somewhat narrower and more shallow than they used to be.'

In *Our Mutual Friend* (1865) he returned to the theme, and in his postscript he wrote of the Poor Law workhouse system: 'I believe there has been no law so often infamously administered, no law so often openly violated, no law habitually so ill-supervised. In the majority of the shameful cases of disease and death from destitution, that shock the public and disgrace the country, the illegality is quite equal to the inhumanity . . . '

Anyone who feels that he overdramatised the horrors of the workhouse should read the records and minute books of the various Boards of Guardians in Ireland to understand the dark night of Irish history, because conditions in Ireland were even worse than those in England.

# 17

# Phasing out the Workhouse

*'The Irish Republic fully realises the necessity of abolishing the present odious, degrading and foreign poor law system.'*

FROM THE FIRST PROGRAMME OF DÁIL ÉIREANN

*'It will be good to remember these things.'*

COMMEMORATIVE PLAQUE ON MAGHERAFELT HOSPITAL

The Local Government Board was established by an Act of 1872 and all powers and duties vested in or imposed on the Poor Law Commissioners for administering the laws for the relief of the poor in Ireland were transferred to it. This meant that the overall administration of the poor law and of the workhouses was carried out centrally by the Local Government Board while the actual day-to-day running of the workhouses and provision of relief continued to be carried out by the Boards of Guardians (the Poor Law Commission formally ceased to exist under a further Act of 1898).

Towards the end of the nineteenth century it was clear that the whole system needed radical reform and it came under increased scrutiny. Public interest became deeply aroused and the Irish Workhouse Association was founded in 1896 with the object of improving conditions.

A Vice-Regal Commission on Poor Law Reform was set up in 1903 to investigate whether expenditure could be reduced without impairing efficiency, and at the same time see if the method of affording relief could be improved. The Commission visited and inspected all the 159 workhouses then in operation (four of the original 163 had been closed), as well as other institutions maintained wholly or in part out of local rates, and examined 743 witnesses. The principal recommendations included in its report of 1906 were:

1. The workhouse system should be abolished.
2. The poverty of Ireland could not be dealt with adequately by any poor relief law, such as that of 1838 which established the workhouses; only by the development of the country's resources.
3. The various classes of inmates in the workhouses should be segregated into separate institutions.
4. The infirm or aged should be removed from the workhouses to county institutes to be known as County Alms-houses.

A further commission – the Royal Commission on the Poor Laws, which reported in 1909 – was in general agreement with the findings and recommendations of the Vice-Regal Commission. As a cardinal principle of all proposals for reform it held that there should be classification *by* institution and not merely *within* institutions, and stressed that effective classification could not be attained as long as all classes of inmates were housed within the walls of a single institution.

No effective steps were taken to implement the recommendations of either the Vice-Regal Commission or of the Royal Commission, and the workhouses continued in use as before.

Perhaps this is an appropriate point to mention various Acts passed in the early decades of the century which, through not poor law acts, and administered apart altogether from the poor laws and the workhouses, made an important contribution towards relieving the hardship and sufferings of the poor and undoubtedly saved large numbers from being forced into the workhouse. The concept of the State as the promoter of social welfare dates from the introduction of these Acts, the most important being the Old Age Pensions Act of 1908, which came into operation the following year. Prior to this Act, the aged poor whose relatives or friends were unable to support them, and for whom outdoor relief was inadequate, had no option but the workhouse – still regarded by most as the very last resort. Other Acts which may be mentioned are the first Tuberculosis Prevention (Ireland) Act 1908, the National Insurance (Health) Act and the National Insurance (Unemployment) Act 1911, the Notification of Births Act 1915, under which Maternity and Child Welfare Schemes were organised, the Public Health (Medical Treatment of Children) Act 1919, and the Blind Persons Act 1920.

But although many Acts had been passed in the years between 1838 and 1921, the principal features of the poor law and the workhouse system, with its Unions and Boards of Guardians, remained unchanged. In fact, between 1850 and the outbreak of World War I in 1914, only five workhouses were closed. Four others shut down between 1914 and 1921. This left a total of 154 for the whole country, 127 of these being in the present area of the Republic of Ireland and 27 in Northern Ireland. The total number receiving relief in workhouses at this time was in the region of 25,000.

The law provided for the relief of the sick and destitute poor in the following manner:

(i)   The able-bodied, male and female: only in the workhouse.

(ii)  The old and infirm: in the workhouse or through the medium of restricted outdoor relief.

(iii) The sick: through outdoor relief or in the workhouse or workhouse infirmary or, if necessary, in an extern hospital. (Growing use was made of the latter power and a practice grew up where the case was admitted nominally to the workhouse and then transferred to an extern hospital. Under the Medical Charities Act 1851, the sick poor were also provided with free medical treatment, either in their own homes or at the dispensaries, and with free medicines and medical appliances.)

(iv) The deaf and dumb and blind: in the workhouse, from which they could be sent to special institutions. Those classified as idiots and imbeciles were similarly transferred.

(v) Widows with two or more legitimate children: in the workhouse or through the medium of outdoor relief. Widows, if able-bodied, and widows with only one legitimate child, only in the workhouse.

(vi) Unmarried mothers, orphans and deserted children under 15 years of age: in the workhouse or by boarding-out or by being placed in a certified school.

Meanwhile another chapter was being added to the history of Ireland. The Easter Week Rising of 1916 appeared at first to be a failure; it was ruthlessly crushed and its leaders executed. But the spark lit could not be extinguished. The movement for self-government grew and in the General Election of December 1918 the people gave Sinn Fein, the nationalist party, an overwhelming mandate to set up an independent Irish parliament in Dublin. It met for the first time on 21 January 1919. The first Dáil Éireann unanimously adopted the democratic programme founded on the Easter Week proclamation. It included the following declaration:

The Irish Republic fully realises the necessity of abolishing the present odious, degrading, and foreign poor law system, substituting therefore a sympathetic native scheme for the care of the nation's aged and infirm, who shall no longer be regarded as a burden but rather entitled to the nation's gratitude and consideration. Likewise it shall be the duty of the Republic to take measures that will safeguard the health of the people and ensure the physical as well as the moral well-being of the nation.[1]

By strange coincidence 21 January was also the day on which the first shots of what came to be known as the War of Independence were fired; during an ambush at Solo-headbeg in County Tipperary two members of the Royal Irish Constabulary were shot dead, thus starting the guerilla war which lasted until the Truce in July 1921.

During the War of Independence, the system of admin-istering the poor laws and the poor laws themselves became to a large extent inoperative in many parts of the country. The British authorities still maintained the Local Government Board in Dublin as the central authority but as a result of local elections held in January and June 1920 Sinn Fein supporters found themselves on many local County Councils and Boards of Guardians. A Department of Local Government, set up as part of the Provisional Government by the first Dáil at its meeting in January 1919, was increasingly recognised by County Councils throughout the country. So for a while there were two central authorities. During the years 1921 and 1922 the councils of several counties, in conjunction with the Minister for Local Government of Dáil Éireann, took steps to alter the poor law and reorganise the administration in their respective counties. Under these 'county schemes', the County Councils undertook responsibility for the relief of the poor in that county, the most important priority being the dismantling of the workhouse system, symbolic as it was of the social degradation associated with the British occupation.

The Anglo-Irish Treaty, signed on 6 December 1921, set up the Irish Free State for twenty-six counties; the re-maining six counties – Armagh, Antrim, Derry, Down, Fermanagh and Tyrone – remained part of Britain under the name of Northern Ireland. In the Irish Free State the Boards of Guardians were replaced by Council Boards of Health or County Boards of Public Assistance. The odious 'workhouse test' as a system of relief was abolished; any person who was eligible could now be granted outdoor relief. The county schemes introduced in 1921 and 1922 were given legal sanction by the Local Government (Temporary Provisions) Act of 1923.

The Anglo-Irish Treaty of 1921 which ended the War of Independence contained the seeds of another war – the Civil War. A breakaway army group (which became known as the Irish Republican Army) opposed the Treaty and challenged the authority of Dáil Éireann, beginning a bitter armed conflict that began in June 1922 and ended in May 1923, with the victory of the Government side.

During the struggle for independence and the ensuing Civil War, a large number of workhouses had been occupied by military, in the early part by British forces, subsequently by the pro- and anti-Treaty factions. Some of these workhouses had been burnt, others had deteriorated and become dilapidated. These that remained were temporarily utilised as follows: thirty-three became County Homes to provide institutional relief for the aged, the infirm and chronic invalids eligible for relief; thirty-two were converted to District or Fever Hospitals, nine to County Hospitals, and most of the others were closed.

A Commission on Poor Relief was appointed by the Minister for Local Government and Public Health in 1925. Its terms of reference were: 'To enquire into the adequacy and the suitability of the County Homes and to make recommendations.'

The Commission reported in 1927. It found that the County Homes (which had been created from converted and upgraded workhouse buildings) were not fit and proper places for the reception of the various classes that were then being sent there. It recommended that the original plan to reserve the County Homes for the aged, the infirm poor and chronic invalids should be revived, that the homes should be brought up to a satisfactory standard, and that separate specialised accommodation should be provided for unmarried mothers, children, and mental defectives. In general these recommendations were left in abeyance.

Over an extended period of many decades, following the reports and recommendations of the Government's Hospitals Commission of 1933, new District, County and Regional Hospitals, and Welfare Homes were provided throughout the country under the Hospitals' Development Programme, financed partly from the proceeds of the Hospitals' Sweepstakes and partly by grants from the Exchequer. Voluntary hospitals were also grant-assisted.

Most of the workhouses which had served as hospitals were demolished or partly adapted for community uses. One exception was the South Dublin Union workhouse, which was upgraded and became St Kevin's Hospital. Later it was completely modernised and extended and renamed St James's Hospital; with the addition of new hospital blocks in recent times it is now the largest public hospital in the country, providing a complete range of medical, surgical and specialist hospital services. Thus ended the link between the Poor Law, the workhouses and hospital care which is explored more fully in Appendix 15.

Traditionally the institutional care of the aged was provided in the County Homes, which were adapted from some of the nineteenth-century workhouses. The Inter-Departmental Committee on the Care of the Aged, which reported to the Minister for Health in 1968, recommended that the concept of these homes should be abandoned and that a system should be developed under which the need of the aged for institutional care would be carefully assessed. Steps would be taken to assign patients to the most appropriate form of care and every effort made to rehabilitate them and restore them to the community. These recommendations formed the basis of the policy adopted for the development of these services.[2] Special new assessment centres were provided and a programme for the erection of new forty-bed Welfare Homes in major towns and cities through the country was undertaken to provide accommodation of modern standards for the elderly within their own community areas. Religious orders and voluntary bodies also provided residential homes for the elderly and local authorities undertook special housing schemes for senior citizens.[3]

## Workhouse Lands

The lands on which the workhouses were built under the Poor Relief (Ireland) Act 1838 were vested at the time in the English Poor Law Commissioners. The intention was that ownership would eventually pass to the Boards of Guardians when they had repaid the capital loans raised for the acquisition of the lands and the erection of the workhouses. The loans had been advanced by the Government and were to have been repaid from the poor rates of each Union by equal instalments spread over twenty years, without interest for the first ten years.

Repayment of these instalments was actually made only by a few Boards of Guardians and then only for a limited period. Towards the close of the famine period £1,321,366 was due from Boards of Guardians of all the Unions in Ireland to the British Exchequer, on foot of workhouse loans and other loans for relief expenditure incurred during the famine years. These debts were consolidated and the Boards of Guardians were placed under an obligation to pay the collective debts to the Imperial Treasury in London, the poor rate being chargeable. Because of their constrained financial circumstances, the local Boards of Guardians were unable to meet these capital repayments, in addition to repayment of loans for providing relief for the poor. In the end, the Government had to cancel the capital debt in 1853, and the workhouse lands remained vested in the central State authorities.

Ownership eventually became vested in the Irish Poor Law Commissioners (from 1847), then the Local Government Board (from 1898), and with the partition of Ireland in 1921, in the Government of the Irish Free State (the twenty-six counties) and the Government of Northern Ireland under the Government of Ireland Act of 1920.

The Minister and local health authorities of the new Irish republic had limited powers of disposal of such lands, namely by way of lease or licence under the provisions of the State Lands (Workhouses) Act 1930. However, the State Lands (Workhouses) Act of 1962 transferred from that date the State's interest in the workhouse lands to the local health authorities in whose functional areas the lands were situated, and conferred on those authorities much wider powers of control and disposal of workhouse lands. The health authorities were deemed to have acquired the lands for the purposes of the Health Acts, and if they did not require them for their own purposes were empowered to sell or let them, subject to the consent of the Minister. Each health authority was strongly recommended to take early steps to ensure that such lands as were not being utilised were suitably used or developed for local authority purposes or, alternatively, were sold or otherwise disposed of.

In Northern Ireland the transfer and disposal of the workhouses and lands were covered by the Health Services Act (NI) 1948 and the Welfare Services Act (NI) 1949.

The Minute Books and reports of the proceedings of the Boards of Guardians for the period 1839–1924, now in the keeping of various local authorities and county libraries give invaluable and detailed information on the workhouse system and are an essential source of material for social and local history chronicling as they do all the details of everyday life – numbers admitted and discharged, in hospital, deaths, punishments, 'petty disbursements', transportations. (See Appendix 16.)

## Northern Ireland

After the setting up of the Northern Ireland state, under the Government of Ireland Act 1920, the following work-houses were adapted for use as District Hospitals during the 1920s and 1930s: Antrim, Armagh, Ballycastle, Bally-mena, Ballymoney, Banbridge, Castlederg, Clogher, Cole-raine, Dungannon, Enniskillen, Kilkeel, Larne, Lima-vaddy, Lisburn, Londonderry, Magherafelt, Newry, New-townards, Omagh.

Although most of the workhouses throughout Northern Ireland were converted into hospitals, additions and alterations to many of them have changed their app-earance. Fortunately, examples of the original workhouse architecture have been preserved in some cases. In Cathal Dallat's *Caring by Design*, Hugh Dixon of the Historic Buildings Council of Northern Ireland observes:

> In Northern Ireland now we really only have four ex-amples which have their full layout still intact – Armagh, Newtownards, Lisnakea and Limavaddy. A good example of a workhouse is the one at Limavaddy, now the Roe Valley Hospital, which has not only got all its buildings but they are not cluttered with modern additions. The exterior of the building has not changed a lot since the days when it was a workhouse. A lot may have happened inside but the main layout has been very well preserved.

As a result of its special history within the context of health care and the architectural style in which it was designed, combined with the fact that it is one of the few workhouse buildings of the period, the building has been listed by the Historic Buildings Council as being of special architectural and historic interest.

Another good example of workhouse architecture is the Social Services Office at Antrim. Originally it was the Admission or Administration Block of the workhouse.

No workhouse in any other part of the country has been preserved as a historic building, though the inscription on a commemorative plaque on the Mid-Ulster Hospital, Magherafelt, ends with the words, 'It will be good to remember these things.'[4]

In Northern Ireland the poor law survived until 1946 when the Boards of Guardians were replaced by eight Health and Welfare Authorities under the Public Health and Local Government (Administrative Provisions) Act 1946. The old survivals of the poor law disappeared. Statutory Health and Welfare Committees were set up for each authority. The Welfare Committees set to work providing homes for old people, first by converting country mansions and eventually by a network of new purpose-built Old People's Homes in single-storey construction, within easy reach of shops and other facilities in towns and villages.

As an integral part of a comprehensive hospitals development programme many of the District Hospitals were later extensively reconstructed to become modern General Hospitals.

In Belfast a modern hospital complex was developed on the workhouse site to become the Belfast City Hospital, aptly described as 'the ugly duckling that grew up to be a beautiful swan.' This was in addition to the city's existing major hospitals – the Royal Victoria and the Mater. And, following the introduction of the National Health Services Act (NI) 1948, a number of new major hospitals were built by the Hospitals Authority set up under the Act to provide up-to-date multi-purpose and specialist hospital services for the entire province.

All hospitals (including workhouses, infirmaries and District Hospitals) passed to the Northern Ireland Hospitals

Authority under Section 3 of the 1948 Act; all other work-house property and lands were dealt with under Section 3 of the Welfare Services Act (NI) 1949.

The records of the poor law Unions and Boards of Guardians in Northern Ireland are held in the Northern Ireland Public Records Office, Belfast.

*The admissions block of the Antrim workhouse*

# 18

# The Poor Law in England, Wales and Scotland

*'In England and Wales the problem mainly centred round fears that the able-bodied might abuse the system; the Scottish Commissioners, on the contrary, wanted to secure that poor persons entitled to relief should receive it.'*

POOR LAW COMMISSION FOR SCOTLAND, 2 MAY 1844

In England and Wales, the inadequacies of the poor law system had long been recognised and they were increasingly exposed by progressive social concern and public opinion. Notwithstanding the developments of social assistance and insurance which Parliament had brought about in the first two decades of the twentieth century, the poor law was still the most important of the social services. It was the last refuge of the destitute, though a more enlightened attitude to the granting of outdoor relief removed reliance on the old workhouse system. A Royal Commission on the Poor Law in England and Wales was appointed in 1905 and reported in 1909. Nevertheless, it took the trade slump and large-scale unemployment of the twenties to hasten the implementation of its main recommendations.

The poor law, in its legislative aspects, now under the control of the new Ministry of Health which had come into being in 1919, remained virtually unchanged until an alteration in the administrative system occurred in 1929, twenty years after the Royal Commission's Report, when the Local Government Act of that year was passed. The abolition of the Boards of Guardians, as recommended in the Report, effected by this Act, made it possible to transfer the ordinary poor law functions such as poor relief, in cash or in kind, to local Public Assistance Boards. It also transferred to local authorities, a vast system of poor law hospitals and workhouses, as well as public health functions generally.

From 1 April 1930, the date on which the Act came into operation, the councils of the counties and county boroughs assumed responsibility for the administration of the diverse types of poor law hospitals as well as the workhouses. The existing workhouses were integrated into the new system as mixed institutions possessing hospital facilities, and containing beds for long-stay chronic invalids, the elderly and the physically infirm. The mixed institution was no longer administered by a workhouse master; he was replaced as official superior by a Senior Medical Officer.

The Local Government Act of 1929 merely effected a change in the administrative machinery which operated the poor law. A Poor Law Act was passed in 1930 but the system, though somewhat modernised and humanised, remained in being until the end of the Second World War. But the steady continuity of social progress, which had begun in the thirties with the improvement of social services and the enhancement of status of general and special hospitals and residential institutions, resumed in the mid-forties, culminating in the coming into operation of six major Acts of Parliament in the period 1944-48, which revolutionised the care and provision for the poor, the unemployed, the sick, the aged, and the workers in Britain. These Acts were: the Ministry of National Insurance Act 1944; the Family Allowances Act 1945; the National Insurance (Industrial Injuries Act 1946; the National Health Service Act 1946; the National Insurance Act 1946; and the National Assistance Act 1948. These Acts effectively, *inter alia*, dismantled the last vestiges of the poor law, substituting for it the social security system of the welfare state, which protected the beneficiaries from the stigma of being pauperised.

The statutory transfer of workhouses and workhouse lands to hospital authorities was finally dealt with by Sections 6 and 9 of the National Health Service Act 1946, and paragraphs 7 and 8 of the Sixth Schedule to the National Assistance Act 1948.

A complete list of the 689 workhouses provided in England and Wales is at Appendix 17. The first workhouse, completed in 1836 in Abingdon, Berkshire, was based on the plans of an architect named Sampson Kempthorne. His workhouse plans were functional to the point of severity, the emphasis being on meeting the specifications at the lowest possible cost. Other architects, including George Wilkinson, were later engaged for this work.

None of the 689 workhouses has been preserved as a historic building.

## *Poor Law and Poor-houses in Scotland*

Ten years after the passing of the English Poor Law (Amendment) Act 1834, establishing the workhouse system in England and Wales, the Poor Law Inquiry Commission for Scotland was set up, in January 1844.

The system of poor relief then existing in Scotland was entirely based on parochial relief, mainly financed by charity supplemented by voluntary contributions. This system was of long standing, dating back beyond 1707, when Scotland became part of the United Kingdom. The parish formed the basis of administration; the system of poor relief was not subject to supervision by a central authority. The duty of administering relief was entrusted to the following authorities:

1. In burghal parishes, the Magistrates of the Borough;
2. In landward parishes, the Kirk Session and Heritors (ie, landowners) – landward was an old Scots expression to denote districts outside boroughs;

3. In partly landward and party burghal parishes, the Kirk Session, the Heritors and the Magistrates.

Under the law then operating in Scotland, 'an able-bodied man has no right to parochial relief for himself or his family though unable to find employment and destitute of the means of subsistence.'

Broadly stated, the English poor law problem of 1834 was the opposite to that which confronted the Poor Law Commission for Scotland. In England and Wales the problem mainly centred round fears that the able-bodied might abuse the system; the Scottish Commissioners, on the contrary, wanted to secure that poor persons entitled to relief should receive it, and that, where given, it should be adequate to the needs of the individual.

The Report of the Commission, dated 2 May 1844, contained no revolutionary proposals. The aim of the Commissioners was to preserve what were 'deemed to be the peculiar merits of the Scottish system.' That system they declared to be 'essentially one of outdoor relief.'

However, they recommended the establishment of poor-houses, but this was not to be made compulsory; they had no wish to do away with outdoor relief to helpless persons. The area of administration was the parish; this they proposed to continue. The adoption of a poor rate was to be compulsory only if charitable and voluntary funds proved insufficient.

The Poor Law Amendment (Scotland) Act 1845 gave legislative effect to the main proposals. It was described at the time as the Charter of the Scottish Poor. Before the 1845 Act there were practically no poor-houses, as such, in Scotland. There were some hospitals of old standing and a few alms-houses and houses of refuge. But these were the exception in a system which aimed at keeping the poor in their own homes. The existence of these institutions was 'for those who, by reason of friendlessness, disease, or excessive helplessness, could not be properly attended to in their homes.'

Nor did the Act of 1845 make any essential change in the poor law machinery for Scotland. The term 'poor-house' was adopted as there was no intention of using a 'workhouse test' as in the English and Irish Poor Law Acts of 1834 and 1838 as a test of destitution, as it was not proposed to provide relief for the able-bodied. The purpose of the Scottish poor-house, as stated in the Act, was 'for more effectually administering to the wants of the aged and other friendless impotent poor, and also for providing for those poor persons who, from weakness or infacility of mind or by reason of dissipated or improvident habits, are unable to take charge of their own affairs.'

This was in stark contrast to the criteria laid down in the 1834 Act which established the workhouse system in England and Ireland. This specified that the workhouses were for the purpose of 'relieving and *setting to work therein*' the destitute poor.

The staffing approved under the Act was: the Inspector of the Poor, who dealt with all applications for relief; the Medical Officer of the poor-house; the poor-house Governor or Matron; the outdoor or parish Medical Officer; the superintendent nurse, and such other staff as required. No able-bodied person being eligible for relief, every applicant for either indoor or outdoor relief had first to be examined by the parish doctor, and receive a certificate from him before the Inspector of the Poor could deal with the case. However, it appears that there was a compassionate approach to this certification, to ensure that all applications for relief were dealt with in a flexible and liberal manner.

Although not compulsory, poor-houses – seventy, with accommodation for 18,800 inmates – were provided for the whole of Scotland. There was a reasonable degree of classification and segregation of inmates in the poor-houses; they were not, as a rule, used as a method of relieving widows and children, except as sick persons in the infirmary wards. The number of poor-houses proved to be surplus to requirements. This was mainly due to the fact that there was no overall central controlling authority to co-ordinate planning such as, for example, the Poor Law Commissioners in England and Wales and Ireland. This also resulted in costly buildings being designed and poor-houses being unnecessarily provided in sparsely populated areas. In course of time various reports were made by the Medical Officers recommending rationalisation of the poor-houses but it was not until the passing of the Local Government Act 1929 that effective steps were taken to close redundant poor-houses and to adapt the remainder for other public and community needs, such as hospitals and residential homes. This resulted in an upgrading and improvement in the standard of comfort in the institutions generally. The system of poor relief was also updated and restructured, and was finally phased out under the National Health and Social Security Statutes of 1946 and 1948, which introduced a new social security system.

# Appendix 1

## Standard Contract for the Building of Workhouses

**To the Guardians** of the          UNION, and
to all Others whom it may concern.

**Whereas**

it appears expedient to US, **The Poor Law Commissioners,** for the due execution of the Provisions of an Act passed in the Session of Parliament held in the 1st and 2nd years of the Reign of Her present Majesty Queen Victoria, intituled, "An Act for the more Effectual Relief of the Destitute Poor in Ireland," that a Workhouse should be built within the Union of      for the Reception, Employment, Classification, and Relief of Destitute Poor Persons therein.

AND WHEREAS we have determined to build such Workhouse, and in the execution of the said determination, have testified our approval of certain Plans of a Workhouse, by affixing our Seal thereto, such Workhouse being designed for the Reception, and proper Accommodation of     Hundred Destitute Poor Persons, Men, Women, and Children, properly classified.

AND WHEREAS it appears to us expedient, that such part only of the said Plans should, in the first instance, be executed, as may be requisite for the Reception and Classification of     Hundred Destitute Poor; and that the completion of the said Workhouse should be deferred, until it shall appear to us necessary to complete the same.

AND WHEREAS it has been represented to us, that the cost of erecting, according to the Plans aforesaid, such portion of the said Workhouse as we have determined, in the first instance, to complete, and of the fitting and furnishing the same, and of providing Utensils, Instruments, and Machinery for setting the Poor to work therein, will amount to the sum of £    sterling, or thereabouts.

212

**Now know ye,** that We, the Poor Law Commissioners, in pursuance of the Powers given to Us by the said Act, and for the purpose of enabling Us to defray the expense of Building such part of the said Workhouse, as is, in the first instance, intended to be built, and for the other hereinbefore recited purposes, do Order and Direct the Guardians of the said Union, to Assess, Raise, and Levy the said sum of

sterling, as a Poor Rate on the rateable Hereditaments, in or arising within the said Union, or to borrow the said sum, according to the provisions of the said Act, and to charge the same, together with all interest that may accrue thereon, on the future Poor Rate of the said Union; and We do hereby authorise the said Guardians to borrow the said sum, and charge the said Rate accordingly.

AND WE FURTHER ORDER AND DIRECT the said Guardians, out of the Poor Rate, and at the common charge of the several Electoral Divisions of the said Union, at all times to uphold and maintain the said Workhouse in good and substantial Repair.

> Given under the Hands and Seal of Us, the POOR LAW COMMISSIONERS, this        day of
> in the Year of Our Lord One Thousand Eight Hundred and
>
> *(Signed)*

J. G. S Lefevre

G. C. Lewis

*Forward by Post,*

184 .

*(Signed)*

Geo Nicholls

# Appendix 2

## Barney's Report on the Execution of Contracts for Certain Union Workhouses in Ireland

---

### Sites

The very important duty of the selection of sites for the workhouses appears to have been generally carried out with great judgment: with the exception of three or four, which are probably rather too distant from the townships, the sites are extremely well chosen; the important points of salubrity, drainage, supply of water, local position with reference to the convenience of the guardians as well as the general interests of the unions, have been kept in view. The greater number of sites are on commanding ground; there are, however, a portion on low ground, and a few in the immediate vicinity of marches or bogs; but I cannot learn that such positions are injurious to the health of the inmates.

The sites considered most inconvenient in point of distance from townships, or difficulty of access, are those of Caherciveen, Tralee, Carrick-on-Shannon, and Balrothery; several others have been objected to on account of locality, cost, or rental; but the explanation afforded by the parties who selected the sites and arranged the purchase or rental, appears to be generally satisfactory.

### Accommodation

Workhouses for the accommodation of 700 paupers and upwards do not afford the desired extent of day-room either for males or females; for instance, in a building for 1,000 paupers, the day-rooms, one for each class, measure 40 feet by 17 feet. With a full house, there would be 170 males and an equal number of females, and admitting one-half of that number to be so infirm as not to be able to leave their beds, the day-rooms will be found totally inadequate to the accommodation of the remainder. It has been observed that the dining-room is intended to be used as a day-room in case of necessity; in such view, a fireplace should be built in each division of the room.

In the workhouses for 200 paupers, up to 600 inclusive, the day-rooms are of better arrangement, and afford the desired space.

The nurseries, for every class of workhouses, are deficient in accommodation, and various measures have been resorted to for

214

obviating this defect; but no general arrangement has been adopted, neither do I see that the buildings afford any means of meeting this want satisfactorily, and it will probably be necessary to erect separate buildings for this purpose. This measure has been carried into effect in a few instances.

The kitchens and wash-houses in buildings for 700 paupers and upwards are very confined, and frequently badly lighted and ventilated. In the buildings accommodating under 700 the kitchens and wash-houses are more commodious and better in every respect than those of the larger class of workhouse; they are quite equal to the wants of the establishments.

The infirmary accommodation has proved insufficient in the more populous unions, more particularly where there is not any fever hospital in the town; in such cases it has been found necessary to occupy the dormitories of the idiot wards, and even those of the probationary wards. However, fever hospitals are now generally in progress, either within the boundary walls of the workhouses or in their immediate vicinity; and as necessity arises, this arrangement will probably be extended to every union.

In the accommodation for idiots the cells and day-room attached are sufficient for the purpose of securing idiots of violent character. In the smaller workhouses this is the only accommodation afforded; in the larger establishments the dormitories for the inoffensive idiots are sufficient, but the day-rooms are very confined and badly ventilated: however, there does not appear to be any objection to allowing this class to resort to the common day-rooms of the establishment.

The idiot wards are totally unfit for the confinement of lunatics.

The airing yards afford the desired space for exercise, and to the rear of the buildings the privies in these yards are sufficient and well situated; this, however, is not the case in the front, or boys and girls' yards, where the privies are a nuisance, more particularly in the summer.

Stabling has been erected at many of the workhouses, and is generally required at the remainder. The distance of the Board-rooms from the townships average from one to two miles, and the guardians must be put both to inconvenience and expense for want of this accommodation on the spot.

The workhouses in the larger towns have been in some cases already filled with paupers, and should an unfavourable season occur, either by failure of crops or severe winter, many of the establishments will certainly prove inadequate to the wants of the unions. The buildings, however, are so arranged as to admit of the wing accommodation being extended, both for males and females, should it be found necessary at any period.

## Ventilation

The main buildings of the workhouses are ventilated upon one uniform principle; viz. by means of towers, within which are the stairs leading to the upper wards. The ventilation is carried out by openings over the doors of the dormitories, and by the passages leading to the landings on the different floors, the foul air passing out either by windows or *louvres* immediately under the roof of the towers. Independent of this ventilation and of the windows in the dormitories, &c., iron ventilators have been introduced in the walls of the building, and occasionally an opening left in the upper parts of the gables. This ventilation seems to be sufficient, with the following exceptions: the day-rooms in buildings for 700 paupers and upwards, and the rear dormitories adjoining the wings on the first floor; the only ventilation in these rooms consists of one door and window in each. The use of stoves led to the closing of the chimney openings in the day-rooms; they are, however, being generally replaced by grates, and the ventilation will in consequence be improved, but still insufficient.

The application of the iron ventilators has led to much discussion and complaint. No general arrangement for placing these ventilators appears to have been made; occasionally they are on a level with the beds, sometimes three or four feet above; it is only in the gables that any uniformity of arrangement is shown. As a means of ventilation, they are of little use, being generally neglected; in some cases they have been removed by order of the guardians, as admitting wet into the walls; and in the later erected buildings they have been altogether omitted in the outside wing-walls. In this situation I think they should be removed, and the openings carefully built up, leaving those in the gables, which are well placed, and if properly attended to, of undoubted advantage.

The infirmaries generally require improved ventilation. At present, in the lower wards, the front windows and side door are the only openings; in the upper wards the same, with the addition of an opening immediately under the roof, leading to the ventilating cupola: in both cases the openings are confined to the front and side of the rooms, leaving the remainder without any means by which the foul air can escape. At several of the infirmaries the ventilation has already been improved by opening the rear walls immediately under the ceilings, and which may be closed or otherwise under the medical officer's instruction, and some such arrangement is generally required. The removal of a party wall on the upper floor of several of the buildings has much improved the ventilation and added very considerably to the accommodation: this is a great improvement applicable to every infirmary.

## Supply of Water

Of the 130 workhouses, 30 are now deficient in the supply of water, principally confined to the summer months. Originally only one well was sunk at each workhouse; and although usually tested before the building was occupied, by pumping for a certain period, which gave a satisfactory result, it soon became apparent, as the occupation of the buildings proceeded, and a general and daily drain upon the wells took place, that the supply would be insufficient, originating a necessity for either sinking second wells or further deepening the original ones: the result is as above stated. The necessity for sinking a second well at every workhouse is obvious. One pump, subject to constant work, must be liable to wear and accident; and many of the workhouses are in localities where competent workmen are not to be had, and at a distance from a supply of water. In such cases the inmates must be put to great inconvenience, and expense must be incurred, the latter soon amounting to sums equal to the cost of a second well; indeed this has already occurred at two or three of the workhouses. In addition to the supply of water from the wells, rain-water tanks have been formed, two usually at the larger stations, and one at the smaller. These are intended for the use of the wash-houses, and the supply afforded has generally proved sufficient during the greater portion of the year. A failure occasionally takes place during the summer months. The supply, however, may be increased to a great extent by leading water (which now runs to waste) to the tanks, or by constructing other tanks, for which the roofs afford ample means of supply.

It has been said that the terms of the contracts, as relating to the supply of water, have not been carried out; and that, in consequence, expense has been incurred for deepening wells, &c. I do not see that such statement can be borne out. It is clear that, generally, there was every reason to believe that the wells afforded a sufficient supply when the buildings were taken off the contractors' hands, having been tested as before stated. Whenever there appeared fair grounds for compelling contractors to deepen wells, it seems to have been taken advantage of; and it is only under peculiar circumstances that such work has formed an extra charge upon the building.

## Drainage

The general system of drainage adopted is that of overflow from the privy-pits, as well as drains from the kitchens and wash-houses, leading in the greater number of cases merely through the inner enclosure wall, leaving the completion of the work as employment for the paupers, or otherwise, as might be found advisable. At some of the workhouses dry cesspools have been built in convenient places, between the inner and outer enclosures; in others advantage has been taken of natural hollows or quarries, to which the drainage has been conveyed. In these cases, the cesspools, &c. are satisfactorily used for the purpose of making manure. This system, no doubt, will be generally adopted; it is the most economical in arrangement, and the larger portion of the work may be affected by pauper labour. In addition to the manure required for the purposes of the cultivated ground of the establishment, sums have been realized by the sale of the surplus, varying from £15 to £25. per annum.

It is quite evident that no better arrangement for drainage generally can be devised. At the same time an absolute necessity will exist for the closest attention to the leading and overflow drains, and more particularly to the periodical cleansing of the privy-pits. These arrangements have already been carried out by the Boards of Guardians at many of the workhouses, generally with judgment, and certainly at a less cost than had the work been provided for in the original contracts. In some cases the drainage has been carried to rivers and natural outlets off the premises; but I apprehend, as the value of the manure comes to be understood, that the drainage will be intercepted and applied as above. At present, also, there are cases where the privy soil runs upon the public roads, and into streams which afford supply of water to cottages. Manure pits have also been sunk in front of the buildings, and adjoining public roads. These are cases of nuisance which should and may be avoided.

## Enclosure

The original plan of enclosure was confined to an inner boundary wall, embracing the airing yards only, leaving the outer spaces to be enclosed by a bank and ditch. This arrangement, applied to the workhouses in the vicinity of large towns, soon proved insufficient, and has led to the outer boundary being also enclosed by a wall, and which appears to be necessary in such positions generally. For workhouses in the less populous neighbourhoods the ditch, and bank planted with quicks, will be found sufficient, except where boundaries abut upon public roads, in such positions a wall becomes of absolute necessity. The enclosure of ditch and bank will require uninterrupted attention, which may be met by the masters of the workhouses with pauper labour.

The rear enclosure and division walls of the infirmary and idiot wards are usually too low, seven feet in height, which is insufficient; at many of the workhouses these walls have been raised from two to three feet, and this seems to be necessary at all the workhouses where the outer boundary consists of ditch and bank.

## Wet Penetrating the Walls

This has been a general source of complaint, and apparently with good cause. However, circumstances connected with the material and execution of the work require to be taken into consideration, and the result of the late inspection is much more favourable than that of the preceding year; indeed there seems but little doubt that the workhouses, with few exceptions, will become dry in the course of another year. The cause of wet penetrating the walls may be ascribed to various circumstances: the dispatch with which it was considered necessary to complete the buildings led to the conducting of the work through winter and summer, wet and dry; in consequence, the walls became repeatedly saturated before the buildings could be covered in. The nature of the material of necessity made use of in many of the buildings is such as to retard the drying process, and such buildings receive a fresh accession of moisture into the interior of the walls on every fall of rain, until the outside mortar joints become set: these also have generally been much injured either by rain or frost, and thus the drying operation becomes lengthened. It has been found necessary, in numerous instances, to protect the walls either by cement rendering or pointing, or by roughcast; this necessity, however, does not arise from defective work, but from the causes above stated. The difficulty attending the building operations will be understood when it is explained, that of 860 working days, when nearly every workhouse was in progress, 436 were wet. Another cause of wet walls is the neglected state of the spouting; the only wet observable in several of the buildings is entirely attributable to this neglect. A further source of wet originates in the want of eaves, gutters, and down spouts. In a country so proverbially wet, it seems absolutely necessary that the walls be fully protected. The want of spouting has been observed by the guardians of several of the workhouses, and in consequence eaves, gutters, and down pipes have been added, so as to complete the whole of the buildings, the good effect of which is evident in the increased dryness of the walls.

All the unoccupied buildings, as well as those allowed to remain in that state a long time previous to occupation, are extremely damp; some of these buildings have been completed for periods varying from one to nearly three years. The airing of them has been neglected, and it is well known that unoccupied building soon assume a damp which requires a long period of occupation to overcome. In these buildings also and in some others, the yards have not been properly levelled, and the surface-water is thrown against the walls and into the foundations, causing the lower parts of the walls to be wet, alike injurious to the building and to the occupants.

It should be understood, with reference to wet walls, that the usual precautions adopted in Ireland for the prevention of damp have not been resorted to, except in a few cases. Taking this into consideration, the buildings, as a general question, may be considered fairly dry. The favourable summer now passed has had an evident good effect; several of the buildings reported wet last year are now dry. The different masters of the workhouses state that the walls are becoming more dry every season; still, from causes before explained, a considerable number of the buildings will require to be repointed or other precautions taken to prevent wet penetrating the walls.

Wet penetrating by the windows has also been much complained of; this has partly arisen from the shrinking of the wood-work and absence of secure pointing round the frames, also from neglect in the application of paints. The two first may be remedied by pointing round the frames, and the latter by painting the casements, and stopping the glass and openings between iron work and frame, which ought to have been done within a certain period after the completion of the building. It is usual and necessary to paint outside work periodically: this being carefully done, and the stopping of the glass made perfect, I do not consider that the small portion of wet which will penetrate by the opening part of the casement, and which cannot be well avoided, can be of any consequence or worthy of complaint.

The absence of lead flashings, and for which cement fillets and weather-slating has been substituted, and which has frequently failed, has certainly admitted wet down the chimney breasts; and when applied to lower buildings abutting against higher, occasioned by the shrinking of the roofs, and settlement of masonry, causing the cement to crack, in some cases lead flashings have been already applied as the remedy; and perhaps, under the difficulty of obtaining workmen in many of the localities accustomed to the use of cement, this may be the more safe proceeding: however, I am aware that many public buildings in Ireland are entirely without lead flashings, and yet perfectly dry. The application of lead flashings after the building has been completed, will of course create a greater expenditure than if used in the regular course of building.

## Extra Work

The subject of extra work does not seem to be clearly understood by the guardians, who have confounded it with fixtures, fittings, &c. Extra work embraces only such as foundations and alterations made during the progress of the building, which could not be foreseen, and consequently not embraced in the original contract. Such work as this should not be mixed up with fixtures,&c., which are of absolute necessity, foreseen and calculated upon. In the returns of expenditure published by the Poor Law Commissioners, fixtures and fittings are embraced in the accounts, under the head of extra work, which has evidently led to an erroneous impression, and swelled the apparent cost of extra work to a large amount. The original contract provided for what may be termed the shell of the building, without reference to fixtures, fittings, or furniture, or any of the items introduced in the extra bills. This arrangement has arisen out of a want of maturity in the plans, probably caused by the necessity stated to have existed for carrying out the completion of the workhouses with the utmost dispatch. The non-introduction of the fixtures, &c. into the original contract, and the omission to act upon the clause in the agreement which provides that, "in the extra works a list of prices be attached to the articles of agreement; all prices of such additional work, being first approved by the architect, must be attached to the contract previous to the execution of it," has unquestionably not only led to the complaints of the guardians on the score of extra work, but also to much additional expense. This, however, must not be taken as an admission that the contractors have been overpaid for the work done by them, but that such work would have been performed by the same parties at a less expense had the fixtures, fittings, &c., comprised in the extra bills been provided for in the original contract. This is fully admitted by several of the most practical and extensive contractors, and also by other competent parties whose' opinion I have thought it advisable to obtain: the average of the opinions give $12^{1}/2$ per cent, excess upon the paid accounts for extra works, and this per-centage agrees with the cost of the extra works framed at Ordnance prices, giving the contractors the advantage of numerous amounts carried out on the bills which it has been found impossible to check or compare.

I should observe, with reference to the extraordinary amount of charges by various contractors for extra work, and the confused and improper manner in which the bills are made out, in numerous cases admitting of deductions varying from one quarter to three quarters of the total amount of the bills, I have learned that several of the contractors are not practical builders, and persons have been employed to measure work and prepare accounts who have been totally incompetent to the duty. In justice to the contractors who have furnished correct and properly detailed accounts, I put forward this observation.

## Construction

From a careful consideration of the plans of the workhouses, without reference to the alterations and improvements effected during the progress of the buildings, they appear to have been prepared under the most economical arrangements, and no unnecessary work can be traced in any part; indeed, I am inclined to consider that economy has been carried to an extreme not desirable in public buildings where durability becomes a leading and important consideration. There are two points in the construction upon which I entertained a doubt: first, whether the wing walls of the main buildings are of sufficient thickness to ensure durability; second, whether the wing roofs are of proper construction to ensure durability. Not relying on my own judgment, I have taken the opinion of competent parties. The most favourable opinion is: "I consider the wing walls to be of sufficient thickness to sustain the weight of the roof, and the construction of the roof sufficient for the purpose, if executed with good material." Other opinions state, "The walls are of sufficient thickness, under a roof of proper construction:" also, "Taking the height of the walls and exposed situations into consideration, the walls should be one-fifth thicker, and the wing roofs are not of proper construction to ensure durability." Under a careful consideration of the subject, I am of opinion, that had the wing walls been given an extra thickness of four or five inches, and a trussed roof applied to the wings, the additional expense would have been amply repaid by the increased durability of the buildings, which I have before alluded to as a most important feature in the character of public buildings. I should here observe, that although a large portion of the buildings exhibit numerous fractures, there are at present only two or three settlements of at all serious character observable; in several instances, the wing walls in the upper dormitories show an inclination to spread, evidently arising from the weak construction of the roof. I am borne out in the opinion, that neither the wing walls nor roof are of a character to ensure durability, by some of the most experienced contractors who carried out the plans; these parties concur in the opinion as to the absence of durability to a certain extent, and more particularly in the exposed situations of many of the workhouses, where they do not receive protection from adjoining buildings. In conclusion, there can be no doubt that had the wing walls been given an extra thickness, and a king or queen post roof applied to the wings, that a period of many years would have been added to the durability of the buildings.

The extreme economy attending the plans and building arrangements, and the haste with which it has been deemed necessary to carry the works to completion, has evidently led to a want of maturity in the plans to be carried out, and from which have arisen all the defects and complaints. That the plans had not been matured is made evident by the numerous and beneficial alterations carried out during the progress of the buildings, more particularly those under the later contracts. I need only observe, the position and construction of the towers, enlarged day-rooms, substitution of gangways and sleeping platforms in lieu of bedsteads, the enlargement of kitchens and wash-houses, substitution of grates for stoves, wood for iron casements, and improved ventilation, all being improvements of valuable character. Had circumstances permitted a more mature consideration of the plans, the above improvements would have formed parts of the arrangement brought into the original contracts, and also to the introduction into such contracts of all the work now embraced under the head of extra work, with the exception of extras upon foundations, which must always be open to such charges.

The application of rubble work to the walls of the workhouses, in addition to economy, became a matter of necessity, arising out of the nature of the material afforded in the localities of the various buildings. This description of work is exhibited in all the buildings in Ireland of ages past, as well as of modern times, with the exception in the latter of ornamental buildings, public and private, of large cost. I have, however, observed throughout Ireland that buildings of rubble masonry are invariably protected by rough-cast or plaster, &c. In addition to this precaution against wet, the interior of buildings of a certain character are further protected by brick linings, or other methods. I allude to this to show that the question of wet walls, so much complained of, is not to be attributed to defective work in the walling, but to the absence of those precautions natural to the moist climate of Ireland.

The arrangement of the window frames would have been more satisfactory had reveals been used; and had this work been embraced in the original contracts, probably but little more than the sum now required to be expended in securing the frames would have been introduced in the builders' charges.

With reference to the different material used in the carpentry, the general character is fair, and the construction appears sufficient, subject to the remarks on the wing roofs. An inferior description of material has in some cases been used, but the locality of the buildings rendered it difficult, if not impracticable, to obtain the material provided by the contract, unless at extreme prices. On the substitution of inferior material, the difference of value has always been deducted from the contractor's accounts. It is hardly necessary to observe that the introduction of inferior material operates against the durability of the building.

The substitution of gangways and sleeping platforms in lieu of bedsteads and flooring, as originally contemplated, is a measure of very great advantage, not only as a better means of accommodation, but also originating a large amount of saving both in the first outlay and in the repair of bedsteads, which in a few years would have become necessary from fair wear. The saving arising from this alteration may be fairly estimated at £25,000. In carrying out this alteration, some expense had been incurred in laying floors under the original plan; but the cases are few, and do not affect the amount of saving referred to.

The earth or mortar floors have generally failed; in but few instances are the original floors now in use: this will suffice to show that the composition has been generally defective. However, I am of opinion, that had these floors been made of proper material, and carefully laid down, they would have been found durable, and preferable either to flagging or other material now being made use of to replace them. I consider the original intention good, and would have been successful if carried out as provided for in the contracts.

Stoves, where used, have been objected to, and are now being generally replaced by grates, which are more applicable, more durable, and less expensive.

The slating has generally been well done; Welch slates in most cases have been used; in a few instances, however, Killaloe slates have been applied; these are not so durable as the former, and have caused complaint; the contracts, however, admitted of the use of them under certain circumstances, with the sanction of the Commissioners' architect.

The ironmongery and plumbers' work is generally good.

(signed) *Geo. Barney,*
Lieutenant-colonel Royal Engineers.

# Appendix 3

## Duties of the Master

---

The following shall be the duties of the Master of the Workhouse :—

No. 1. To admit Paupers into the Workhouse in obedience to any Order made under Article 1, and also persons applying for admission, who may appear to him to require relief through any sudden and urgent necessity; or who shall be named in any written recommendation from a Warden, and shall appear to the Master to be destitute and proper objects for admission ; and to cause every Pauper upon admission to be examined by the Medical Officer, as is directed in Article 4.

No. 2. To register the name and religious persuasion of every Pauper, upon his admission ; and to cause every Male Pauper above the age of seven years, upon admission, to be searched, cleansed, and clothed, and to be placed in the ward appropriated to the class to which he appears to belong.

No. 3. To enforce industry, order, punctuality, and cleanliness and the observance of the several Rules herein contained, by the Paupers in the Workhouse, and by the several Officers, Assistants, and Servants therein employed.

No. 4. To read prayers to the Paupers before breakfast and after supper every day, or cause prayers to be read—at which all the inmates must attend, excepting those who are incapacitated through sickness, infirmity, or infancy, and those who object to such attendance on account of their religious principles ; and to the Paupers making such declaration, the Master shall, if practicable, cause prayers to be read by some one of their own religious persuasion.

No. 5. To cause the Paupers to be inspected, and their names called over, immediately after morning prayers every day, in order that it may be seen that each individual is clean and in a proper state.

No. 6. To provide for and enforce the employment of the ablebodied adult Paupers, during the whole of the hours of labour ; to assist in training the youth in such employment as will best fit them for gaining their own living ; to keep the partially disabled Paupers occupied to the extent of their ability ; and to allow none who are capable of employment to be idle at any time.

No. 7. To visit the Sleeping Wards of the Male Paupers at ELEVEN o'CLOCK in the forenoon of every day, and to see that such Wards have been all duly cleansed and properly ventilated.

No. 8. To see that the meals of the Paupers are properly dressed and served, and to superintend the distribution thereof, in accordance with Articles 16, 19, and 20.

No. 9. To say, or cause to be said, Grace before and after meals.

No. 10. To see that the dining halls, tables, and seats are cleansed after each meal.

No. 11. To visit all the Wards of the Male Paupers at or before NINE o'CLOCK every night, and see that all the Male Paupers are in bed, and that all fires and lights are extinguished.

No. 12. To receive from the Porter the keys of the entrance to the Workhouse at NINE o'CLOCK every night, and to deliver them to him again at SIX o'CLOCK every morning, or at such hours as shall from time to time, be fixed by the Board of Guardians, and approved by the Commissioners.

No. 13. To see that the Male Paupers are properly clothed, and that their clothes are kept in proper repair.

No. 14. To send for the Medical Officer of the Workhouse in case any Pauper is taken ill, or becomes insane ; and to take care that all sick and insane Paupers are duly visited by the Medical Officer, and are provided with such medicines and attendance, diet, and other necessaries, as the Medical Officer shall in writing direct, and to apprise the nearest relation in the Workhouse of the sickness of any Pauper. And in the case of dangerous sickness, to send for the Chaplain or other licensed Minister of the persuasion of the Pauper, as well as for any relative or friend of such Pauper, resident within a reasonable distance, whom he may desire to see.

No. 15. To give immediate information of the death of any Pauper in the Workhouse to the Medical Officer, and to the nearest relations of the deceased who may be known to him, and who may reside within a reasonable distance ; and if the body be not removed within a reasonable time, to provide for the interment thereof.

No. 16. To take charge of the clothes, and other articles, if any, of such deceased Pauper, and deliver an inventory thereof to the next Meeting of the Board of Guardians, who shall give the necessary directions respecting the same.

No. 17. To keep all Books of Accounts which he is, or hereafter may be, by any Order under the seal of the Commissioners, directed and required to keep* ; to allow the same to be constantly open to the inspection of any of the Guardians of the Union, and to submit the same to the Guardians at their Meetings.

No. 18. To keep a Book in the Form (B) to this Order annexed, to be entitled " The Diet Class Book," in which he shall every evening enter the numbers of the several classes of Healthy and Sick Inmates, as ascertained by the daily roll-call in each department of the Workhouse, as directed in Article 15.

No. 19. To keep a Daily Diet Book in the Form (C) to this Order annexed, and for the better regulation of the issues of provisions from store, to ascertain and enter in the said book, before each meal the numbers of each of the several classes who are to partake thereof, and the quantities of each article of diet which, according to the existing dietary, shall be required for each class, and likewise to enter the quantities of each article to be taken from store for consumption at such meal by the healthy inmates of the Workhouse.

No. 20. In like manner to keep and daily enter up a Daily Diet Book in the Form (D) to this Order annexed, for the sick inmates.

No. 21. To submit to the Board of Guardians at every Ordinary Meeting an estimate of such provisions and other articles as are required for the use of the Workhouse, and to receive and execute the directions of the Board of Guardians thereupon.

No. 22. To receive all provisions and other articles purchased or procured for the use of the Workhouse, and before placing them in store, to weigh the same, and examine and compare them with the bills of parcels or invoices severally relating thereto ; and after having proved the accuracy of such bills or invoices, to authenticate the same with his signature, and submit them to the Board of Guardians at their next Ordinary Meeting.

No. 23. To receive and take charge of all provisions, clothing, linen, and other articles, belonging to the Workhouse, or confided to his care by the Board of Guardians, and issue the same to the Matron or other persons as may be required ; and such articles shall be applied to such purposes as shall be authorized or approved of by the Board of Guardians, and to no other.

No. 24. To take stock of Provisions, Clothing, Linen, and other articles belonging to the Workhouse once, at the least, in every half-year, that is to say, on the 25th day of March and the 29th day of September respectively, in the presence of two Guardians, to be named a Committee for this special purpose, and the Clerk of the Union.

No. 25. To obtain the order in writing of the Board of Guardians, duly entered in the ORDER BOOK provided for that purpose, and signed by the Chairman before purchasing or procuring any articles for the use of the Workhouse, or ordering any alterations or repairs of any part of the premises, or of the furniture, or other articles belonging thereto.

No. 26. To read over to the Paupers such of the Regulations herein contained, and at such times, as the Board of Guardians shall direct.

No. 27. To report to the Board of Guardians, from time to time, the names of such Children as may be fit to put out to service, or other employment, and to take the necessary steps for carrying into effect the directions of the Board of Guardians thereon.

No. 28. To keep a book to be called "The Master's Journal"; to enter therein every important occurrence in the Workhouse, other than those entered in the book required by Article 54 to be kept, and to cause such book to be laid before the Board of Guardians at every Ordinary Meeting.

No. 29. To take care that the wards, rooms, larder, kitchen, and all other offices of the Workhouse, and all the utensils and furniture thereof, be kept clean and in good order; and as often as any defect in the same, or in the state of the Workhouse, shall occur, to report the same in his Journal to the Board of Guardians, at their next. Ordinary Meeting.

No. 30. To inform the Visiting Committee and the Board of Guardians of the state of the Workhouse in every department; and to report in his Journal to the Board of Guardians at their next Ordinary Meeting any negligence or other misconduct on the part of any of the subordinate officers or servants of the establishment; to offer suggestions to the Board of Guardians for the correction of abuses, and the introduction of improvements in the management of the Workhouse; and generally to observe and fulfil all lawful orders and directions of the Board of Guardians suitable to his office.

# Appendix 4

## DRAWING FOR AN

## ECONOMICAL BEDSTEAD,

### PREPARED FOR THE

## CENTRAL BOARD of HEALTH _ IRELAND.

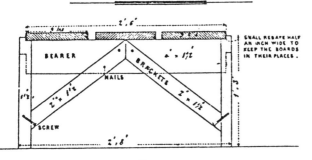

END VIEW.

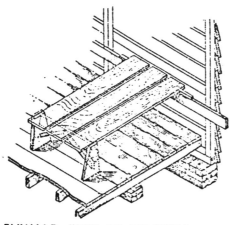

FAMILIAR VIEW OF BEDSTEAD.

MARCH. 1847.                                    GEO. WILKINSON. ARCHT

# Appendix 5

Potato Crop – Abstract of Replies received from Clerks of
Unions in Ireland, to Queries addressed, in August 1846,
to the Boards of Guardians by the Poor Law
Commissioners

---

1. Has the Potato Disease reappeared in your Union?
2. If Yes, in how many Electoral Divisions, and which, has it
   appeared?
3. In what Electoral Division has it not appeared?
4. What proportion of the crop has been affected in your Union?
5. For how many months' consumption would the healthy portion
   of the crop supply food?
6. What proportion of the Potato Crop on the Workhouse land is
   found diseased?

| NAME OF UNION. | 1. Has the Potato Disease reappeared in your Union? | 2. If Yes, in how many Electoral Divisions, and which, has it appeared? |
|---|---|---|
| | *Answers.* | *Answers.* |
| Abbeyleix . . . | Yes. | In every Division of the Union. |
| Antrim . . . | Yes. - | The disease has appeared in all the Electoral Divisions. |
| Ardee . . . . | Yes. | In all. |
| Armagh . . . | It has. | In all. |
| Athlone . . . | It has. | In all. |
| Athy . . . . | It has. | In all. |
| Bailieborough. . | It has. | In all. |
| Ballina . . . | To a great extent. | Every Electoral Division throughout the Union. |
| Ballinasloe . . | Yes. | In every one of them. |
| Ballinrobe . . | | |
| Ballycastle . . | It has. | In all. |
| Ballymena. . . | Yes. | In all. |
| Ballymoney . . | Yes. | In all the Divisions. |
| Ballyshannon . . | Yes. | In all. |
| Balrothery. . . | Yes. | In all. |
| Baltinglass . . | It has. | In all the Electoral Divisions of the Union. |
| Banbridge . . | Yes. | In all. |
| Bandon . . . | Yes, to a much greater extent than last year. | In all the Electoral Divisions. |
| Bantry . . . | Yes. | All. |
| Belfast . . . | Yes. | In all. |
| Boyle . . . . | Yes. | All. |

230

| NAME OF UNION. | 3. In what Electoral Division has it not appeared ? | 4. What proportion of the Crop has been affected in your Union ? |
|---|---|---|
| | *Answers.* | *Answers.* |
| Abbeyleix . . . | It has appeared in every division, not a field has escaped. | Seven-eighths. |
| Antrim . . . | None exempt. | Impossible to state with any degree of accuracy. |
| Ardee . . . . | None. | Cannot be ascertained at present. |
| Armagh . . . | None. | The entire crop. |
| Athlone . . . | In none. | The disease having checked the growth of the crop, it is far below average, and half of what are, being diseased, I may say that there are not two parts of a crop according to an average year. |
| Athy . . . . | None. | Cannot be ascertained as yet. |
| Bailieborough. . | In none. | The whole generally. |
| Ballina . . . | None exempt. | About the five-sixths. |
| Ballinasloe . . | It has made its appearance in every field of potatoes in every division throughout the Union. | The Guardians concur in saying the entire of it, and that a solitary exception cannot be made. |
| Ballinrobe. . . | | |
| Ballycastle. . . | In none. | All the crop. |
| Ballymena. . . | In none. | Almost all. |
| Ballymoney . . | In none. | The entire crop is considered affected. |
| Ballyshannon . . | None. | Nearly the whole. |
| Balrothery . . | In none. | Nearly the entire. |
| Baltinglass . . | No Electoral Division has escaped. | It is feared all the crop is affected, certain it is all the tops are blasted. |
| Banbridge . . | No reply to this query, but in reply to No. 2, it is stated to have appeared in all the divisions. | The one-half or more. |
| Bandon . . . | In none. | We have reason to fear that scarcely any portion will be saved. |
| Bantry. . . . | None. | Impossible to state, the failure is so general. |
| Belfast . . . | None. | The whole. |
| Boyle . . . . | None. | All. |
| Cahirciveen . . | In none. | Nearly the entire. |
| Callan . . . . | | |
| Carlow . . . | In none. | About five-sixths from present appearances. |
| Carrickmacross . | Not any. | From present appearances the whole crop is injured. |
| Carrick-on-Shan-non . . . . | None. | At least three-fourths of a very deficient crop diseased. |
| Carrick-on-Suir . | It has appeared in all the divisions. | Nineteen-twentieths, more or less. |
| Cashel . . . . | None. | Nearly all. |
| Castlebar . . . | None. | All. |

| NAME OF UNION. | 5. For how many Months' consumption would the healthy portion of the Crop supply food ? | 6. What proportion of the Potato Crop on the Workhouse land is found diseased ? |
|---|---|---|
| | *Answers.* | *Answers.* |
| Abbeyleix    . . | Not more than a month or six weeks. | They are not as yet dug out, but all the stalks are affected, some of the potatoes are not at present diseased, but they are unusually small. |
| Antrim    . . . | Not more than one month's consumption. | Almost the entire of it. |
| Ardee .    . . . | See reply to 4th query (cannot be ascertained at present.) | About one-half. |
| Armagh    . . . | About two months, certainly not more. | Fully three-fourths, and they are much better than the average in the neighbourhood. |
| Athlone    . . . | About three months. | The potato crop on the Workhouse ground is so damaged, that with much difficulty six men can, by digging from morning till evening, furnish a day's meal (about five and a-half cwt.) |
| Athy .    . . . | Cannot be ascertained as yet. | Scarcely any of the potatoes diseased as yet, although the stalks are all blackened and appear to be withering. |
| Bailieborough.    . | As the disease is in a progressive state, they could not form a correct opinion. | None growing thereon. |
| Ballina    . . . | According as the disease is spreading, there will not be a sufficient quantity for three months. | There is about one acre of potatoes on the Workhouse land, and from their present appearance there will not be more than one-fifth of them fit for use. I fear that they will be entirely lost from the rapidity of the disease ; their appearance day after day is an awful spectacle, and every other part of the Union equally so. |
| Ballinasloe    . . | The disease is so rapid in its destruction, that it cannot be exactly stated, but there may be about two months. | The potatoes growing on the Workhouse ground were up to Saturday last apparently sound, but since that time they have shown indications of the disease, and present now the same appearance as other diseased crops ; and as the disease progresses daily |

# Appendix 6i

## Statement showing the Amount of Workhouse Accommodation in Ireland – 1st May, 1847

| UNIONS | No. of inmates for which the Workhouse was originally designed. | No. of inmates for which Additional Accommodation has been otherwise provided. | OBSERVATIONS Showing the manner in which additional accommodation has been provided |
|---|---|---|---|
| Abbeyleix | 500 | 100 | Hiring a house for fever patients. |
| Antrim | 700 | 95 | Straw shed converted into nursery (40). Sheds constructed which accommodate (55). Idiot wards to be raised. |
| Ardee | 600 | 400 | A malt-house hired capable of affording the increased accommodation. |
| Armagh | 1,000 | 350 | Wards provided over dining hall (100). Sheds (100). Addition to fever hospital hired (100). Nurseries built (50). |
| Athlone | 900 | – | |
| Athy | 600 | 110 | Straw shed converted into sick ward (30). Sheds in boys' and girls' yards appropriated to the use of children under 4 (80). Tenders for raising idiot wards accepted. |
| Bailie-borough | 600 | – | Additional building in course of erection. |
| Ballina | 1,200 | – | |
| Ballinasloe | 1,000 | – | |
| Ballinrobe | 800 | – | |

| | | | |
|---|---|---|---|
| Ballycastle | 300 | 30 | One of the fuel stores converted into a day room. Tender for affording additional accommodation accepted. |
| Ballymena | 900 | 80 | Sleeping galleries erected. Accommodation for 60 additional inmates in course of erection. |
| Ballymoney | 700 | 50 | Female probationary ward altered. |
| Ballyshannon | 500 | – | |
| Balrothery | 400 | 197 | Officers' apartments appropriated and sleeping galleries erected. |
| Baltinglass | 500 | 40 | |
| Banbridge | 800 | 160 | Sleeping galleries erected to accommodate 120. Sheds erected (40); further accommodation in course of erection. |
| Bandon | 900 | 150 | Idiot wards raised and sheds erected. Plans for additional buildings requested. A loan of £3000 requested from Public Works Loan Commissioners. |
| Bantry | 600 | 50 | Coal and straw store fitted up for convalescent patients. |
| Belfast | 1,000 | 747 | Rooms in workhouse appropriated; sheds and sleeping galleries erected. |
| Boyle | 700 | – | Wooden sheds erected. |
| Cahirciveen | 400 | – | Guardians have determined on building a large addition to the workhouse. |
| Callan | 600 | 190 | Sleeping galleries erected; stores, stables, and idiot cells appropriated. |
| Carlow | 800 | 160 | Sheds erected and used as dormitories. Addition to infirmary, &c., contemplated. |
| Carrickma-cross | 500 | 240 | Two houses hired, sleeping galleries erected. |
| Carrick-on-Shannon | 800 | 11 | Shed appropriated to fever patients. |
| Carrick-on-Suir | 500 | 400 | Store hired, and sleeping galleries erected. |
| Cashel | 700 | 130 | Hired house. |
| Castlebar | 700 | – | |
| Castleblayney | 800 | – | |

| | | | |
|---|---|---|---|
| Castlederg | 200 | 56 | Alterations for the accommodation of fever patients in workhouse hospital, and providing for other patients. |
| Castlerea | 1,000 | – | |
| Cavan | 1,200 | 40 | Sheds for convalescent patients. |
| Celbridge | 400 | – | |
| Clifden | 300 | – | |
| Clogheen | 500 | 80 | Sheds used as stores, converted into dormitories. |
| Clogher | 500 | – | Plans for additional buildings under consideration. |
| Clones | 600 | 220 | Hired houses. |
| Clonmel | 600 | 1,000 | Hiring of a large concern formerly used as a brewery. |
| Coleraine | 700 | 60 | Lofts raised over boys' dormitories. |
| Cookstown | 600 | – | Guardians have determined on building an addition to the workhouse, capable of accommodating 400. |
| Cootehill | 800 | – | |
| Cork | 2,000 | 3,250 | Portions of old house of industry hired (800). Additions by way of sheds, &c. (2450). |
| Donegal | 500 | 10 | House hired. |
| Downpatrick | 1,000 | 20 | Enlargement of nursery. |
| Drogheda | 800 | 40 | Sleeping galleries erected. |
| Dublin, Nth | 2,000 | 1,466 | Hiring of houses (2), and erection of sheds. |
| Dublin, Sth | 2,000 | 360 | Erection of buildings in connexion with workhouse. |
| Dundalk | 800 | 120 | School-rooms converted into day-rooms and sleeping galleries erected. |
| Dunfanaghy | 300 | – | |
| Dungannon | 800 | 200 | House hired. Extension of the buildings at the workhouse contemplated. |
| Dungarvan | 600 | 50 | Stabling converted into a fever hospital. |
| Dunmanway | 400 | 120 | House hired, stable sheds appropriated. |
| Dunshaugh-lin | 400 | 71 | Stables and probationary wards converted into sleeping apartments. House hired as fever hospital. |
| Edenderry | 600 | – | Erection of additional buildings under consideration. |
| Ennis | 800 | – | |

| | | | |
|---|---|---|---|
| Enniscorthy | 600 | 200 | Two store-houses have been hired capable of accommodating 150 and 50 respectively. |
| Enniskillen | 1,000 | 120 | Hired house and sheds appropriated to the accommodation of fever patients. |
| Ennistymon | 600 | – | |
| Fermoy | 900 | 200 | Store-house hired capable of accommodating 150; shed erected, affording accommodation for 50. |
| Galway | 1,000 | 100 | Erection of sheds. |
| Glenties | 500 | – | |
| Gorey | 500 | 210 | Erection of sleeping galleries, (80). Dining hall converted into dormitory, (80). Hired house, for fever patients (50). |
| Gort | 500 | – | |
| Gortin | 200 | 8 | Erection of a shed. |
| Granard | 600 | 48 | Turf-house, straw-house, and sheds adjoining, converted into dormitories. Sleeping galleries erected. |
| Inishowen | 600 | – | |
| Kanturk | 800 | 250 | A store-house capable of accommodating 200. Sheds capable of accommodating 50, erected. |
| Kells | 600 | 200 | Enclosing and fitting up sheds attached to idiot wards. |
| Kenmare | 500 | – | |
| Kilkeel | 300 | – | |
| Kilkenny | 1,300 | 600 | Hiring houses, erecting sleeping galleries and sheds. |
| Killarney | 800 | – | |
| Kilmallock | 800 | 200 | Erection of sheds in workhouse yard and in front of fever ward. |
| Kilrush | 800 | – | Addition to infirmary in course of erection. |
| Kinsale | 500 | 442 | Old jail rented (200). Sheds erected (200). Sheds for fever patients (42). |
| Larne | 400 | 130 | Erection of sleeping galleries. |
| Letterkenny | 500 | – | |
| Limerick | 1,600 | 912 | Additions to workhouse and erection of temporary sheds. |
| Lisburn | 800 | 160 | Sleeping galleries erected, accommodation for 100. Coal store appropriated, (60). |

| | | | |
|---|---|---|---|
| Lismore | 500 | 100 | A store-house hired for the purpose. |
| Lisnaskea | 500 | 130 | Permanent buildings erected in addition to workhouse. |
| Listowel | 700 | 100 | Sleeping galleries erected. |
| Londonderry | 800 | 100 | Permanent buildings in women's yard, (40). Temporary sheds for fever patients, (60). |
| Longford | 1,000 | – | |
| Loughrea | 800 | – | |
| Lowtherstown | 400 | – | |
| Lurgan | 800 | 24 | Sheds enclosed. Additional sheds are nearly finished, calculated to accommodate 1200. |
| Macroom | 600 | 60 | Store hired as addition to workhouse. |
| Magherafelt | 900 | 160 | Temporary wooden sheds. |
| Mallow | 700 | 90 | Sheds. |
| Manor-hamilton | 500 | 12 | Sheds altering with a view to afford additional accommodation. |
| Midleton | 800 | 200 | Additional wing added, and stables appropriated. |
| Milford | 400 | – | |
| Mohill | 700 | – | |
| Monaghan | 900 | 300 | Additions being made to workhouse, to accommodate 300 inmates. |
| Mount-mellick | 800 | 400 | A store has been hired until the 29th September next to accommodate 400, and has been occupied. |
| Mullingar | 800 | – | Sleeping galleries erecting. |
| Naas | 530 | 150 | A house hired to accommodate 100. Stables fitted up, affording accommodation for 50. |
| Navan | 500 | 30 | Coal store appropriated. |
| Nenagh | 1,000 | 260 | Erection of sheds and sleeping galleries. |
| Newcastle | 550 | 360 | Houses hired and alterations made in the rooms in the workhouse. |
| New Ross | 900 | 108 | Hired house (80). Sheds erected (28). |
| Newry | 1,000 | 100 | Stabling converted into day-rooms, and sheds erected. |
| Newtownards | 600 | 200 | Erection of sheds and sleeping galleries. |
| Newtown Limavady | 600 | – | |
| Oldcastle | 600 | – | |
| Omagh | 800 | 200 | Sleeping galleries erected. |

| | | | |
|---|---|---|---|
| Parsonstown | 800 | – | |
| Rathdown | 600 | 25 | Stables have been appropriated to afford workhouse accommodation. |
| Rathdrum | 600 | 260 | Part of Flannel Hall, granted by Earl Fitzwilliam, accommodates 200; hired house for fever patients, 60. |
| Rathkeale | 660 | 247 | Additional buildings and sleeping galleries erected. A house hired for fever patients. |
| Roscommon | 900 | 92 | House hired for the accommodation of fever patients, and stable fitted up also for the reception of patients. |
| Roscrea | 700 | 200 | Sleeping galleries erected, stables appropriated. |
| Scariff | 600 | 40 | Stables have been fitted up for the purpose of affording additional accommodation. |
| Shillelagh | 400 | 40 | Idiot wards raised a story each (in course of erection.) |
| Skibbereen | 800 | 40 | Stables fitted up to afford additional accommodation. |
| Sligo | 1,200 | 70 | Sheds erected in infirmary yards. |
| Strabane | 800 | 36 | Store taken for fever patients. |
| Stranorlar | 400 | – | |
| Swinford | 700 | – | |
| Thurles | 700 | 60 | Straw and turf sheds appropriated to the accommodation of fever patients. |
| Tipperary | 700 | 200 | Sleeping galleries, accommodating 150, erected. House hired for fever patients 50. |
| Tralee | 1,000 | 186 | Sleeping galleries (150), sheds (36). |
| Trim | 500 | 52 | Hired house. |
| Tuam | 800 | – | Tenders for sheds to accommodate 100 have been advertised for. |
| Tullamore | 700 | 50 | A house has been hired for the accommodation of 50 fever patients. |
| Waterford | 900 | 200 | Sleeping galleries and sheds. |
| Westport | 1,000 | – | |
| Wexford | 600 | – | |

# Appendix 6ii

Fever Hospitals in connexion with Workhouses: –
Statement of the Unions in which Fever Wards have been
Built or Hired, or are in course of Erection; Numbers to be
Accommodated; and Arrangements reported for the
Reception of Fever Cases: – 1st May, 1847

| | | | |
|---|---|---|---|
| Abbeyleix | Hired | 100 | Arrangements for increasing the accommodation have been made with the trustees of the fever hospital, and the workhouse infirmary appropriated. |
| Antrim | New building | 40 | Open. |
| Ardee | – | 40 | Open. |
| Armagh | – | 40 | Open. A house has been hired in addition to the fever hospital; 100 accommodated. |
| Athlone | – | 46 | In course of erection. |
| Athy | Sheds | 30 | Sheds, formerly used for straw and turf stores, fitted up for fever patients. |
| Bailieborough | | 45 | Sheds in course of erection to afford temporary accommodation. |
| Ballina | New shed/ buildings | 30 | In course of erection. Guardians have determined on erecting further sheds according to Board of Health plans. |
| Ballinasloe | – | 64 | In course of erection. Idiot wards used as convalescent wards. |
| Ballinrobe | – | | An application has been made to the Lords of the Treasury for a loan for the purpose of building a fever hospital; – a consent to the expenditure of £700 to build a fever hospital has been signed by Guardians. |
| Ballycastle | New building | 40 | Open. |

| | | | |
|---|---|---|---|
| Ballymena | – | 40 | Building in course of erection. A house has ben procured from Sir Shafto Adair, as a temporary fever hospital. |
| Ballymoney | – | 32 | Open. |
| Ballyshannon | – | | Plan of fever hospital accepted – Tenders for erection of sheds invited. |
| Balrothery | New building | 48 | Open. |
| Baltinglass | Hired | 36 | Open. |
| Banbridge | New building | 48 | Open. Kitchen and store-rooms to be added. Guardians have resolved to extend the accommodation for patients. |
| Bandon | Shed | 50 | Erected in infirmary yard; accommodation for 70 additional persons to be provided. |
| Bantry | New building | 44 | Open. |
| Belfast | – | 159 | Open. Extension of, contemplated. Temporary increased accommodation erected (350). |
| Boyle | – | 44 | Finished. Idiot wards to be enlarged to afford additional accommodation. Loan of £800 applied for. |
| Cahirciveen | Sheds | 100 | In course of erection. |
| Callan | New building | 69 | In course of erection. A temporary fever hospital has been hired in Ballingary under 9th Vict. cap. 6 to accommodate 20. |
| Carlow | Hired | 70 | Temporary fever hospital hired. |
| Carrick-macross | – | | Fever cases sent to a hospital unconnected with the workhouse. |
| Carrick-on-Shannon | Shed building | 34 | Open. Sheds have been erected in men's yard. |
| Carrick-on-Suir | Sheds | 100 | In course of erection. A temporary fever hospital at Portlaw, under 9th Vic. c. 6. |
| Cashel | New building | 44 | Open. Additional accommodation for 100 provided; idiot wards converted into convalescent wards. |
| Castlebar | – | | Portion of workhouse appropriated; idiot wards to be raised. |
| Castleblayney | New building | 60 | Open. |

| | | | |
|---|---|---|---|
| Castlederg | New building | 36 | Open. Workhouse hospital raised and separated from main building for treatment of fever patients. |
| Castlerea | Hired 2 | 24 | Probationary wards have been adopted. |
| Cavan | – | | Idiot and probationary wards used for the treatment of fever patients. Tenders for permanent hospital invited. |
| Celbridge | – | | Cases sent to fever hospital in town. |
| Clifden | – | | Workhouse opened 8th March. |
| Clogheen | Addition to workhouse | 45 | Addition made to infirmary sufficient for the accommodation of 45 patients. |
| Clogher | New building | 32 | Open. |
| Clones | – | | Erection of fever hospital under consideration. |
| Clonmel | Hired | | House hired for the reception of fever patients. |
| Coleraine | New building | 60 | In course of erection; works to be completed 1st September next. |
| Cookstown | – | 75 | Guardians have determined on erecting a fever hospital. |
| Cootehill | – | 40 | Finished. |
| Cork | Hired houses | | Houses have been hired in different parts of the city for the treatment of fever patients. |
| Donegal | – | | Guardians have resolved to build a fever hospital on procuring a loan; plans sent to Guardians. Tender forwarded for Commissioners' consideration. |
| Downpatrick | New building | 60 | Plans have been sent to Guardians. Sheds to accommodate 30 in course of erection. |
| Drogheda | – | 50 | Finished. Temporary hospital hired, accommodation for 20 patients. |
| Dublin, Nth | Hired | 60 | Not yet occupied. Patients are sent to the Hardwicke Fever Hospital also. |
| Dublin, Sth | Hired | 75 | Open. Hired for four months. |
| Dundalk | New building | 48 | Open. A house has been taken in addition. |

| | | | |
|---|---|---|---|
| Dungannon | New building | 40 | Open. |
| Dungarvan | Sheds | | |
| Dunmanway | New building | 60 | Tender for erection of fever hospital accepted. Portion of workhouse appropriated to the treatment of fever patients. |
| Dunshaugh-lin | Hired | 25 | The stables have been fitted up for the reception of patients. Erection of hospital for 60 patients agreed on. |
| Edenderry | New building | 40 | A tender for the erection of a fever hospital has been accepted, and a consent for the expenditure signed by Guardians. |
| Ennis | – | | Patients sent to County Fever Hospital. |
| Enniscorthy | – | | Patients sent to Enniscorthy Fever Hospital. |
| Enniskillen | Hired, &c. | 120 | Sheds for convalescent patients have been erected on workhouse grounds. |
| Ennistymon | New building | 30 | Open. |
| Fermoy | New building | 75 | In course of erection. Temporary fever hospitals have been hired under 9th Vict. c. 6. |
| Galway | Sheds | 100 | Erected in workhouse yards. |
| Glenties | – | | |
| Gorey | Hired | 50 | Tenders for erection of temporary fever hospital accepted. |
| Gort | – | | Plans of sheds for the accommodation of 100 selected. |
| Gortin | Sheds | 8 | Occupied. |
| Granard | New building | 40 | Finished. |
| Inishowen | – | | Part of infirmary at workhouse appropriated to the reception of fever patients. |
| Kanturk | New building | 74 | Open. An addition is in course of erection which will afford accommodation for 50. |
| Kells | – | | Patients sent to Kells Fever Hospital. |
| Kenmare | New building | 40 | Open. |
| Kilkeel | New building | 40 | Open. |
| Kilkenny | Hired | 80 | Portion of County Fever Hospital hired. Patients also treated in part of the workhouse. |

| | | | |
|---|---|---|---|
| Killarney | – | | |
| Kilmallock | New building | 40 | Convalescent wards have been added. |
| Kilrush | – | | Tenders for the erection of sheds accepted. |
| Kinsale | Sheds | 42 | Shed building in course of erection. Patients also sent to Carrigaline Fever Hospital. |
| Larne | New building | 40 | Open. |
| Letterkenny | Temporary sheds | 40 | In course of erection. |
| Limerick | New building | 96 | Open. Erection of further accommodation under consideration. |
| Lisburn | New building | 60 | Tender for building accepted. House hired as a temporary fever hospital. |
| Lismore | – | | Patients sent to Lismore Fever Hospital, where the Guardians contemplate providing additional accommodation. |
| Lisnaskea | – | | Guardians intend to build a fever hospital. |
| Listowel | New building | 46 | In course of erection. A house has been hired as a temporary fever hospital. |
| Londonderry | Sheds | 60 | In course of erection. |
| Longford | New building | 64 | Open. Addition to fever hospital contemplated. |
| Loughrea | Sheds | 100 | Patients sent to fever hospital in town, and treated also in part of workhouse. Plan of fever hospital and sheds approved, and tender accepted. |
| Lowtherstown | New building | 40 | In course of erection. |
| Lurgan | New building | 40 | Open. An addition is being added which will accommodate 50 more. Temporary sheds to accommodate 300 in course of erection. |
| Macroom | New building | 40 | Open. Houses have been hired to afford additional accommodation. |
| Magherafelt | New building | 40 | Open. Wooden sheds calculated for 60 or 100 fever patients erected. Erection of further sheds to accommodate 200 proposed. |

| | | | |
|---|---|---|---|
| Mallow | New building | 60 | Arrangement for erection of fever hospital under consideration. House hired at Doneraile under 9 Vict. c. 6. |
| Manor-hamilton | Sheds | | In course of erection. Idiot wards to be raised. |
| Midleton | Hired | 32 | Additional accommodation for 200 patients has been provided, by appropriating additions lately made to workhouse. |
| Milford | – | | Tender for the erection of a temporary fever hospital accepted. |
| Mohill | – | | Tender for the erection of fever hospital accepted. |
| Monaghan | Hired | 30 | Guardians are about building a fever hospital. A loan has been obtained for the purpose. |
| Mount - mellick | New building | 44 | Open. An additional shed in course of erection. |
| Mullingar | New building | 60 | Finished. |
| Naas | New building | 44 | Open. |
| Navan | – | | Patients sent to County Fever Hospital. Building of fever ward in connexion with workhouse contemplated. |
| Nenagh | New building | 70 | In course of erection. |
| Newcastle | – | | Sheds in connexion with Newcastle Fever Hospital, where the patients from the workhouse are treated, in course of erection. |
| New Ross | New building | 72 | Open. An additional ward, to accommodate 22 patients, in course of erection. Portion of workhouse appropriated. |
| Newry | – | | Erection of fever hospital contemplated. |
| Newtownards | New building | 60 | Open. |
| Newtown Limavady | New building | 30 | Open. |
| Oldcastle | New building | 44 | Open. |
| Omagh | – | | Patients treated in Omagh Fever Hospital. Sheds in course of erection. |

| | | | |
|---|---|---|---|
| Parsonstown | – | | Patients sent to town fever hospital. Plans of sheds have been sent to Guardians. |
| Rathdown | – | | Patients sent to Rathdown Fever Hospital. |
| Rathdrum | Hired | 60 | Open. Arrangements for the erection of fever hospital under consideration. House hired as a temporary fever hospital (60). |
| Rathkeale | Hired | 100 | Arrangements for building a fever hospital are under consideration. |
| Roscommon | – | 40 | Open. Tender for erection of fever hospital sheds accepted. Stables fitted up for patients. |
| Roscrea | – | | Patients sent to Roscrea Fever Hospital. |
| Scariff | – | | Erection of fever hospital under consideration. |
| Shillelagh | – | | Tender for erection of fever hospital accepted. Patients sent at present to Carnew Fever Hospital. |
| Skibbereen | New building | 44 | Open. Additional accommodation has been provided at the workhouse. |
| Sligo | Hired | 60 | Fever sheds calculated to accommodate 40 in course of erection. |
| Strabane | Hired | 36 | Guardians have resolved to build a fever ward for 70 patients. House hired as temporary hospital to accommodate 36. |
| Stranorlar | – | | Plans sent and approved by Guardians for 60 patients. Portion of workhouse at present appropriated to the treatment of fever patients. |
| Swinford | – | | Guardians have resolved to build a fever ward, and advertised for tenders. Portion of workhouse appropriated to the treatment of fever patients. |
| Thurles | New building | 70 | In course of erection. |
| Tipperary | New building | 56 | In course of erection. House hired as temporary fever hospital. |

| Tralee | New building | 60 | In course of erection. |
|---|---|---|---|
| Trim | – | | Patients treated in Trim Fever Hospital. |
| Tuam | Sheds | 50 | In course of erection. |
| Tullamore | New building | 40 | Open. A house has been hired, which affords accommodation for 50 additional patients. |
| Waterford | – | | Patients sent to Waterford Fever Hospital. Additional sheds provided by Fever Hospital Committee. |
| Westport | – | | |
| Wexford | – | | |

# Appendix 7

## From the Poor Law Commissioners Report published 25 March, 1847

The statistics (from the 2,000 localities) referred to present no adequate notion of the disastrous state of certain individual Unions in Ireland, and the harrowing details which fill the Minutes of the Boards of Guardians, and our other correspondence from such Unions, in cases where the means at the disposal of the Guardians have been found to be utterly inadequate to meet the pressure of applications from persons in the last extremities of destitution. We cannot, without entering too much into detail particularise each Union in which these events have taken place; neither, at the same time, is it right to omit all record of such suffering as the people have undergone on the one hand, and of the difficulties and embarrassments which the Guardians have had to encounter. There are few situations more painful and afflicting than that of a Board of Guardians, established to administer relief, yet finding themselves in the midst of an appalling state of distress, without funds to relieve the sufferers effectively, or to alleviate in any material degree the universal distress. Possessed of a workhouse, capable of holding only a few hundred inmates at one time, the Guardians are looked to with hope by thousands of famishing persons, and are called on to exercise, for a time, the mournful task of selection from the distressed objects who present themselves for admission as their last refuge from death . . . We regret to say that in many of the workhouses, more especially in Connaught and in the south of Ireland, such has been the frightful state of distress, that all precautions have been borne down, and the workhouses crowded to an extent far beyond their calculated capacity, and the consequences have been in some cases most disastrous. In all these cases the seeds of contagious disease have been introduced by persons suffering under dysentery or fever when first admitted; and the diseases so introduced have spread to inmates previously healthy, and also to officers of the workhouse.

# Appendix 8

## Soup
### – Instructions issued by the Commissariat Relief Office

---

It is recommended to Relief Committees to establish Soup Kitchens; and also provide ingredients for Soup to be sold to persons who can prepare it according to printed directions.

The Soup, No. 1 in Count Rumford's Essay on Food, appears to be the best adapted for general use, as not containing any green or unseasoned Vegetables, and may consist only of Barley, Peas, Salt, Water, with cuttings of Wheaten Bread, or Biscuit.

A Land Proprietor in the County of Waterford, whose Labourers use this Soup for dinner, has supplied the following practical information in recommending its general adoption:-

"The Soup, No. 1 in Count Rumford's Essay, has been used in the Lismore Union Workhouse for many months, and has been adopted in the Fermoy Union, and I believe in Macroom also.

"For the last year I have given this Soup, one quart each, to my Labourers for Dinner. Each quart is about *two pounds four ounces* in weight, and costs *three farthings*.

"It is composed of Barley, ground whole, with all the Bran, whole Peas, Pepper, Salt and Water. [See proportions below.]

"In each quart are placed small cuttings of Wheaten Bread, on which the boiling soup is poured, so as to fill each quart.

"The whole-meal of Barley answers as well as pearl Barley, and is much cheaper.

"Of course, Meat would improve the Soup, but then the price would be greatly increased; and the object is to produce a nutritious Food at the lowest price.

"A quantity of Peas and Barley, used in Soup, will support a much greater number of persons than if cooked separately.

"The Soup used in Lismore Workhouse is composed of pearl Barley, Peas, Pepper and Salt, in the proportion of one pound of Peas, and one one pound of Barley, to one gallon of water.

"For dinner, each adult gets thirty ounces of this Soup, with six ounces of Bread, as only two meals are given in the day; and the Bread is given separately.

"Count Rumford's Essay is sold by W. and G. Robertson, 35 Lower

248

Sackville Street, Dublin, and by Hamilton, Youghal."

In preparing this Soup, the Peas should be soaked in Cold Water for some hours, not less than two, before being put into the boiler; and the Soup must be made with Soft Water, as Peas will not mix with Hard Water, unless a small lump of soda is put into it. The Water should be boiling when the Peas are put in; and they must be let boil separately until tender. Do not add the salt until they are boiled, or they will not become soft. They should be stirred occasionally to keep them from the bottom of the boiler. When they are quite soft, stir in the Barley, and let the Soup simmer gently for a couple of hours. In the meantime put some pepper into a vessel with a little of the soup, mix them well, and pour them into the boiler – then stir the Soup thoroughly and season it with salt.

If Biscuit is to be used with the Soup instead of Bread, put it separately into the vessel like the cuttings of Bread, otherwise it cannot be equally distributed.

The cost must vary, as the ingredients are obtained under favorable circumstances or the contrary.

*Commissariat Relief Office, Dublin Castle,*
*31 December, 1846*

# Appendix 9

## Rules governing dietaries according to the General Order of the Poor Law Commissioners issued 5 February 1849

Inmates were divided into seven classes:

(i)   Able-bodied working males.
(ii)  Able-bodied working females.
(iii) Aged and infirm persons of either sex, and adult persons of either sex, above fifteen years of age, but not working.
(iv)  Boys and girls above nine and under fifteen years of age.
(v)   Children above five and under nine years of age.
(vi)  Children above two and under five years of age.
(vii) Infants under two years of age.

Adults were to have two meals a day, one consisting of not less than: Class (i): Eight ounces of Indian meal and half a pint of new milk; Class (ii): Seven ounces of Indian meal and half a pint of new milk; Class (iii): Six ounces of Indian meal and half a pint of new milk.

The other meal was to consist of not less than: Class (i): Fourteen ounces of brown bread and two pints of soup; Class (ii): Twelve ounces of brown bread and one and a half pints of soup; Class (iii): Ten ounces of brown bread and one and a half pints of soup.

Where three meals a day were allowed, 'the amount of nutriment to be at least equal to that contained in the two meals as set forth'.

Children, classes (iv), (v) and (vi), were to get three meals a day, similar to those given to adults but of smaller proportions.

The allowance for infants under two years of age was 'not less than eight ounces of white bread and a pint of new milk daily'.

The soup was to be made of peas-meal or oatmeal, or both, in the proportion of eight ounces of meal to one gallon of water, 'well seasoned with onions, pepper and salt, and thickened at all commencement seasons with turnips and carrots or other such vegetables'.

These, of course, were recommended diets. Given the limited financial resources of the workhouses and the severe overcrowding that still pertained in 1849, it is scarcely credible that workhouse staffs, dealing with unprecedented numbers, and trying to cope with fever and death in addition, would have had the time to sort out the twelve-ouncers from the ten-ouncers or to worry about the seasoning of soup.

# Appendix 10

This account of assisted emigration from Lord Lansdowne's estate in Kenmare, County Kerry, comes from *Realities of Irish Life* by W.S. Trench; his agent. (His preamble outlining the condition of the estate in Kenmare is quoted in chapter fourteen, page 150).

---

I therefore resolved to put into practice a scheme which I had mediated for a long time previously, namely to go myself to Lord Lansdowne at Bowood, to state to him the whole circumstance of the case, and to recommend him to adopt an extensive system of voluntary migration as the only practicable and effective means of relieving this frightful destitution. This plan I carried into effect. I went over to England (and) during my stay I had frequent and lengthened interviews with that most enlightened and liberal statesman.

The broad sketch of the plan I laid before him was as follows: I showed him by the poor-house returns, that the number of paupers off his estate and receiving relief in the workhouse amounted to about three thousand. That I was wholly unable to undertake the employment of these people in their present condition on reproductive works; and that if left in the workhouse, the smallest amount they could possibly cost would be £5 per head per annum, and thus that the poor rates must necessarily amount, for some years to come, to £15,000 per annum, unless these people died or left – and the latter was not probable. I stated also, that hitherto the people had been kept alive in the workhouse by grants from the rates-in-aid and other public money; but that this could not always go on. That the valuation of his estate in that district scarcely reached £10,000 per annum; and thus that the poor rates necessary to be raised in future off the estate to support this number of people, would amount to at least thirty shillings in the pound. I explained further to him, that under these circumstances, inasmuch as the poor rates were a charge prior to the rent, it would be impossible for his lordship to expect any rent whatever out of his estate for many years to come.

The remedy I proposed was as follows: that he should forthwith offer free emigration to every man, woman and child now in the poor-house or receiving relief and chargeable to his estate. That I had been in communication with an Emigration Agent, who had offered to contract

251

to take them to whatever port in America each pleased, at a reasonable rate per head. That even supposing they all accepted this offer, the total, together with a small sum per head for outfit and a few shillings on landing would not exceed from £13,000 to £14,000, a sum less than it would cost to support them in the workhouse for a single year. That in the one case he would not only free his estate of this mass of pauperism which had been allowed to accumulate upon it, but would put the people themselves in a far better way of earning their bread hereafter; whereas by feeding and retaining them where they were, they must remain as a millstone around the neck of his estate, and prevent its rise for many years to come; and I plainly proved that it would be cheaper to him, and better for them, to pay for their emigration at once, than to continue to support them at home.

His lordship discussed the matter very fully, and with that kindness, good sense, and liberality which characterised all his acts; and on my leaving Bowood he gave me an order for £8,000 wherewith to commence the system of emigration, with a full understanding that more should be forthcoming if required.

I shall not readily forget the scenes that occurred in Kenmare when I returned, and announced that I was prepared at Lord Lansdowne's expense to send to America everyone now in the poor-house who was chargeable to his lordship's estate, and who desired to go; leaving each to select what port in America he pleased – whether Boston, New York, New Orleans, or Quebec.

The announcement at first was scarcely credited; it was considered by the paupers to be too good to be true. But when it began to be believed and appreciated, a rush was made to get away at once. The organisation of the system required, however, much care and thought.

The mode adopted was as follows: two hundred each week were selected of those apparently most suited for emigration; and having arranged their slender outfit, a steady man, on whom I could depend, Mr. Jeremiah O'Shea, was employed to take charge of them on their journey to Cork, and not to leave them nor allow them to scatter, until he saw them safely on board the emigrant ship. This plan succeeded admirably; and week after week to the astonishment of the good people of Cork, and sometimes not a little to their dismay, a batch of two hundred paupers appeared on the quays of Cork, bound for the Far West.

A cry was now raised that I was exterminating the people. But the people knew well that those who now cried loudest had given them no help when in the extremity of their distress, and they rushed from the country like a panic-stricken throng, each only fearing that the funds at my disposal might fail before he and his family could get their passage.

So great was the rush from the workhouse to emigrate, and so great was the influx into the workhouse to qualify (as I generally required the application of that sure test of abject poverty before I gave an order for emigration) that the Guardians became uneasy, and said the poor-house would be filled with those seeking emigration, even faster than it could be emptied. But I told them not to be alarmed – that all demands should be met. And thus, two hundred after two hundred, week after week, departed from Cork, until the poor-house was nearly emptied of paupers chargeable to the Lansdowne estate; and in little more than a year 3,500 paupers had left Kenmare for America, all free emigrants, without any ejectments having been brought against them to enforce it, or the slightest pressure put upon them to go.

Matters now began to right themselves; only some fifty or sixty paupers remained in the workhouse, chargeable to the property over which I had the care and Lord Lansdowne's estate at length breathed freely.

It must be admitted that the paupers despatched to America on such a sudden pressure as this were of a very motley type; and a strange figure these wild batches of two hundred each – most of them speaking only the Irish language – made in the streets of Cork as well as on the quays of Liverpool and America. There was great difficulty in keeping them from breaking loose from the ship, not only in Cork but in Liverpool, where the ship's touched before they left for the West.'

The Trench plan aroused mixed feelings. One who did not approve was Father O'Sullivan, parish priest of Kenmare, who engaged in rather acrimonious controversy with Mr Trench in the matter. Another was the patriot O'Donovan Rossa, who was at that time doing business in west Cork. He wrote some vigorous verses, which Trench (who never discovered the identity of the author) regarded as dangerous incitement against him. In his *Recollections* Rossa recalled: 'Stewart Trench, the land agent of Lord Lansdowne, was at that time in his glory evicting the tenantry. The stories I heard about him moved me to write this poem:

> *O Kerry! where now is the spirit*
> *That ever distinguished thy race.*
> *If you tolerate Trench you will merit*
> *A stigma of shame and disgrace.*
>
> *Persecution by law he can preach*
> *He can nicely "consolidate" farms;*
> *He can blarney and lie in his speech*
> *And exterminate the Irish in swarms.*

*No hope for a comfort in life*
*While crouchingly quiet and obedient,*
*The weal of your child or your wife*
*Is naught to Trench the tyrannical agent*

The Kenmare men asked me to get what I wrote about Trench printed for them in some slips of paper. I got them printed and sent them to the Kerry men. Trench got hold of one of them, and was mad to find out who was the writer; he said it was inciting people to murder him. But the Kerry men did not give me away.'

One reason why Trench was viewed with some suspicion and distrust was because of his opposition to the Ribbonmen (an anti-landlord secret society, 1835-55, so called because of its badge – a green ribbon) and other secret agrarian societies in the district. Another was his known contacts with the police.

## ÉTÉ 1847 / SUMMER OF 1847

| No. Rég. Reg. No. | Nom Name | Âge Age | Date d'entrée Date of Entry | Père Father | Mère Mother | Paroisse Parish | Comté County | Bateau Vessel | Adopté par Adopted by |
|---|---|---|---|---|---|---|---|---|---|
| 407 | DORION, William | 8 | 10/26/47 | Daniel | Cicily Dorion | ? | Armagh | Rankin | Person in Rimouski |
| 93 | DORNION, Daniel | 6 | 08/06/47 | Michael | Catherine Love | Fannoth | Donegal | Rankin | Rev. Mr. Faucher Lotbinière |
| 331 | DOYLE, Lawrence | 12 | 08/29/47 | Lawrence | Mary Flinn | Glinnigal | Carlow | Industry | Mr. Lemieux St. Roch |
| 446 | DUNN, Margaret | 14 | 04/06/48 | John | Judith Gaffny | Dorah | Queens | Juverna | Mrs. Ferguson St. John Street |
| 309 | EGAN, Bridget | 6 | 09/20/47 | Bryan | Bridget Casy | Hillglass | Roscommon | Erin's Queen | Died Feb. 3, 1848 |
| 308 | EGAN, Peter | 16 | 09/20/47 | Bryan | Bridget Casy | Hillglass | Roscommon | Erin's Queen | Agapit Belanger Rimouski |
| 222a | FEENEY, ANNE | 8 | 09/02/47 | Thomas | Mary Lyons | Bumblin | Roscommon | Virginius | Mr. Kelly St. Sylvester |
| 222 | FEENEY, Catherine | 18 | 09/02/47 | Thomas | Mary Lyons | Bumblin | Roscommon | Virginius | Mr. Kelly St. Sylvester |
| 249 | FEENY, Catherine | 14 | 09/07/47 | Michael | Ellen Kelly | Bumblin | Roscommon | Naomi | Died Oct. 1 |
| 82 | FINNERTY, Hannah | 14 | 08/06/47 | Patrick | Catherine Coffy | Foghany | Galway | Blonde | ? |
| 334 | FITZGERALD, John | 10 | 09/29/47 | Edward | Catherine Lehey | ? | Kerry | Bridgetown | Died Oct. 7 Brother is in Montreal |
| 5 | FITZPATRICK, Anne | 13 | 07/47 | Patrick | Mary Forestal | the Rower | Kilkenny | Progress | Jean Bouvette St. Grégoire |
| 99 | FITZPATRICK, Bridget | 18 | 08/09/47 | Patrick | Mary Forestal | the Rower | Kilkenny | Progress | Norbert Beliveau St. Grégoire |
| 6 | FITZPATRICK, Edward | 15 | 07/47 | Patrick | Mary Forestal | the Rower | Kilkenny | Progress | Jean Prince St. Grégoire |
| 458i | FITZPATRICK, Ellen | 8 | 07/01/48 | Patrick | Mary Forestal | the Rower | Kilkenny | ? | Returned to mother St. Grégoire |
| 187 | FLYNN, Bridget | 2½ | 08/27/47 | John | Onah Bradley | near Rovishtown | Sligo | Wanderer | Died Sept. 24 |
| 186 | FLYNN, Margaret | 13 | 08/27/47 | John | Onah Bradley | near Rovishtown | Sligo | Wanderer | Died Sept. 30 |

## ÉTÉ 1847 / SUMMER OF 1847

| No. Rég. Reg. No. | Nom Name | Âge Age | Date d'entrée Date of Entry | Père Father | Mère Mother | Paroisse Parish | Comté County | Bateau Vessel | Adopté par Adopted by |
|---|---|---|---|---|---|---|---|---|---|
| 202 | HYLER, Mary (or Hilliard) | 13 | 08/28/47 | Andrew | Nancy Fitzpatrick | Hinch | Clare | Champion | Luc Reau (went 1858 to St Grégoire Longueuil) |
| 201 | HYLER, Michael (or Hilliard) | 15 | 08/28/47 | Andrew | Nancy Fitzpatrick | Hinch | Clare | Champion | Louis Beauloricr Nicolet |
| 120 | HYNES, Edward | 14 | 08/14/47 | James | Mary Hines | Megorna | Mayo | Rankin | Eusège Lepage Rimouski |
| 119 | HYNES, Patrick | 12 | 08/14/48 | James | Mary Hines | Megorna | Mayo | Rankin | Luc St. Laurent Rimouski |
| 348 | KENNEDY, Anne | 5 | 10/05/47 | John | Margaret Howe | Burris | Tipperary | Sir. R. Peel | Died |
| 384 | KENNEDY, Anne | 20 | 10/15/47 | Denis | Margaret O'Hara | Kiluren | Clare | Manchester | Left for Boston |
| 227 | KENNEDY, Bridget | 17 | 09/04/47 | Francis | Mary Kenny | Monaghan | Tipperary | Albion | Returned to parents |
| 303 | NOONAN, Mary m. her adoptive brother, d. TB 1851 | 15 | 09/20/47 | Patrick | Mary Coleman | Lamon Valley | Westmeath | Odessa | Fran. Bergeron St. Grégoire |
| 302 | NOONAN, Pat | 5 | 09/20/47 | Patrick | Mary Coleman | Lamon Valley | Westmeath | Odessa | Louis Leblanc St. Grégoire |
| 428 | NUNN, Augustus | 12 | 12/17/47 | Augustus | Suzan Wafer | Ardamine | Wexford | Royalist | Died Jan 13, 1848 |
| 429 | NUNN, Letitia | 9 | 12/17/47 | Augustus | Suzan Wafer | Ardamine | Wexford | Royalist | Given March 6 |
| 393 | RIELY, Mary | 18 | 10/18/47 | James | Catherine Moore | Tomrasin | Fermanagh | Superior | Person in St. Thomas |
| 370 | RIELY, Margaret | 6 | 10/06/47 | James | Catherine Moore | Tomrasin | Fermanagh | Superior | Person in St. Thomas |
| 257 | RODRICK, Mary | 11 | 09/07/47 | Michael | Honora Burgan | Rathdowny | Queens | Naparima | ? |
| 258 | RODRICK, Pat | 5 | 09/07/47 | Michael | Honora Burgan | Rathdowny | Queens | Naparima | ? |
| 245 | ROURKE, Hugh | 16 | 09/07/47 | Hugh | Ann Maguire | Curan | Monahand | Coromandel | J.B. Mottard Ste. Croix |
| 420 | RYAN, Thomas | 8 | 11/25/47 | James | Biddy | Nockevally | Galway | Thistle | Died Dec: 24 |
| 58 | RYAN, Thomas | 10 | 07/47 | Michael | Catherine Hogan | ? | Tipperary | Avon | William Breen* Cap Blanc- |
| 431b | RYAN, Thomas | 10 | 12/20/47 | Michael | Catherine Hogan | * Child was sent to Chateauguay, New York in 1848 | Leitrim | | |
| 254 | RYAN, William | 13 | 09/07/47 | Edward | Eliza McGaurin | Annanduff | Leitrim | John Munn | Nick Wheeler Frampton |
| 271 | SANDERS, Jane | 16 | 09/07/47 | James | Rebecca Carson | Clunelochar | Leitrim | Ellen Carr | Protestant |

# Appendix 12

| UNIONS. | Number of such Emigrants sent out, to date of last annual Report (14 July, 1849.) | Numbers since sent out. | Total number of this class of emigrants since the Spring of 1848. | UNIONS. | Number of such Emigrants sent out, to date of last annual Report (14 July, 1849.) | Numbers since sent out. | Total number of this class of emigrants since the Spring of 1848. |
|---|---|---|---|---|---|---|---|
| Abbeyleix, | 17 | 11 | 28 | Carrickmacross, | 14 | 24 | 38 |
| Antrim, | 13 | 18 | 31 | Car.-on-Shannon | 40 | 20 | 60 |
| Ardee, | 22 | — | 22 | Carrick-on-Suir, | 12 | 11 | 23 |
| Armagh, | 28 | 29 | 57 | Cashel | 40 | 30 | 70 |
| Athlone, | 25 | 28 | 53 | Castlebar, | — | 15 | 15 |
| Athy, | 20 | 17 | 37 | Castleblayney, | 14 | — | 14 |
| Ballina, | 47 | 40 | 87 | Castlederg, | 6 | — | 6 |
| Ballinasloe, | 53 | — | 53 | Castlerea, | 20 | — | 20 |
| Ballinrobe, | — | 25 | 25 | Cavan, | 60 | — | 60 |
| Ballycastle, | 3 | 3 | 6 | Celbridge, | 8 | — | 8 |
| Ballymena, | 11 | 3 | 14 | Clogheen, | 26 | 7 | 33 |
| Ballymoney, | — | 10 | 10 | Clogher, | 15 | — | 15 |
| Ballyshannon, | 20 | — | 20 | Clones, | 17 | 12 | 29 |
| Balrothery, | 10 | — | 10 | Clonmel, | 43 | 16 | 59 |
| Baltinglass, | 16 | — | 16 | Coleraine, | 12 | 8 | 20 |
| Banbridge, | 19 | 17 | 36 | Cookstown, | 22 | 11 | 33 |
| Bandon, | — | 20 | 20 | Cootehill, | — | 15 | 15 |
| Belfast, | 64 | — | 64 | Cork, | — | 61 | 61 |
| Boyle, | 30 | 21 | 51 | Dingle, | — | 20 | 20 |
| Callan, | 18 | 10 | 28 | Donegal, | 23 | 8 | 31 |
| Carlow, | 22 | 30 | 52 | Downpatrick, | 12 | 11 | 23 |
| Dublin, North, | 28 | 18 | 46 | Loughrea, | 48 | 25 | 73 |
| Royal Hibernian Military School . | 24 | — | 24 | Macroom, | — | 13 | 13 |
|  |  |  |  | Magherafelt, | 21 | 6 | 27 |
|  |  |  |  | Mallow, | 20 | — | 20 |
| Dublin, South, Dublin Mendicity Institution . | 41 | 15 | 56 | Midleton, | — | 26 | 26 |
|  | 5 | — | 5 | Milford, | 9 | — | 9 |
|  |  |  |  | Mohill, | 25 | 20 | 45 |
| Dundalk, | — | 7 | 7 | Monaghan, | 7 | 9 | 16 |
| Dunfanaghy, | 7 | — | 7 | Mountmellick, | 22 | 15 | 37 |
| Dungannon, | 31 | — | 31 | Mullingar, | 40 | 30 | 70 |
| Dungarvan, | 18 | 22 | 40 | Naas, | 15 | — | 15 |
| Dunmanway, | — | 14 | 14 | Navan, | 25 | — | 25 |
| Dunshaughlin, | 16 | — | 16 | Nenagh, | 40 | 45 | 85 |
| Edenderry, | 18 | — | 18 | Newcastle, | 18 | 38 | 56 |
| Ennis, | — | 40 | 40 | New Ross, | 16 | 18 | 34 |
| Enniscorthy, | 25 | 16 | 41 | Newry, | 10 | 25 | 35 |
| Enniskillen, | — | 107 | 107 | Newtownards, | 7 | — | 7 |
| Ennistymon, | — | 23 | 23 | Newtownlimavady, | 9 | 8 | 17 |
| Fermoy, | 30 | 25 | 55 | Oldcastle, | — | 22 | 22 |
| Galway, | 22 | 25 | 47 | Omagh, | — | 19 | 19 |
| Gorey, | 15 | 6 | 21 | Parsonstown, | 30 | 35 | 65 |

| UNIONS. | Number of such Emigrants sent out, to date of last Annual Report (14 July, 1849). | Numbers since sent out. | Total number of Emigrants of this class since the Spring of 1848. | UNIONS. | Number of such Emigrants sent out, to date of last Annual Report (14 July, 1849). | Numbers since sent out. | Total number of Emigrants of this class since the Spring of 1848. |
|---|---|---|---|---|---|---|---|
| Gort, | — | 16 | 16 | Rathdown, | — | 19 | 19 |
| Gortin, | — | 4 | 4 | Rathdrum, | 15 | — | 15 |
| Granard, | 12 | 12 | 24 | Rathkeale, | — | 60 | 60 |
| Kanturk, | — | 30 | 30 | Roscrea, | 60 | 30 | 90 |
| Kells, | — | 26 | 26 | Scariff, | — | 20 | 20 |
| Kenmare, | — | 25 | 25 | Shillelagh, | 10 | 12 | 22 |
| Kilkeel, | 4 | 7 | 11 | Skibbereen, | 85 | 25 | 110 |
| Kilkenny, | — | 59 | 59 | Sligo, | 46 | 22 | 68 |
| Killarney, | 35 | — | 35 | Strabane, | 18 | 11 | 29 |
| Kilmallock, | — | 30 | 30 | Stranorlar, | — | 8 | 8 |
| Kilrush, | 30 | — | 30 | Thurles, | 30 | — | 30 |
| Kinsale, | — | 29 | 29 | Tipperary, | 62 | 25 | 87 |
| Larne, | 8 | 11 | 19 | Trim, | 12 | — | 12 |
| Letterkenny, | 20 | 10 | 30 | Tuam, | 37 | 20 | 57 |
| Limerick, | 74 | — | 74 | Tullamore, | 18 | 35 | 53 |
| Lisburn, | 12 | — | 12 | Waterford, | 25 | 23 | 48 |
| Lismore, | 25 | 12 | 37 | Westport, | — | 10 | 10 |
| Lisnaskea, | 20 | 24 | 44 | Wexford, | 20 | 41 | 61 |
| Listowel, | — | 37 | 37 | | | | |
| Londonderry, | 27 | 13 | 40 | Total | 2,219 from 66 Unions, * | 1,956 from 98 Unions, † | 4,175 from 118 Unions. *† |
| Longford, | 50 | 27 | 77 | | | | |

\* Including 24 sent from the Royal Hibernian Military School, and 5 from the Dublin Mendicity Institution; also, 20 from Wexford Workhouse, who were sent out to the Cape of Good Hope.
† Including 41 sent from Wexford Workhouse as Emigrants to the Cape of Good Hope.

SUMMARY.—Twenty ships have been dispatched in the two years from May, 1848, to April, 1850, with Orphan Girls from Workhouses in Ireland, as Emigrants to the Australian Colonies. Of these vessels, 11 were dispatched from time to time to Sydney, conveying 2,253 Emigrants; 6 to Port Philip, conveying 1,265 Emigrants; and 3 to Adelaide, conveying 600 Emigrants. Total of such Emigrants to Australia, 4,114. The remaining 61 (from the Wexford Union) were sent out to the Cape of Good Hope.

# Appendix 13

## Complete list of the Workhouses (163) in Ireland

| Name of the workhouse | Workhouse cost | | Area of site and land* | Number of persons | Date of first admissions to workhouse |
| | Building £ | Fittings etc. £ | | | |
|---|---|---|---|---|---|
| Abbeyleix | 5,850 | 1,020 | 5.5.11 | 500 | 6 June 1842 |
| Antrim | 5,580 | 1,474 | 6.0.15 | 700 | 19 Sept 1843 |
| Ardee | 5,175 | 1,975 | 5.3.24 | 600 | 13 May 1842 |
| Armagh | 7,200 | 1,554 | 7.0.27 | 1,000 | 14 Jan, 1842 |
| Athlone | 7,500 | 1,801 | 7.2.24 | 900 | 22 Nov, 1841 |
| Athy | 5,600 | 1,030 | 6.2.4 | 600 | 9 Jan, 1844 |
| Bailieborough | 6,000 | 1,160 | 6.1.3 | 600 | 20 June 1842 |
| Ballina | 9,400 | 1,980 | 9.1.17 | 1,200 | 3 Nov, 1843 |
| Ballinasloe | 7,600 | 1,882 | 5.3.33 | 1,000 | 1 Jan, 1842 |
| Ballinrobe | 7,000 | 1,400 | 6.1.36 | 800 | 26 May, 1842 |
| Ballycastle | 3,875 | 812 | 5.3.28 | 300 | 3 Jan, 1843 |
| Ballymahon | 6,250 | 1,370 | 6.0.0 | 600 | 1852 |
| Ballymena | 6,600 | 1,800 | 6.0.4 | 900 | 17 Nov, 1843 |
| Ballymoney | 6,785 | 1,240 | 6.0.0 | 700 | 6 March, 1843 |
| Ballyshannon | 5,850 | 1,100 | 5.0.0 | 600 | 6 May, 1843 |
| Ballyvaughan | 5,150 | 980 | 5.2.7 | 500 | 1852 |
| Balrothery | 4,945 | 905 | 24.3.13 | 400 | 15 March, 1841 |
| Baltinglass | 5,750 | 1,050 | 7.2.11 | 500 | 28 Oct, 1841 |
| Banbridge | 6,300 | 1,280 | 5.1.11 | 800 | 22 June 1841 |
| Bandon | 6,600 | 1,462 | 6.2.20 | 900 | 17 Nov, 1841 |
| Bantry | 6,850 | 1,350 | 6.0.0 | 800 | 24 April, 1845 |
| Bawnboy | 4,900 | 945 | 12.0.0 | 500 | 1852 |
| Belfast | 7,000 | 2,869 | 12.0.0 | 1,000 | 11 May, 1841 |
| Belmullet | 5,700 | 1,145 | 7.2.4 | 500 | 1852 |
| Borrisokane | 6,550 | 1,330 | 8.3.1 | 600 | 1853 |
| Boyle | 6,885 | 1,414 | 6.0.0 | 700 | 31 Dec, 1841 |

*In acres, roods and perches – statute measure

| Name of the workhouse | Workhouse cost | | Area of site and land* | Number of persons | Date of first admissions to workhouse |
| | *Building* £ | *Fittings etc.* £ | | | |
|---|---|---|---|---|---|
| Cahirciveen | 7,500 | 1,350 | 6.0.0 | 800 | 17 Oct, 1846 |
| Callan | 5,500 | 1,140 | 6.1.36 | 600 | 25 March, 1842 |
| Carlow | 9,000 | 1,470 | 7.2.19 | 800 | 18 Nov, 1844 |
| Carrickmacross | 5,000 | 977 | 5.3.2 | 500 | 11 Feb, 1843 |
| Carrick-on-Shannon | 7,050 | 1,350 | 6.3.2 | 800 | 21 July, 1842 |
| Carrick-on-Suir | 5,168 | 1,032 | 6.3.12 | 500 | 8 July, 1842 |
| Cashel | 5,500 | 950 | 6.3.8 | 700 | 28 Jan, 1842 |
| Castlebar | 6,300 | 1,259 | 7.0.0 | 700 | 22 Oct, 1842 |
| Castleblayney | 6,150 | 1,289 | 8.1.20 | 800 | 15 Dec, 1842 |
| Castlecomer | 6,400 | 990 | 7.2.0 | 500 | 1853 |
| Castlederg | 2,100 | 484 | 3.1.34 | 200 | 2 March, 1841 |
| Castlerea | 8,485 | 1,815 | 6.0.0 | 1,000 | 30 May, 1846 |
| Castletownbere | 6,300 | 1,240 | 9.1.14 | 600 | 1852 |
| Castletown-devlin | 5,200 | 885 | 12.0.0 | 400 | 1853 |
| Cavan | 10,500 | 2,000 | 9.0.0 | 1,200 | 17 June, 1842 |
| Celbridge | 4,600 | 900 | 5.0.0 | 400 | 9 June, 1841 |
| Claremorris | 6,500 | 1,435 | 8.0.0 | 800 | 1852 |
| Clifden | 3,600 | 900 | 4.3.17 | 300 | 8 March, 1847 |
| Clogheen | 5,230 | 935 | 6.0.31 | 500 | 29 June, 1842 |
| Clogher | 4,900 | 885 | 9.2.13 | 500 | 9 March, 1844 |
| Clonakilty | 6,900 | 1,400 | 7.0.0 | 700 | 1852 |
| Clones | 5,750 | 1,207 | 6.0.0 | 600 | 23 Feb, 1843 |
| Clonmel | 1,505 | 794 | (1) | 600 | 1 Jan, 1841 |
| Coleraine | 6,870 | 1,270 | 6.3.20 | 700 | 19 April, 1842 |
| Cookstown | 5,250 | 1,050 | 6.1.6 | 600 | 31 May, 1842 |
| Cootehill | 7,360 | 808 | 6.0.2 | 800 | 2 Dec, 1842 |
| Cork | 12,800 | 8,000 | 12.0.0 | 2,000 | 1 March, 1840 |
| Corofin | 5,700 | 915 | 12.0.0 | 500 | 1852 |
| Croom | 6,200 | 1,150 | 3.0.31 | 600 | 1852 |
| Dingle | 6,850 | 1,380 | 10.3.12 | 700 | 1849 |
| Donaghmore | 4,750 | 775 | 6.0.0 | 400 | 1853 |
| Donegal | 5,785 | 910 | 6.2.10 | 500 | 21 May, 1843 |
| Downpatrick | 7,500 | 2,123 | 11.1.36 | 1,000 | 17 Sept, 1842 |

(1) House of Industry adapted.

| Name of the workhouse | Workhouse cost | | Area of site and land* | Number of persons | Date of first admissions to workhouse |
| | Building £ | Fittings etc. £ | | | |
| --- | --- | --- | --- | --- | --- |
| Drogheda | 7,100 | 1,450 | 7.2.11 | 800 | 16 Dec, 1841 |
| Dromore West | 4,650 | 815 | 6.0.0 | 400 | 1852 |
| Dublin, North | 4,819 | 3,180 | (1) | 2,000 | 4 May, 1840 |
| Dublin, South | 5,608 | 4,591 | (2) | 2,000 | 24 April 1840 |
| Dundalk | 5,690 | 1,387 | 8.1.17 | 800 | 14 March, 1842 |
| Dunfanaghy | 4,350 | 855 | 6.0.0 | 300 | 24 June, 1845 |
| Dungannon | 6,650 | 1,350 | 6.0.0 | 800 | 23 June, 1842 |
| Dungarvan | 6,480 | 1,600 | 4.3.29 | 600 | 4 July, 1844 |
| Dunmanway | 5,210 | 990 | 5.0.0 | 400 | 2 Oct, 1841 |
| Dunshaughlin | 4,938 | 912 | 5.0.0 | 400 | 17 May, 1841 |
| Edenderry | 5,300 | 1,110 | 6.1.36 | 600 | 19 March, 1842 |
| Ennis | 6,500 | 2,100 | 6.0.0 | 800 | 15 Dec, 1842 |
| Enniscorthy | 5,600 | 1,082 | 5.0.22 | 600 | 11 Nov, 1842 |
| Enniskillen | 8,750 | 1,415 | 9.2.35 | 1,000 | 1 Dec, 1845 |
| Ennistymon | 6,600 | 1,800 | 6.0.0 | 600 | 5 Sept, 1845 |
| Fermoy | 3,251 | 1,148 | 5.2.28 | 900 | 6 July, 1841 |
| Galway | 8,162 | 1,637 | 7.3.38 | 1,000 | 2 March, 1842 |
| Glenamaddy | 5,250 | 995 | 6.0.0 | 500 | 1852 |
| Glenties | 5,100 | 940 | 8.2.0 | 500 | 24 July, 1846 |
| Glin | 5,900 | 1,115 | 6.0.0 | 600 | 1852 |
| Gorey | 5,675 | 1,025 | 7.0.0 | 500 | 22 Jan, 1842 |
| Gort | 5,350 | 1,150 | 7.1.12 | 500 | 11 Dec, 1841 |
| Gortin | 2,689 | 711 | 3.0.19 | 200 | 19 Feb, 1842 |
| Granard | 5,925 | 1,225 | 6.1.20 | 600 | 30 Sept, 1842 |
| Inishowen | 6,350 | 1,010 | 6.0.0 | 600 | 2 Oct, 1843 |
| Kanturk | 6,800 | 1,400 | 6.0.0 | 800 | 18 July, 1844 |
| Kells | 5,970 | 939 | 8.3.9 | 600 | 23 May, 1842 |
| Kenmare | 6,550 | 1,380 | 9.0.0 | 500 | 25 Oct, 1845 |
| Kildysart | 5,450 | 975 | 6.0.0 | 500 | 1852 |
| Kilkeel | 4,050 | 767 | 7.2.33 | 300 | 1 Sept, 1841 |
| Kilkenny | 9,700 | 2,050 | 9.3.21 | 1,300 | 21 April, 1842 |
| Killala | 4,500 | 885 | 6.0.0 | 500 | 1852 |
| Killarney | 7,350 | 1,200 | 8.0.0 | 800 | 5 April, 1845 |
| Kilmallock | 7,000 | 1,212 | 7.0.0 | 800 | 29 March, 1841 |
| Kilmacthomas | 5,650 | 955 | 6.0.0 | 500 | 1853 |
| Kilrush | 6,800 | 1,350 | 6.0.0 | 800 | 9 July, 1842 |

(1) House of Industry adapted.    (2) Foundling Hospital adapted.

| Name of the workhouse | Workhouse cost | | Area of site and land* | Number of persons | Date of first admissions to workhouse |
| | Building £ | Fittings etc. £ | | | |
|---|---|---|---|---|---|
| Kinsale | 5,900 | 1,000 | 6.0.0 | 500 | 4 Dec, 1841 |
| Larne | 4,989 | 333 | 5.0.37 | 400 | 4 Jan, 1843 |
| Letterkenny | 6,450 | 1,475 | 6.0.0 | 500 | 14 March, 1845 |
| Limavady | 5,982 | 1,309 | 7.0.14 | 500 | 15 March, 1842 |
| Limerick | 10,000 | 2,830 | 11.1.14 | 1,600 | 20 May, 1841 |
| Lisburn | 6,200 | 1,358 | 6.0.0 | 800 | 11 Feb, 1841 |
| Lismore | 5,500 | 1,000 | 4.0.0 | 500 | 18 May, 1842 |
| Lisnaskea | 5,443 | 1,021 | 6.1.36 | 500 | 25 Feb, 1843 |
| Listowel | 5,980 | 1,276 | 6.0.0 | 700 | 13 Feb, 1845 |
| Londonderry | 6,780 | 1,157 | 6.0.6 | 800 | 10 Nov. 1840 |
| Longford | 7,000 | 1,580 | 6.3.22 | 1,000 | 24 March, 1842 |
| Loughrea | 6,960 | 1,740 | 6.2.2 | 800 | 26 Feb, 1842 |
| Lowtherstown (Irvinestown) | 6,710 | 1,216 | 5.0.0 | 400 | 1 Oct, 1845 |
| Lurgan | 8,581 | 1,319 | 6.0.0 | 800 | 22 Feb, 1841 |
| Macroom | 8,359 | 1,010 | 6.0.0 | 600 | 13 May, 1843 |
| Magherafelt | 6,600 | 1,460 | 6.0.0 | 900 | 11 March, 1842 |
| Mallow | 6,090 | 1,160 | 6.0.0 | 700 | 2 Aug, 1842 |
| Manorhamilton | 5,372 | 1,015 | 5.1.16 | 500 | 8 Dec, 1842 |
| Midleton | 6,853 | 1,347 | 6.2.5 | 800 | 21 Aug, 1841 |
| Milford | 6,250 | 1,150 | 6.0.0 | 400 | 6 April, 1842 |
| Millstreet | 5,950 | 1,215 | 6.0.0 | 600 | 1852 |
| Mitchelstown | 6,100 | 1,150 | 7.3.12 | 600 | 1852 |
| Mohill | 6,700 | 1,280 | 6.1.3 | 700 | 8 June, 1842 |
| Monaghan | 6,350 | 1,457 | 7.2.5 | 900 | 25 May, 1842 |
| Mount Bellew | 5,150 | 920 | 6.0.0 | 500 | 1852 |
| Mountmellick | 6,915 | 1,381 | 6.0.0 | 800 | 3 Jan, 1845 |
| Mullingar | 7,250 | 1,400 | 10.2.11 | 800 | 8 Dec, 1842 |
| Naas | 5,550 | 950 | 5.1.14 | 550 | 4 Aug, 1841 |
| Navan | 5,700 | 1,081 | 6.2.22 | 500 | 4 Aug, 1842 |
| Nenagh | 8,320 | 1,580 | 7.0.0 | 1,000 | 28 April, 1842 |
| Newcastle | 6,680 | 920 | 5.0.0 | 550 | 15 March, 1841 |
| Newport | 5,000 | 965 | 12.0.0 | 500 | 1852 |
| New Ross | 7,600 | 1,550 | 10.0.5 | 900 | 6 July, 1842 |
| Newry | 7,100 | 1,727 | 7.0.25 | 1,000 | 16 Dec, 1841 |
| Newtownards | 4,835 | 1,035 | 8.1.8 | 600 | 4 Jan, 1842 |
| Oldcastle | 5,975 | 1,119 | 7.1.6 | 600 | 12 Aug, 1842 |
| Omagh | 6,557 | 1,343 | 6.0.0 | 800 | 24 Aug, 1841 |

| Name of the workhouse | Workhouse cost | | Area of site and land* | Number of persons | Date of first admissions to workhouse |
|---|---|---|---|---|---|
| | *Building* £ | *Fittings etc.* £ | | | |
| Oughterard | 5,950 | 1,055 | 7.3.0 | 600 | 1852 |
| Parsonstown (Birr) | 6,900 | 1,384 | 6.3.5 | 800 | 2 April, 1842 |
| Portumna | 6,700 | 1,175 | 8.2.39 | 600 | 1852 |
| Rathdown | 6,500 | 1,100 | 8.0.0 | 600 | 12 Oct, 1841 |
| Rathdrum | 6,600 | 1,200 | 5.1.34 | 600 | 8 March, 1842 |
| Rathkeale | 6,686 | 864 | 6.0.0 | 660 | 26 July, 1841 |
| Roscommon | 7,500 | 1,488 | 7.1.6 | 900 | 4 Nov, 1843 |
| Roscrea | 6,700 | 1,296 | 6.0.0 | 700 | 7 May, 1842 |
| Scariff | 6,400 | 1,050 | 6.0.0 | 600 | 11 May, 1842 |
| Shillelagh | 5,300 | 1,000 | 6.1.36 | 400 | 18 Feb, 1842 |
| Skibbereen | 7,083 | 1,217 | 10.2.27 | 800 | 19 March, 1842 |
| Schull | 6,000 | 1,115 | 11.1.28 | 600 | 1852 |
| Sligo | 9,100 | 1,900 | 9.0.0 | 1,200 | 17 Dec, 1841 |
| Strabane | 6,885 | 1,355 | 5.0.17 | 800 | 18 Nov, 1841 |
| Stranorlar | 7,300 | 1,330 | 7.1.14 | 400 | 3 May, 1844 |
| Strokestown | 6,500 | 1,075 | 12.3.1 | 600 | 1852 |
| Swinford | 7,100 | 1,300 | 6.0.0 | 700 | 14 April, 1846 |
| Thomastown | 6,250 | 1,215 | 7.3.13 | 600 | 1853 |
| Thurles | 5,840 | 1,260 | 6.2.0 | 700 | 7 Nov, 1842 |
| Tipperary | 6,240 | 1,110 | 6.0.0 | 700 | 3 July, 1841 |
| Tralee | 8,557 | 1,643 | 10.0.0 | 1,000 | 1 Feb. 1844 |
| Trim | 5,750 | 1,040 | 6.1.36 | 500 | 11 Oct, 1841 |
| Tuam | 6,700 | 1,400 | 7.1.3 | 800 | 4 May, 1846 |
| Tubbercurry | 5,150 | 1,220 | 12.0.0 | 500 | 1852 |
| Tulla | 5,000 | 1,085 | 4.0.10 | 500 | 1852 |
| Tullamore | 5,950 | 1,265 | 6.1.7 | 700 | 9 June, 1842 |
| Urlingford | 5,300 | 1,200 | 12.0.0 | 500 | 1853 |
| Waterford | 7,850 | 1,577 | 6.0.25 | 900 | 20 April, 1841 |
| Westport | 7,800 | 2,000 | 7.1.6 | 1,000 | 5 Nov, 1845 |
| Wexford | 5,780 | 1,120 | 7.0.0 | 600 | 25 July, 1842 |
| Youghal | 6,950 | 1,375 | 11.3.0 | 700 | 1853 |

Following the opening of the workhouses, additional adjoining lands, ranging from a few roods up to as many as ten or twelve acres, were acquired at almost all workhouses as sites for ancillary buildings to provide work for the inmates, or as workhouse burial grounds.

## *Summary:*

## Number of workhouses provided in each county:–

### CONNAUGHT

Galway   10
Leitrim   3
Mayo   9
Roscommon   4
Sligo   2

### MUNSTER

Clare   8
Cork   18
Kerry   6
Limerick   5
Tipperary   8
Waterford   4

### LEINSTER

Carlow   1
Dublin   4
Kildare   3
Kilkenny   5
Laois   2
Longford   3
Louth   3
Meath   5
Offaly   4
Westmeath   3
Wexford   4
Wicklow   3

### ULSTER

Antrim   7
Armagh   2
Cavan   4
Derry   4
Donegal   7
Down   6
Fermanagh   3
Monaghan   4
Tyrone   9

# Appendix 14

## Number of Young Persons in the Workhouses of Ireland on 2nd April, 1853

| | |
|---|---|
| From   9 to 15 years of age | 50,188 |
| From 15 to 21 years of age | 26,250 |
| Total from 9 to 21 years of age | 76,438 |

Of the above persons there have been in gaol

| | No. from 9 to 15 Years of Age | No. from 15 to 21 Years of Age | Total Persons from 9 to 21 Years of Age | Per Centage | | |
|---|---|---|---|---|---|---|
| | | | | 9 to 15 Years | 15 to 21 Years | 9 to 21 Years |
| 1. For Offences committed in the Workhouse | 511 | 1,165 | 1,676 | 1.0 | 4.4 | 2.2 |
| 2. For Offences under Vagrant Act | 182 | 330 | 512 | .4 | 1.3 | .7 |
| 3. For other Offences | 102 | 413 | 515 | .2 | 1.6 | .6 |
| Total who have been in Gaol | 795 | 1,908 | 2,703 | 1.6 | 7.3 | 3.5 |

The state of their education is thus shown:

| | No. from 9 to 15 Years of Age | No. from 15 to 21 Years of Age | Total Persons from 9 to 21 Years of Age | Per Centage | | |
|---|---|---|---|---|---|---|
| | | | | 9 to 15 Years | 15 to 21 Years | 9 to 21 Years |
| 1. Can neither read nor write | 6,596 | 10,567 | 17,163 | 13.1 | 40.3 | 22.5 |
| 2. Know the Alphabet and Spelling | 10,705 | 4,324 | 15,029 | 21.3 | 16.4 | 19.7 |
| 3. Read imperfectly | 13,177 | 5,609 | 18,786 | 26.3 | 21.4 | 24.5 |
| 4. Read and write | 19,710 | 5,750 | 25,460 | 39.3 | 21.9 | 33.3 |
| Total | 50,188 | 26,250 | 76,438 | 100. | 100. | 100. |

The number of illegitimate children in the Workhouses of Ireland, under 15 years of age, on the 2nd April, 1853, in comparison with the total number of children of the same age,

| | |
|---|---|
| Number of Illegitimate Children | 5,710 |
| Total Number of Children under 15 years of age | 76,724 |
| Percentage of Illegitimate Children | 7.4 |

# Appendix 15

## Medical and Hospital Services

In England, under Elizabeth's legislation (the 1601 Act), the system of rate-supported public parochial assistance had included provision for the sick and infirm poor but this Act had not been extended to Ireland.

It was not until the beginning of the eighteenth century that the sad state of the sick poor excited the compassion and conscience of their fellow-citizens to the extent that groups came together to establish voluntary hospitals. Because of the penal restrictions of the period on religious communities, the Irish voluntary hospital movement was initially entirely lay in character, and in the beginning was confined to the city areas, particularly Dublin. It was a form of charity to the public that had not been available in Ireland since the closure of the monasteries following the Reformation.

The first voluntary hospital actually opened was planned and financed by six Dublin surgeons who, in 1718, acquired and equipped at their own expense, a house in Cook Street for the reception of poor patients. This became known as The Charitable Infirmary and, after several changes of address, was finally located in Jervis Street. The hospital, which provided free medical services for the poor, was administered by a Managing Committee or Board of Governors.

Though the Cook Street hospital was the first to be opened, the distinction of being the founder of the first voluntary hospital in these islands belongs to Dr Richard Steevens, a medical practitioner in Dublin who left, in his death-bed will in 1710, all his property in trust to his sister and, on her death, to provide a hospital for the sick poor of the city. But there was a delay of ten years before the building was put in hands and it was not ready for the reception of patients until 1733.

The establishment of other general hospitals on a voluntary basis followed, and in addition there were hospitals for special purposes such as St Patrick's in James's Street, founded in 1747 by Dean Jonathan Swift for the mentally afflicted, and the Lying-In Hospital for Woman (the Rotunda), founded in 1745 by Dr Bartholomew Mosse.

In the north of the country, the Belfast Charitable Society, set up in 1752, arranged for the building of a poor-house and infirmary in 1752. Unfortunately, after the Rebellion of 1798 the Society was given forty-eight hours to have the poor house evacuated. Although the order caused great resentment, the Society had no option but to comply.

Among the first voluntary hospitals in the provinces was Barrington's Hospital in Limerick, founded in 1827.

A significant influence on voluntary hospital development was the lifting of restrictions on the Catholic community, thus allowing the foundation of a number of new Irish religious orders dedicated to the care of the sick poor. The Irish Sisters of Charity opened St Vincent's Hospital in Dublin in 1834, while the Sisters of Mercy opened the Mercy Hospital in Cork in 1857, the Mater Misericordiae Hospital in Dublin in 1861, and the Mater Infirmorum Hospital in Belfast in 1883. These, and other orders from then on, resulted in a most important contribution to the Irish hospital system.

The public hospital system in Ireland evolved from the workhouses, where some accommodation for hospital services had been provided (see page 179), and together with County Infirmaries (twenty-seven in number) and County Fever Hospitals (twelve in number), established under enactments of 1763, 1805, 1806, 1814 and 1817 which were administered apart from the Poor Law, provided a framework which went some way towards meeting the medical needs of the poor.

However it was not until 1851 that the Medical Charities Act laid the foundation of what became known as the Poor Law Medical Service. The Boards of Guardians were empowered to divide each Union into dispensary districts, appoint medical officers, and supply the necessary medicines and appliances. The medical officer was required to give free medical advice, treatment and medicines to poor persons resident in the dispensary district. (This system was eventually replaced by the 'Choice of Doctor' scheme for medical card-holders under the Health Act of 1970). Midwives were also provided under the Act in a tentative attempt at a system of public health nursing. These 'midwives' received no formal training and were popularly known as 'handy-women'. It was not until 1885 that midwives appointed by the Boards of Guardians were required to have a certificate from a recognised Lying-in Hospital as to their competency in midwifery, or produce satisfactory evidence of approved practical knowledge of midwifery.

In the meanwhile, sanitary authorities were evolving. They were to play an important part in developing the preventive side of the health services. The bigger towns had sanitary authorities since the early nineteenth century, their work consisting mainly of the provision of sewers, water supplies, wash-houses, street lighting and other amenities conducive to comfort and public health. The administration of the sanitary services was reorganised and codified under the Public Health

(Ireland) Acts of 1874 and 1878. Under these Acts the municipal corporations and town commissioners were appointed sanitary authorities for the larger urban areas; the Boards of Guardians became the sanitary authorities for the rural areas and smaller towns. The final change in the nineteenth-century administration came with the Local Government (Ireland) Act, 1898; which established elective County Councils, Urban District Councils and Rural District Councils – the latter took over the sanitary functions of the Boards of Guardians, who, however, continued their original functions of providing relief (including medical relief) for the poor.

# Appendix 16

## Workhouse Records

---

The collection of surviving workhouse drawings is housed in the Irish Architectural Archive, by whose kind permission the list (document 85/138) is reproduced.

Surviving papers of the Poor Law Guardians provide extensive though uneven information on the administration of relief within the workhouse and through outdoor relief. These records of the Boards of Guardians, the major state agency for the relief of the poor, are of primary importance for studies of the famine. The records, where extant, are now generally located in the local county libraries in the Irish Republic and in the Public Records Office in Northern Ireland. Some records are in the National Archives, Dublin.

The main records are as follows:

The *Indoor Workhouse Registers* (available for 23 Unions) provide unique documentation of the social condition of inmates under the following headings: (1) date of admission; (2) name and surname; (3) sex; (4) age; (5) if adult, whether married, single, deserted or bastard; (6) occupation; (7) religion; (8) name of wife or husband and number of children; (9) electoral division or townland of residence; (10) date when left the workhouse or died; (11) date of birth if born in workhouse.

*Outdoor Relief Registers* (available for 8 Unions) give the name of each person relieved: sex, age, whether married or single, etc.

*Rate Books* (available for 5 Unions).

*Minute Books* (sometimes typed) or *Rough Minute Books* (which are better records, being handwritten) record information under the headings stipulated by the Poor Law Commissioners.

Other sources of information are the Master's Journal which contains weekly handwritten reports from the workhouse master to the Board of Guardians; the District Court Records which list Committal Orders of orphans to industrial schools and workhouses; and the reports of the Poor Law Commissioners' Inspectors who visited each workhouse twice a year and submitted detailed accounts of conditions in the workhouse to the Poor Law Commissioners.

## Workhouse Drawings: 85/138

The collection in the Irish Architectural Archive is divided into three distinct parts:

*Part 1:* Drawings from Union workhouses and Union fever hospitals dating from 1839 on, from the office of George Wilkinson, architect to the Poor Law Commissioners in Ireland. The drawings are arranged alphabetically by individual workhouse or hospital.

*Part 2:* Drawings for work on Union workhouses and Union fever hospitals but unconnected with the original construction of the workhouses, together with drawings relating to other local government projects. The material dates from the later part of the nineteenth and early part of the twentieth centuries. Arranged alphabetically by individual building of project.

*Part 3:* Reports of the Commissioners in Lunacy, found with the above material.

*Abbreviations:* UW, Union workhouse; UFH, Union fever hospital; UCW, Union convalescent wards; UIS, Union industrial school.

## Part 1

1. Ballina, Co Mayo (UW); 2. Ballinrobe, Co Mayo (UW); 3. Ballymahon, Co Longford (UW); 4. Baltinglass, Co Wicklow (UW); 5. Baltinglass, Co Wicklow (UFH); 6. Balrothery, Co Dublin (UW); 7. Balrothery, Co Dublin (UFH); 8. Bandon, Co Cork (UW); 9. Bantry, Co Cork (UW); 10. Bantry, Co Cork (UFH); 11. Caherciveen, Co Kerry (UW); 12. Carlow, Co Carlow (UW); 13. Carrick-on-Suir, Co Tipperary (UW); 14. Castleblayney, Co Monaghan (UW); 15. Castlecomer, Co Kilkenny (UW); 16. Castlerea, Co Roscommon (UW); 17. Castlerea, Co Roscommon (UFH); 18. Claremorris, Co Mayo (UW); 19. Clifden, Co Galway (UW); 20. Cootehill, Co Cavan (UFH); 21. Cork, Co Cork (UW); 22. Croom, Co Limerick (UW); 23. Croom, Co Limerick (UFH); 24. Dingle, Co Kerry (UW); 25. Donaghmore, Co Laois (UW); 26. Donegal, Co Donegal (UW); 27. Donegal, Co Donegal (UFH); 28. Drogheda, Co Louth (UFH); 29. Dungannon, Co Louth (UW); 30. Dungarvan, Co Waterford (UW); 31. Dunshaughlin, Co Meath (UW); 32. Ennis, Co Clare (UW); 33. Enniscorthy, Co Wexford (UW); 34. Ennistymon, Co Clare (UW); 35. Glenamaddy, Co. Donegal (UFH); 36. Glenamaddy, Co Donegal (UW); 37. Gorey, Co. Wexford (UW); 38. Killarney, Co Kerry (UW); 39. Kilkenny, Co Kilkenny (UW); 40. Kilmallock, Co Limerick (UW); 41. Kinsale, Co Cork (UW); 42. Lismore, Co Waterford (UW); 43. Listowel, Co Kerry (UW); 44. Longford, Co Longford (UFH);

45. Macroom, Co Cork (UW); 46. Mallow, Co Cork (UW); 47. Manorhamilton, Co Leitrim (UW); 48. Manorhamilton, Co Leitrim (UFH); 49. Millstreet, Co Cork (UW); 50. Mitchelstown, Co Cork (UW); 51. Mohill, Co Leitrim (UW); 52. Mount Bellew, Co Galway (UW); 53. Mountmellick, Co Laois (UW); 54. Mullingar, Co Westmeath (UW); 55. Naas, Co Kildare (UW); 56. Naas, Co Kildare (UFH); 57. Navan, Co Meath (UW); 58. Nenagh, Co Tipperary (UW); 59. Newport, Co Mayo (UW); 60. New Ross, Co Wexford (UW); 61. Oldcastle, Co Meath (UFH); 62. Oughterard, Co Galway (UW); 63. Birr (Parsonstown), Co Offaly (UW); 64. Portumna, Co Galway (UW); 65. Rathdrum, Co Wicklow (UFH); 66. Rathkeale, Co Limerick (UW); 67. Roscrea, Co Tipperary (UW); 68. Shilleagh, Co Wicklow (UW); 69. Skibbereen, Co Cork (UW); 70. Strokestown, Co Roscommon (UW); 71. Strokestown, Co Roscommon (UFH); 72. Swinford, Co Mayo (UFH); 73. Tobercurry, Co Sligo (UW); 74. Tralee, Co Kerry (UCW); 75. Tuam, Co Galway (UW); 76. Tullamore, Co Offaly (UW); 77. Urlingford, Co Kilkenny (UW); 78. Waterford, Co Waterford (UW); 79. Wexford, Co Wexford (UW); 80. Youghal, Co Cork (UIS); 81. Unidentified (UFH).

## *Part 2:*
(Only those documents relating to workhouses are listed.)

85. Ballymena, Co Antrim – alterations to UW; 88. Carlow, Co Carlow – alterations to County Home 1923; 89. Castlebar, Co Mayo – alterations to UW 1929; 91. Cavan, Co Cavan – County Home plans; 94. Clonmel, Co Tipperary – alterations to UW 1929; 96. Donegal, Co Donegal – alterations to UW 1924; 100. Enniscorthy, Co Wexford – alterations to UW; 103. Glenties, Co Donegal – alterations to UW; 104. Keadue, Co. Roscommon – alterations to hospital; 107. Killarney, Co Kerry – map of UW; 108. Letterkenny, Co Donegal – alterations to UW; 111. Longford, Co Longford – alteration to UW 1928; 113. Navan, Co Meath – alterations to UW 1925; 118. Rathdrum, Co Wicklow – alterations to UFH 1922; 119. Roscommon, Co Roscommon – alterations to UW 1924–27; 122. Skibbereen, Co Cork – ground plan UW, early 20th century; 127. Tullamore, Co Offaly – alteration to UW 1922–23; Wexford, Co Wexford – conversion of former UW 1924.

*Note:* A number of drawings in this collection are on restricted access due to their extremely fragile condition.

*The Reports of the Master and other Officers were read, and Orders made thereon, as follows*

*Orders That the Master be directed to have James and Patrick McCormick who are at present Inmates of the Workhouse Clothed and forwarded to Dublin immediately in order that they may accompany their Mother who is under Sentence of Transportation to Vandiemans land.—*

Order directing the Master to send two children to Dublin
in order that they might accompany their mother who
was under transportation sentence.

From the Mohill Minute Book
for 14 December, 1850

*The Master reported that after measuring the Sheds in the several Yards he finds that about 9000 yards of Calico would be required to cover them previous to their being tarred*

*Ordered*

*That Advertisements be issued calling upon persons to tender for putting and keeping in perfect repair the Sheds in question till the 1st of May next.—*

*The Master also reported that the Weaver ( a pauper Inmate of the Workhouse ) refuses to Work unless he be allowed Some White Bread*

*Ordered*

*That the Master be directed to stop occasionally the Milk allowed to the Weaver if he refuses to Work in future.—*

The second order concerns a weaver who was refusing to
work unless he was allowed some white bread.
Punishment: that he be deprived of his milk allowance if
he continued to refuse.

From the Mohill Minute Book
for 11 January, 1851

# Appendix 17

Workhouses in Unions and Parishes under the Poor Law Amendment Act, and under Local Acts, in England and Wales &c.

Aberayron
Abergavenny
Aberystwith
Abingdon
Albans, St
Alcester
Alderbury
Alnwick
Alresford
Aiston with Garrigill
Alton
Altrincham
Amersham
Amesbury
Ampthill
Andover
Asaph, St
Ashbourne
Ashby-de-la Zouch
Ashford, East
Ashford, West
Ashton-under-Lyne
Aston
Atcham
Atherstone
Auckland
Austell, St
Axbridge
Axminster
Aylesbury
Aylsham

Bakewell

Bala
Banbury
Bangor and ˗
 Beaumaris
Barnet
Barnstaple
Barrow-upon-Soar
Basford
Basingstoke
Bath
Battle
Beaminster
Bedale
Bedford
Bedminster
Belford
Bellingham
Belper
Berkhampstead
Bermondsey
Berwick-upon-Tweed
Bethnal Green
Beverley
Bicester
Bideford
Biggleswade
Billericay
Billesdon
Bingham
Birmingham
Bishop Stortford
Blaby
Blackburn

Blandford
Blean
Blofield
Blything
Bodmin
Bolton
Bootle
Bosmere and
 Claydon
Boston
Bourn
Brackley
Bradfield
Bradford, Wilts
Bradford, Yorkshire
Braintree
Brampton
Brecknock
Brentford
Bridge
Bridgend and
 Cowbridge
Bridgnorth
Bridgwater
Bridlington
Bridport
Brighton
Bristol, City of
Brixworth
Bromley
Bromsgrove
Bromyard
Buckingham

Buntingford
Burnley
Burton-on-Trent
Bury, Lancashire
Bury St Edmund's

Caistor
Calne
Camberwell
Cambridge
Canterbury, City of
Cardiff
Cardigan
Carlisle
Carmarthen
Carnarvon
Castle Ward
Catherington
Caxton and Arrington
Cerne
Chailey
Chapel-en-le-Frith
Chard
Cheadle
Chelmsford
Chelsea
Cheltenham
Chepstow
Chertsey
Chester, City of
Chesterfield
Chester-le-Street
Chesterton
Chichester, City of
Chippenham
Chipping Norton
Chipping Sodbury
Chorley
Chorlton
Christchurh
Church Stretton
Cirencester
Cleobury Mortimer

Clerkenwell, St
 James
Clifton
Clitheroe
Clun
Clutton
Cockermouth
Colchester
Columb St Major
Congleton
Cookham
Corwen
Cosford
Coventry, City of
Cranbrook
Crediton
Crickhowell
Cricklade and
 Wootton Bassett
Croydon
Cuckfield

Darlington
Dartford
Daventry
Depwade
Derby
Devizes
Dewsbury
Docking
Doncaster
Dorchester
Dore
Dorking
Dover
Downham
Driffield
Droitwich
Droxford
Dudley
Dunmow
Durham
Dursley

Easingwold
Eastbourne
East Grinstead
Easthampstead
East Retford
Eastry
East Stonehouse
East Ward
Ecclesall Bierlow
Edmonton
Elham
Ellesmere
Ely
Epping
Epsom
Erpingham
Eton
Evesham
Exeter, City of

Faith's, St
Falmouth
Fareham
Faringdon
Farnham
Faversham
Festiniog
Flegg, East and West
Foleshill
Fordingbridge
Forehoe
Freebridge Lynn
Frome
Fulham
Fylde, The

Gainsborough
Garstang
Gateshead
George, St, in the
 East
George, St, the
 Martyr

George, St, Hanover
    square
Germans, St
Glanford Brigg
Glendale
Glossop
Gloucester
Godstone
Goole
Grantham
Gravesend and
    Milton
Greenwich
Guildford
Guiltcross
Guisborough

Hackney
Hailsham
Halifax
Halstead
Haltwhistle
Hambledon
Hardingstone
Hartismere
Hartley Wintney
Haslingden
Hastings
Hatfield
Havant
Haverfordwest
Hay
Hayfield
Headington
Helmsley
Helston
Hemel Hempstead
Hendon
Henley
Henstead
Hereford
Hertford
Hexham

Highworth and
    Swindon
Hinckley
Hitchin
Holbeach
Holborn
Hollingbourn
Holywell
Honiton
Hoo
Horncastle
Horsham
Houghton-le-Spring
Howden
Hoxne
Huddersfield
Hungerford
Huntingdon
Hursley

Ipswich
Islington, St Mary
Ives, St

James, St,
    Westminster

Keighley
Kendal
Kensington
Kettering
Keynsham
Kidderminster
Kingsbridge
Kingsclere
King's Lynn
King's Norton
Kingston-on-Thames
Kingston-on-Hull
Kington
Knighton

Lambeth

Lancaster
Lanchester
Langport
Launceston
Ledbury
Leeds
Leek
Leicester
Leigh
Leighton Buzzard
Leominster
Lewes
Lewisham
Lexden and Winstree
Leyburn
Lichfield
Lincoln
Linton
Liskeard
Liverpool
Llandilo Fawr
Llandovery
Llanelly
Llanfyllin
Loddon and
    Clavering
London, City of
London, East
London, West
Longtown
Loughborough
Louth
Ludlow
Luke, St, Middlesex
Luton
Lutterworth
Lymington

Macclesfield
Madeley
Maidstone
Maldon
Malling

Malmsbury
Malton
Manchester
Mansfield
Margaret, St , and St
　John, Westminster
Market Bosworth
Market Drayton
Market Harborough
Marlborough
Martin's, St , in the
　Fields
Marylebone, St
Martley
Medway
Melksham
Melton Mowbray
Mere
Meriden
Midhurst
Mildenhall
Milton
Mitford and
　Launditch
Monmouth
Montgomery and
　Pool
Morpeth
Mutford and
　Lothingland

Nantwich
Narberth
Neath
Neots, St
Newark
Newbury
Newcastle in Emlyn
Newcastle under
　Lyme
Newcastle on Tyne
Newent
New Forest

Newhaven
Newington, St Mary
Newmarket
Newport,
　Monmouthshire
Newport, Salop
Newport Pagnell
Newton Abbot
Newtown and
　Llanidloes
Northallerton
Northampton
North Aylesford
Northleach
Northwich
North Witchford
Norwich
Nottingham
Nuneaton

Oakham
Okehampton
Olave, St
Ongar
Ormskirk
Orsett
Oswestry
Oundle
Oxford, City of

Pancras, St
Pateley Bridge
Patrington
Pembroke
Penkridge
Penrith
Penzance
Pershore
Peterborough
Petersfield
Petworth
Pewsey
Pickering

Plomesgate
Plymouth
Plympton, St  Mary
Pocklington
Pontypool
Poole
Poplar
Portsea Island
Potterspury
Prescot
Preston
Pwllheli

Radford
Reading
Redruth
Reeth
Reigate
Richmond, Surrey
Richmond, Yorkshire
Ringwood
Risbridge
Rochdale
Rochford
Romford
Romney Marsh
Romsey
Ross
Rothbury
Rotherham
Rotherhithe
Royston
Rugby
Ruthin
Rye

Saffron Walden
Salford
Salisbury, City of
Samford
Saviour's, St
Scarborough
Sculcoates

Sedbergh
Sedgefield
Seisdon
Selby
Settle
Sevenoaks
Shaftesbury
Shardlow
Sheffield
Sheppey
Shepton Mallet
Sherborne
Shiffnal
Shipston-on-Stour
Shoreditch, St
   Leonard's
Shrewsbury
Skipton
Skirlaugh
Sleaford
Solihull
Southam
Southampton
Southmolton
South Shields
South Stoneham
Southwell
Spalding
Spilsby
Stafford
Staines
Stamford
Stepney
Steyning
Stockbridge
Stockport
Stockton
Stokesley
Stoke Damerell
Stoke-upon-Trent
Stone
Stourbridge
Stow

Stow-on-the-Wold
Strand, The
Stratford-on-Avon
Stroud
Sturminster
Sudbury
Sunderland
Swaffham
Swansea

Tamworth
Taunton
Tavistock
Teesdale
Tenbury
Tendring
Tenterden
Tetbury
Tewkesbury
Thakeham
Thame
Thanet, Isle of
Thetford
Thingoe
Thirsk
Thomas, St
Thornbury
Thorne
Thrapston
Ticehurst
Tisbury
Tiverton
Tonbridge
Torrington
Totnes
Towcester
Truro
Tunstead and
   Happing
Tynemouth

Uckfield
Ulverstone

Uppingham
Upton-on-Severn
Uttoxeter
Uxbridge

Wakefield
Wallingford
Walsall
Walsingham
Wandsworth and
   Clapham
Wangford
Wantage
Ware
Wareham and
   Purbeck
Warminster
Warrington
Warwick
Watford
Wayland
Weardale
Wellingborough
Wellington, Salop
Wellington, Somerset
Wells
Welwyn
Wem
Weobly
Westbourne
West Bromwich
Westbury-on-Severn
Westbury and
   Whorwelsdown.
West Derby
West Firle
West Ham
Westhampnett
West Ward
Weymouth
Wheatenhurst
Whitby
Whitchurch, Hants

| | | |
|---|---|---|
| Whitchurch, | Wincanton | Burslem |
| Salop | Winchcombe | Wolverhampton |
| Whitechapel | Winchester, New | Woodbridge |
| Whitehaven | Windsor | Woodstock |
| Whittlesey | Winslow | Worcester |
| Wigan | Wirrall | Worksop |
| Wight, Isle of | Wisbech | Wrexham |
| Wigton | Witham | Wycombe |
| Williton | Witney | |
| Wilton | Woburn | Yarmouth, Great |
| Wimborne and | Wokingham | Yeovil |
| Cranborne | Wolstanton and | York |

---

## SUMMARY OF THE FOREGOING TABLE

| | |
|---|---|
| Number of Unions and Parishes under the Poor Law Amendment Act and under Local Acts having 1 workhouse | 541 |
| 2 workhouses | 46 |
| 3 workhouses | 10 |
| 4 workhouses | 4 |
| 5 workhouses | 2 |
| Total Number of Unions and Parishes under the Poor Law Amendment Act and under Local Acts having Workhouses | 603 |

---

## WORKHOUSE ACCOMMODATION

| Number of Unions, & c. having workhouses | Number of Workhouses | Number of inmates they will accommodate | Number of Unions, &c. not having workhouses |
|---|---|---|---|
| 603 | 689 | 184,320 | 23 |

# Appendix 18

## George Nicholls – A Biographical Note

Sir George Nicholls (1781-1865), poor law reformer and administrator, was born in Cornwall in 1781. Before he became involved in the question of the poor laws and their administration which called urgently for reform, he had served for a period in the British Navy and had also spent some time as a banker. Nicholls' leading idea was to abolish outdoor relief and to rely on the 'workhouse test' as a means of relieving the condition of the poor. This was in accord with the 'Benthamite Principle' of denying the poor parish relief except as a last and unpleasant resort. The administrative machinery was also Benthamite. The hitherto independent parishes were grouped into Unions, each under an elected Board of Guardians with a strong central authority – the Poor Law Commission – to enforce a uniform policy. These principles and machinery were accepted and incorporated in subsequent Poor Law legislation and administration. When the English Poor Law Amendment Act was passed in 1834, Nicholls was appointed one of the three Commissioners entrusted with its administration. Edwin Chadwick, who had been Jeremy Bentham's private secretary, was appointed secretary to the Poor Law Commissioners.

Upon the passing of the Poor Law Relief (Ireland) Act, 1838, Nicholls was assigned by the Government to organise and superintend the introduction and implementation of the Act in Ireland. Accordingly he proceeded to Ireland in September 1838, residing with his wife and family in Blackrock, County Dublin. He did not return to London until November 1842, by which time he was satisfied the workhouse system was established in Ireland. The task of directing the working of the measure proved very difficult, as had been forecast by people familiar with Irish attitudes and conditions. The Irish poor law and its administration, based as they were on the workhouse system, were subjected to sharp criticism, both in and out of Parliament, but opponents bore testimony to Nicholls' character and ability. Even today to read his reports and writings on the poor law system is to be impressed by his diligence and capacity. He died in London in 1865.

# Notes

## 1: Breakdown of the Irish System of Care

1 Giraldus Cambrensis, *The Topography of Ireland*, quoted in Edward Ledwich, *Antiquities of Ireland*, p.69.
2 Francis Grose, *The Antiquities of Ireland* (Dublin, 1790), pp. 31-32.
3 Geraldine Carville, *The Heritage of Holy Cross* (Belfast, 1973), pp. 109-10.
4 Edmund Burke, *Letters, Speeches, Tracts on Irish Affairs* (London, 1792), p. 86.
5 Arthur Young, *Tour in Ireland 1776-1779* (London, 1880), p.54.

## 2: Origins of the Poor Law System

1 R. Blakey, *The History of Political Literature* (London, 1858), vol. II, pp.84-85.
2 G. Vanderlint, *Money Conquers All Things* (London, 1734).

## 3: Relief Measures in Ireland in the Eighteenth Century

1 Dean Swift's Works, vol. VI, *Short View of State of Ireland* (Dublin, 1727), pp.281-282.
2 Warburton, Whitelaw, Walsh, *A History of the City of Dublin* (London, 1818), vol. 1, p.578.
3 *Report of the Royal Commission on Poor Laws, Ireland* (1909), p.3.
4 W. D. Wodsworth, *Brief History of the Dublin Foundling Hospital* (Dublin, 1876).
5 Warburton, Whitelaw, Walsh, op. cit., p.580; E. M. Lysaght, *Irish Life in 17th Century*, p.50; J. Robins, *The Lost Children* (Dublin, 1980), p. 16.
6 Royal Dublin Society, *Proposals for a Comprehensive Scheme for Establishing County Poor-Houses throughout Ireland* (Dublin, 1768).
7 *Brief Retrospect of the Poor Laws, Reports of Vice-Royal Commission* (1906) and *Royal Commission* (1909).
8 George Nicholls, *History of the Irish Poor Laws* (London, 1856), p.59.

## 4: *English Legislation Leading to the Introduction of Workhouses*

1 Jeremy Bentham, *Management of the Poor* (Dublin, 1796).

## 5: *Developments Leading to the Irish Poor Laws.*

1 *Report of Select Committee on Legislative Provisions for the Poor of Ireland,* House of Commons 1803-4 (109).
2 *Two Reports of Select Committee on the State of Disease and Conditions of the Labouring Poor in Ireland,* HC 1819 (314-409).
3 *Report of Select Committee on the Labouring Poor in Ireland,* HC 1823 (561).
4 *Report of Select Committee, House of Lords, on State of Ireland 1825,* HC 1826 (40).
5 *Three Reports of Select Committee on the State of the Poor in Ireland,* HC 1830 (589, 654, 665).
6 *Three Reports of Commissioners for Enquiring into the Conditions of the Poorer Classes in Ireland,* HC 1835 (369); HC 1836 (43); HC 1837 (68).
7 Alexis de Tocqueville, *Journey in England and Ireland* (London, 1835).
8 Idem, HC 1836 (43).
9 Gustave de Beaumont, *Ireland, Social, Political and Religious* (London, 1839), p.35.

## 6: *Proposals for Workhouses in Ireland*

1 Nicholls, *First Report on Poor Laws, Ireland* (London, 1836), p.3.
2 Ibid, pp.5-6.
3 Ibid, p.21.
4 Ibid, p.22.
5 Ibid, p.24.
6 *Report of the Viceregal Commission on Poor Law Reform in Ireland,* 1906, (cd. 3202), pp.8-9.
7 Nicholls, *History of Irish Poor Laws,* op. cit., p.188.
8 *Parliamentary Debates 1838* (Hansard, vol. XL, col. 950).
9 Letter from Lord John Russell to Nicholls dated 12 August 1837: 'I think it desirable that you visit the northern counties of Ireland, after which I shall be glad to receive your report as to whether the circumstances or any new matter which you may be now able to

observe or collect, shall have caused you to alter, or in any way modify, the opinions and recommendations set out in your last report.'

10   Nicholls, *Second Report on Poor Laws, Ireland* (London), p.1.
11   *Parliamentary Debates 1838* (Hansard vol. XL11, p.675, col. 680).
     Viscount Castlereagh stated that a great public meeting had been called together at Belfast, at which Dr Cooke, the leader of a large party, proposed three cheers for Mr O'Connell for his determined opposition to this Poor Law Bill. With respect to the hon and learned gentleman, he was delighted to see him present. He knew the hon and learned gentlemen held a power over Her Majesty's Government by which he could prevent them from carrying measures which were obnoxious to the people of Ireland.
         Mr O'Connell said (col. 681) that it was his rule to support ministers when they were right and to oppose them when wrong. He begged the House to consider that he and the noble Lord, for the first time in that House, fully coincided in their views, and represented the almost unanimous opinions of the Irish people.

## 7: The Act of 1838

1   *An Act for the More Effectual Relief of the Destitute Poor in Ireland*, London, 31 July, 1838, section 35.
2   Nicholls, *First Report*, op. cit. p.64.

## 8: The Building of the Workhouses

1   Cahal Dallat, *Caring by Design*, The Department of Health and Social Services, Northern Ireland, 1985, p.24.
2   *Fifth Annual Report of the Poor Law Commissioners 1839*, p. 27.
3   Nicholls, *First Report on Poor Laws for Ireland, 1847*, p.50.
4   Information supplied by the Poor Law Commissioners for Census of 1841, as quoted in the *General Report of the Census Commissioners*, p.xv.
5   George Wilkinson general report – *Thirteenth Annual Report of the Poor Law Commissioners*, 1847, pp.213-219.

## 9: The Building of the Workhouses

1   J. Ginger, *The Notable Man*, p.44, quoting 'The Reformer', from *The Early Life of Edmund Burke* by A.P. Samuels (Cambridge, 1923).

2 *Eighth Annual Report of Poor Law Commissioners*, 1842, appendices C and D.
3 J. Robins, op. cit., p.236, 'An Infernal Contraption'.

## 10: *Life in the Workhouse*

1 General Order of the Poor Law Commissioners, 5 February, 1849. The General Order is quoted in full in T.A. Mooney's *Compendium of Irish Poor Law* (Dublin, 1887), pp.283-310.
2 Ibid.
3 J. H. Kohl, *Travels in Ireland*, 1842, p.280.
4 Thomas Harrington.
5 General Order, ibid.
6 W. M. Thackeray, *Irish Sketch Book* (London, 1844), pp.320-324.

## 11: *Pre-Famine Ireland*

1 Cecil Woodham Smith, *The Great Hunger* (London, 1962), p.31.
2 Gustave Beaumont, op. cit.
3 S. C. and A. M. Hall, *Ireland, Its Scenery, Character, etc.* (London, 1841-1843), vol. I, p.82.
4 James S. Donnelly, *The Land and the People of Nineteenth Century Cork* (London, 1975), p.62.
5 *Midleton Papers*: Charles Bailey's Report on Valuation of the Estate, 6 April, 1840. Quoted in Donnelly, op. cit. p.13.
6 P. Fitzgerald to Lord Cloncurry, 8 December, 1847, quoted in *Cork Examiner*, 22 December, 1847.
7 W. S. Trench, *Realities of Irish Life* (London, 1868).
8 The Halls, op. cit., vol. 1, p.6.
9 Charles E. Trevelyan, 'The Irish Crisis', from the *Edinburgh Review*, 1850, p.2.
10 Lord Palmerston to Lord Monteagle, October 1846. *Monteagle Papers*.

## 12: *The Workhouse in the Famine Years*

1 *Annual Report of Poor Law Commissioners for 1846*, published 1 May, 1847. (Returns relating to some Unions are given in appendix 5).
2 Woodham Smith, op. cit., p.175.
3 *Lismore Papers*, National Library of Ireland, MS.6929, Rent Receipts 1818-1890.

4  J. H. Tuke, *Narrative of Visits to Distressed Districts in Ireland in November and December, 1846* (London, January 1847), pp.3-10.
5  Trench, op. cit.
6  Tuke, *A Visit to Connaught in the Autumn of 1847* (London, 1848).
7  Joseph Crosfield, 'Distress in Ireland', published in a Society of Friends pamphlet (London, 1847), pp.2-4.
8  Board of Works Correspondence, 1846, pp. 434-435.
9  Wilkinson, Report of May, 1850.
10 Tuke, op. cit.,
11 *Annual Report of the Poor Law Commissioners for 1846*, pp.286-289.
12 Isaac Butt, *The Famine in the Land* (Dublin, 1847), p. 10.
13 *Dawson Papers*, Public Records Office of Northern Ireland.
14 *Transactions of the Society of Friends during the Irish Famine, 1846-47*, appendix v, p.219.
15 *Report of the British Association for the Relief of Distress*, 1849, p.171.
16 Sean O'Faolain in *King of the Beggars*, a life of Daniel O'Connell, (Dublin, 1838), has this description of O'Connell's appeal: 'Wearied out, moping, O'Connell comes back to Dublin in January, 1847, and in February 1847 he goes to the House of Commons. Tottering to his place, swaying as he rises, he mumbles out a pitiable appeal for mercy to his dying people,' p.326.
17 The figure for those receiving separate rations was given as 2,226,534 adults and 755,178 children.
18 A. M. Sullivan, *New Ireland* (London, 1877), p.62.
19 The members of the Tralee Board of Guardians in 1847 were: W. Denny (Chairman). R. Bateman, Dr W. Blennerhassett, T. Blennerhasset, R. Chute, C. W. Fairfield, M. Flaherty, R. C. Hickson, G. Hilliard, J. Hurley, E. Hussey, R. Jellicott, J. Keane, J. Lynch, J. McCartie, T. Murphy, J. O'Donnell, J. O'Donovan, C. W. O'Leary, J. Sealy, F. Spring, T. C. Stack, Colonel Stokes, W. Thomson. From the Minutes of the Tralee Board of Guardians, 1846-48, MS.7860, National Library, Dublin.
20 Aine Ní Cheannain, *Heritage of Mayo* (Dublin, 1982), p.92.

## 13: Death in the Workhouse

1  J. O'Rourke, *The Great Irish Famine* (Dublin, 1875), p.365.
2  *Annual Report of the Poor Law Commissioners for 1846*.
3  Sir W. P. MacArthur, 'The Medical History of the Famine', in *The Great Famine*, ed. R. D. Edwards and T. D. Williams (Dublin, 1956), p.265.
4  Tuke, op. cit.

5 Minute Book, Fermoy Board of Guardians, 1847-48, 10 March, 1847, pp.36-29.
6 Minute Book, Dunmanway Board of Guardians, 1846-47, 16 January, 1847, pp.61-62.
7 Minute Book, Bantry Board of Guardians, 1846-47, 2 March, 1847, p.5; 25 May, 1847, p.9.
8 Reports made to the Board of Health by medical officers sent to enquire into the state of the workhouses in Cork, Bantry and Lurgan, Dublin, 27 March, 1847.
9 Trench, op. cit., p.00.
10 Spencer T. Hall, *Life and Death in Ireland* (London, 1849), p.37.
11 MacArthur, op. cit., p.305.
12 *Illustrated London News.*
13 Census of Ireland, 1851, Table of Deaths, p.243.

## 14: The Workhouse and Emigration

1 Donnelly, op. cit., p.52.
2 J. H. Kohl, *A German in Ireland* (London, 1842), p.280.
3 Donnelly, op. cit., p.55.
4 Charles Lever, *The Martins of Cro' Martin* (London, 1856), p.243.
5 Donnelly, op. cit., pp. 55-56.
6 Rev S. C. Osborne, *Gleanings in the West of Ireland* (London, 1850), p.27.
7 *Coollattin Emigration Papers.*
8 Sir William Butler, *An Autobiography* (London 1911), pp.4-11.
9 Trench, op. cit.
10 Donnelly, op. cit., pp.129-130.
11 *Three Reports from the Lords Select Committee on Colonisation from Ireland*, HC, 1847-1848 (415), xvii, and HC, 1849 (86), appendix C, p.201.
12 *Papers Relative to Emigration*, HC, 1847-48 (932), xlvii, pp.157-8. From 1847, emigration began to be more widely used as an alternative to eviction. Sir Robert Gore Booth, a resident landlord in Sligo, was accused by Mr Perley of the Canadian Government Immigration Agent of 'exporting and shovelling out the helpless and infirm to the detriment of the colony'. Sir Robert in reply put forward the landlord's point of view, declaring that it was not right to evict and turn people out on the world and that to emigrate them was the only solution.
13 Ibid., pp.13-14.

14  Marianna O'Gallagher, *Grosse Ile: Gateway to Canada 1832-1937* (Quebec, 1984), pp.50-51.
15  Woodham Smith, op.cit., p.225.
16  O'Gallagher, op.cit., p.55.
17  British Parliamentary Papers, vol. 17, p.217.
18  Article in *The Whig*, published in *The Quebec Mercury* on 26 October, 1847.
19  BPP vol. 17, p.233.
20  O'Gallagher, op. cit., pp.56-57.
21  Ibid., pp.85-86.
22  Woodham Smith, op. cit., p.237.
23  P. Hinchy, *Three Centuries of Emigration*, Seminar, Salt Lake, Utah (USA, 1969), p.9.
24  *Annual Report of Irish Poor Law Commissioners for 1848*, appendix A, no.v, pp.58-60.
25  *Annual Report of Irish Poor Law Commissioners for 1850*, appendix B, no. xvii, pp.133-4.
26  Mr and Mrs Hall, op. cit., vol. 1, pp.27-29.
27  *Annual Report of Irish Poor Law Commissioners for 1847*, p.8.
28  *Report of the Royal Commission on Poor Law, Ireland*, 1909, p.189.
29  F. S. Lyons, *Ireland Since the Famine* (London, 1974), p.33.

## 15: *Later History of the Workhouses*

1  *Report of the Royal Commission on the Poor Laws, Ireland*, 1909, p.20. The average number of inmates was based on the maximum and minimum numbers of inmates per week and the number of weeks' stay recorded in the *Annual Reports of the Poor Law Commissioners*. For example, it reached an all-time high of 267,170 for week ending 21 June, 1851, and was down to 140,031 on 27 September, 1851.
2  *Report of the Poor Law Commissioners for 1857*.
3  George Wilkinson continued in private practice in Dublin, where he was employed by the Board of Works on the planning of district lunatic asylums. His best known work, apart from the workhouses, is the old Harcourt Street station in Dublin, designed in the classical style. He returned to England in 1888 and died in Twickenham in 1890.
4  *Report of the Poor Law Commissioners for 1860*.
5  *Report of the Irish Poor Law Commissioners for 1861*, pp.394-417.
6  *Report of the Royal Commission, 1909*, pp.68-69 (267).
7  *Report of the Poor Law Commissioners for 1853*.

8  *Report of the Royal Commission on Poor Law, Ireland,* 1909, p.72 (287).

9  *Report of the Commissioners on the Relief of Sick and Destitute Poor, 1925-27,* p.69. Stationery Office, Dublin, 1927.

## 16: The Workhouse in Literature

1  Charles Kickham, *Knocknagow* (Dublin, 1869), p.545.

2  Kickham, *Sally Cavanagh,* new ed. (Dublin, 1948), pp.189-196.

3  O'Donovan Rossa, *Recollections* (New York, 1898), pp.166-167.

4  Lady Gregory, *The Workhouse Ward* (Dublin, 1907).

5  Elizabeth Coxhead, *Lady Gregory, A Literary Portrait* (London, 1961), pp.109-110.

6  Colum's father was not apparently the stuff of which stern workhouse masters were made. He was too easy-going, too fond of meeting his cronies down at the local, and not diligent enough for the Poor Law Guardians. He was eventually made to resign his position of security and status in 1889, and the family had to leave their rent-free quarters in the workhouse. These were the circumstances, as Padraic Colum was later to recall, that gave a gloomy ending to the later Longford days. Padraic Colum's Centenary Programme, Dublin, 1981).

7  Translations from *Mo Sceal Féin,* C. T. O Ceirín (Cork, 1970), pp.48-50, and S. O'Sullivan (Dublin, 1973), pp.10-12.

## 17: Phasing out the Workhouses

1  Dorothy MacArdle, *The Irish Republic* (Dublin, 1937), p.275.

2  Inter-Departmental Committee on the Care of the Aged (Dublin SO, 1968), PRL777, p.31.

3  B. Hensey, *The Health Services of Ireland* (Dublin, 1979), p.149.

4  Heritage Centres and Famine Museums are now being developed throughout the country, at Cobh (Queenstown), County Cork; Strokestown House, County Roscommon; The Ulster-American Folk Park, Omagh, County Tyrone; and in other locations.

# Bibliography

Barnes, Jane, *Irish Industrial Schools 1868–1908*. Dublin 1989.

Beaumont, Gustave de. *Ireland, Social, Political and Religious*, London 1839.

Beckett, J.C., *The Making of Modern Ireland 1603-1923*, London 1966.

Bennett, Wm., *Narrative of a Recent Visit to Ireland*, London 1848.

Bentham, Jeremy, *Management of the Poor*, Dublin 1796.

Blakey, Robert, *History of Political Literature*, London 1855.

Burke, Edmund, *Letters, Speeches and Tracts on Irish Affairs*, M. Arnold (ed.), Dublin 1881.

Burke, Edmund, *Life and Times*, A.P. Samuels, Cambridge 1923.

Burke, Helen, *The People and the Poor Laws in Nineteenth-Century Ireland*, Dublin 1987.

Butt, Isaac, *The Famine in the Land*, Dublin 1847.

Carlyle, Thomas, *My Irish Journey in 1849*, London 1850.

Carty, James, *A Documentary Record of Ireland*, Dublin 1949.

Carville, Geraldine, *The Heritage of Holy Cross*, Belfast 1973.

Cobbett, Wm., *History of the Protestant Reformation in England and Ireland*, London 1824.

Crosfield, Joseph, *Distress in Ireland*, Dublin 1847.

Coxhead, E., *Lady Gregory, A Literary Portrait*, London 1961.

Curtis, Edmund, *History of Ireland*, London 1937.

Cusack, M. F., *Father Theobald Mathew (1790-1856)*, Dublin 1874.

Dallat, Cahal, *Caring by Design, Department of Health and Social Services*, Northern Ireland, 1985.

Davitt, Michael, *The Fall of Feudalism in Ireland*, Dublin 1904.

Dickens, Charles, *Oliver Twist*, London 1839. *Our Mutual Friend*, London 1865.

Donnelly, James S., *The Land and the People of Nineteenth-Century Cork*, London 1975.

Doyle, Bishop (J.K.L.), *Legal Provision for the Poor*, 1831.

Edwards, R.D., and Williams, T.D., *The Great Famine*, Dublin 1956.

Farrell, M., *The Poor Law and the Workhouse in Belfast*, Northern Ireland Public Records Office, 1978.

Fitzpatrick, W.J., *Life of J.K.L.* (Bishop Doyle), Dublin 1861.

Fleetwood, John, *History of Medicine in Ireland*, Dublin 1951.

Frazer, W.M., *History of English Public Health*, London 1950.

Ginger, J., *Life and Times of Oliver Goldsmith*, London 1977.

Gregory, Lady, *The Workhouse Ward*, Dublin 1909.

Gwynn, A. and Hadcock, R.N., *Medieval Religious Houses Ireland*, London 1970.

Hall, Spenser, *Life and Death in Ireland as Witnessed in 1849*, London 1849.

Henchy, Patrick, *Three Centuries of Emigration* – Seminar, Salt Lake City, Utah, USA 1969.

Hensey, B.J., *The Health Services of Ireland*, Dublin 1979.

Illustrated London News, 1847, 1848, London.

Irish Workhouse Association, Annual Report, 1907, Dublin.

Johnston, Joseph, *A Tour of Ireland*, London 1844.

Joyce, P.W., *A Social History of Ireland*, London 1903.

Kickham, Charles, *Knocknagow*, Dublin 1869.

Kickham, Charles, *Sally Cavanagh*, Dublin 1948.

Kohl, J.H., *A German Visitor to Ireland*, 1842.

Lecky, W.E.H., *History of Ireland in the Eighteenth Century*, New York 1892.

Lewis, G.C., *Local Disturbances in Ireland*, London 1832.

Lonergan, E., *A Workhouse Story of St Patrick's Hospital*, Cashel 1992.

Lyons, F.S., *Ireland Since the Famine*, London & Edinburgh 1974.

Macardle, Dorothy, *The Irish Republic*, London 1937.

MacArthur, Sir Wm., 'Medical History of the Famine', as quoted in *The Great Famine* – Edwards, R.D. and Williams, T.D. (ed.), New York 1956.

Marx, Karl, *Das Kapital*, Moscow 1954.

Maxwell, Constantia, *A Stranger in Ireland from the Reign of Elizabeth to the Great Famine*, New York 1954.

Mooney, T.A., *Compendium of the Irish Poor Law*, Dublin 1887.

Mitchel, John, *The Last Conquest of Ireland (Perhaps)*, Dublin 1861.

Nicholson, A., *Ireland's Welcome to the Stranger*, London 1847.

Nicholls, George, *History of the English Poor Law*, London 1834.

Nicholls, George, *Poor Laws, Ireland*, Reports, London 1838.

Nicholls, George, *History of the Poor Laws in Ireland*, London 1856.

O'Connor, Denis, *Seventeen Years of Workhouse Life*, Dublin 1861.

O'Donovan, Rossa, *Recollections*, New York 1898.

O'Laoghaire, An t-Athair Peadar. *Mo Sceal Fein*, Dublin 1915.

O'Rourke, John, *History of the Great Irish Famine*, London 1875.

Osborne, S.G., *Gleanings in the West of Ireland*, London 1850.

Prendergast, J.P., *The Cromwellian Settlement of Ireland*, Dublin 1922.

Robins, Joseph, *The Lost Children*, Dublin 1980.

Roberts, George, *Social History of the People of Southern England*, London 1856.

Royal Dublin Society, *Proposals for a Comprehensive Scheme for Establishing County Poor-houses throughout the Kingdom of Ireland*, Dublin 1768.

Senior, Nassau W., *Journals Relating to Ireland*, London 1844.

Smith, Cecil Woodham, *The Great Hunger*, London 1962.

Society of Friends, *Transactions of Central Relief Committee during the Famine in Ireland*, 1846/47, Dublin 1852.

Sullivan, A.M., *New Ireland*, London 1877.

Swift, Jonathan, *Short View of the State of Ireland*, Dublin 1827.

Swift, Jonathan, *Works* (Vol. VI), Scott (ed.) London.

Thackeray, W.M. *Irish Sketch Book*, London 1844.

Tocqueville, A. de, *Journey in England and Ireland*, London 1835.

Trench, W.S., *Realities of Irish Life*, London 1869.

Trevelyan, G.E., *The Irish Crisis*, London 1848.

Tuke, J.H., *A Visit to Connaught in 1847*, London 1848.

Tuke, J.H., *Narrative of Visits to Distressed Districts, Ireland*, London 1847.

Vanderlint, Jacob, *Money Answers All Things*, London 1734.

Warburton (J.W.), Whitelaw (J.) and Walshe (R.), *History of the City of Dublin*, London 1818.

Watt, John, *The Church in Medieval Ireland*, Dublin 1972.

Whately, E.J., *Life and Correspondance of Richard Whately*, London 1886.

Wodsworth, W.D., *Brief History of Dublin Foundling Hospital*, Dublin 1876.

Young, Arthur, *A Tour in Ireland*, London 1780.

# Official Documents and Reports

*(HC = House of Commons Papers)*

---

Annual Reports of the Poor Law Commissioners for England, Wales (with a section on Ireland), 1838-47.

Annual Reports of the Poor Laws Commissioners for Ireland, 1848-72. (Separate Commissioners were appointed for Ireland in 1847).

Annual Reports of the Local Government Board for Ireland 1872-1921.

Annual Reports on the Medical Charities Act 1853-1856 (thereafter these reports were included in the Annual Reports of the Poor Law Commissioners, Ireland).

Board of Work series and correspondance 1846/47 relating to measures for relief of distress in Ireland, HC 1847.

Census of Ireland 1841, 1851, 1861. General Reports and Tables of Death.

Devon Commission Report (1843-45) on occupation of land in Ireland. HC 1845, XIX-XXII.

Hansard Parliamentary Reports 1837, 1938 and 1847.

Health Act 1970, Dublin.

Health Services Act (Northern Ireland) 1948.

Hospitals Commission Report 1933, Dublin.

House of Commons (HC) Papers (various) 1835-50.

House of Lords Select Committee on State of Ireland Report 1825.

National Assistance Act 1948 (6th Schedule), London.

National Health Services Act 1946, London.

Papers relative to emigration, HC 1847 and 1848.

Papers relative to Proceedings for the Relief of Distress and the State of the Unions and Workhouses in Ireland. HC 1846 (37) (50), HC 1847/48 (54-56), HC 1849 (58).

Reports of Select Committees on Conditions of the Labouring Poor in Ireland. HC 1819 and HC 1823.

Four Reports of Select Committee on the State of the Poor in Ireland. HC 1825 (129)

Reports of the Royal Commission of Enquiry (1833-36) into the Conditions of the Poorer Classes in Ireland. HC 1835 (369), HC 1836 (43), HC 1837 (68).

Reports (three) by George Nicholls on Poor Laws for Ireland, HC 1837.

Report of Commission of Enquiry into the Execution of the Contracts for Certain Workhouses in Ireland, HC 1844; and Further Report with Copy of Treasury Minute thereon, HC 1845.

Report of Poor Law Inquiry Commission for Scotland, 1844.

Poor Law Amendment (Scotland) Act 1845.

Report of Vice-Regal Commission on Poor Law Reform in Ireland, HC 1906.

Reports of Royal Commission on Poor Laws and Relief of Distress in Ireland, HC 1909.

Report of Commission on the Relief of the Sick and Destitute Poor, Dublin, 1927.

Report of the Inter-Departmental Committee on the Improvement and Reconstruction of County Homes (Dublin, 1949) and White Paper thereon, 1951.

Report of the Inter-Departmental Committee on the Care of the Aged, Dublin, 1968.

The Years Ahead – A Policy for the Elderly, Stationery Office, 1988.

State Lands (Workhouses) Act 1960, Dublin.

Welfare Services (Northern Ireland) Act 1949.

# Index

JOHN O'CONNOR was born in Killorglin, County Kerry. He started his working life in the National Library of Ireland, where he specialised in historical research and studied the wealth of archive material on the workhouses and the closely related field of poor law. Later in the Department of Health he was involved in the programme for the renovation and replacement of the County Homes (formerly workhouse buildings) and the provision of modern Welfare Homes. Thus his book springs from a deep interest in and knowledge of his subject, which is explored in depth in this first history of the workhouses of Ireland.